# Japan's Policy Trap

# Japan's Policy Trap

*Dollars, Deflation, and the Crisis of Japanese Finance*

Akio Mikuni

R. Taggart Murphy

BROOKINGS INSTITUTION PRESS
*Washington, D.C.*

*Copyright © 2002*
THE BROOKINGS INSTITUTION
*1775 Massachusetts Avenue, N.W., Washington, D.C. 20036*
*www.brookings.edu*

*Library of Congress Cataloging-in-Publication data*
Mikuni, Akio, 1939–
    Japan's policy trap : dollars, deflation, and the crisis of Japanese finance / Akio Mikuni and R. Taggart Murphy.
        p.    cm.
Includes bibliographical references and index.
    ISBN 0-8157-0222-1 (cloth : alk. paper)
    1. Balance of trade—Japan.    2. Japan—Foreign economic relations.
3. Japan—Economic conditions—1989–    4. Political culture—Japan.
I. Murphy, R. Taggart.    II. Title.
    HF3826.5 .M55 2002
    332.4'1'0952—dc21                                        2002008636

9  8  7  6  5  4  3  2  1

The paper used in this publication meets minimum requirements of the American National Standard for Information Sciences—Permanence of Paper for Printed Library Materials: ANSI Z39.48-1992.

Typeset in Minion

Composition by R. Lynn Rivenbark
Macon, Georgia

Printed by R. R. Donnelley and Sons
Harrisonburg, Virginia

# Contents

*Figures*

## Table

# Foreword

Over the past several decades the United States and Japan have pursued strikingly different approaches to exchange rate policy. For the U.S. government, the watchword, by and large, has been "hands off." To be sure, from time to time, even U.S. officials can be convinced that the dollar is either over- or undervalued. But there is no surer way for American officials to be reprimanded by the Secretary of the Treasury than to make an inadvertent public remark about the value of the dollar. In Japan the situation is very different. Government officials comment frequently on the value of the yen, and the government has had a record of relatively frequent intervention in foreign exchange markets to reinforce its verbal message. I listened to such pronouncements about the appropriate level of the yen when I was ambassador to Japan, as did my predecessors and successors. The pattern continues today.

This book argues that the difference in exchange rate policy is much more than a philosophical one about the appropriateness of public comment on exchange rates or direct intervention by the central bank in exchange markets.

It maintains that the starting point has been a determined long-term policy in Japan of suppressing the value of the yen below the value that markets would generate, a policy rooted in a desire to nurture a successful manufacturing sector. The authors analyze how accomplishment of this goal has involved tight regulation and guidance of the financial sector, influenced the conduct of macroeconomic policy, and affected the nature of corporate governance. This unstated policy goal provides a useful explanation for what have seemed to many over the years to be inexplicable regulatory policies. Dedication to this policy also helps to explain, the authors suggest, how Japan got into the economic slump of the past decade and why it has been so difficult for it to resuscitate growth.

Some readers will find this book controversial, both in its presumption of a sustained policy of suppressing the yen and in its analysis of how the policy has been implemented. Whether or not one agrees with the analysis and conclusions, I believe that this study raises a crucially important issue and makes a very strong and original contribution to the debate over Japanese economic policy. The authors bring to this debate backgrounds that are very different from that of the academic economist. R. Taggart Murphy, an American national, spent years in the financial community in Tokyo, observing distortions in the market from the trenches. Akio Mikuni runs the only truly independent Japanese-owned rating agency and has also experienced the unique features of the economic system first hand. They provide a perspective that is as valuable as it is timely.

As with all Brookings publications, the views expressed in this book are those of the authors and should not be ascribed to the trustees, officers, or other staff members of the Brookings Institution.

Michael H. Armacost
*President*

*June 2002*
*Washington, D.C.*

# *Preface*

Japan's economic performance during the forty years after the end of the American Occupation in 1952 so dazzled the world that it acquired the label "miracle." Japan's stumbling since then has confounded analysts both inside and outside Japan. This book argues, however, that one grew out of the other. In particular, we contend that the trade surpluses and export drives that were the hallmarks of Japan's success led directly to the current impasse. In a policy regime that we trace back to 1895, the Japanese bureaucracy treated the accumulation of trade and current account surpluses denominated in the prevailing currency of the day—gold, sterling, dollars—as the be-all and end-all of economic progress in Japan. But that regime has brought with it increasingly perverse monetary side effects. Efforts to cope with these effects led to real estate and equity bubbles and the worst public sector deficits in the developed world, finally landing Japan in a deflationary trap from which we see no easy escape. Further, we maintain that Japan's economic dilemma is inextricably tied up with the global economic hegemony of the United States, which directly depends on the status of the dollar as a universal currency and the ability of the Americans to run what the French economist Jacques Rueff once labeled "deficits without tears."

We come to this conclusion from different perspectives. In 1975, Mikuni founded the first independent, investor-supported ratings agency in Japan, one that has won broad acceptance in the global financial community for the quality of its assessment of Japanese corporate health. With experience in both the Japanese and American financial markets, he had a strong feel for the very different incentive structures within which Japanese and American corporations historically have operated. In particular, well-established Japanese companies did not compete for credit; credit was allocated by a banking system that was itself driven by bureaucratic rather than market norms. A quarter century of closely observing credit allocation in Japan led Mikuni to reflect on the way that the Japanese banking system served as the primary tool of monetary policy in Japan and how monetary policy had become increasingly dominated by the need to cope with an ever-growing hoard of dollars accumulated through Japan's endless trade and current account surpluses.

Meanwhile, as a player in the go-go investment banking world of 1980s Tokyo, Murphy was struck by a perennial imbalance in the Tokyo markets: Japanese institutional investors were desperate for secure returns denominated in yen with which they could pay off policyholders and depositors, yet Japan's growing hoard of claims on the outside world—an inevitable consequence of its trade and current account surpluses—were not being accumulated in yen. Instead, they were being accumulated in the fiat currency of the world's leading debtor nation, the U.S. dollar. While the mismatch provided lucrative opportunities for Tokyo's *gaijin* bankers, Murphy began to fret over the implications. As an American, he was troubled at how little Washington seemed to understand the links between U.S. prosperity, American ability to accumulate trade and current account deficits with impunity, and Japanese willingness and determination to run and sustain countervailing surpluses denominated in dollars.

In a series of books, articles, and conference papers, we independently went public with our analyses and concerns. We had first become friends in the late 1980s through business connections and discovered that we shared a scepticism about the conventional wisdom on the Japanese economy. Much of the analysis we encountered—particularly that emanating from official sources—seemed to us less a product of thoughtful attempts to come to grips with the anomalies of the Japanese economy than a need to produce something plausible to satisfy demanding outsiders. We began to collaborate in the likes of joint appearances at conferences (in particular, one held under the auspices of the University of Amsterdam in March 1998). We resolved to explore together in a more systematic way the ideas we had developed and to treat them at book length. We are pleased that Brookings has given us the opportunity.

We wish to thank the Brookings Institution in general and Mike Armacost in particular for their support. Mike has been a champion of this project since its inception, and it would not have happened without him. He performed many services in bringing this book about, among them reading drafts at various stages of completion and offering us the benefit of his thoughts and experience. We are very grateful. Others also read drafts and kindly offered their suggestions. We wish to thank Karel van Wolferen, John Judis, Bob Cutts, Kumano Masaharu, Robert Angel, Martin Mayer, Robert Litan, Barry Bosworth, Ed Lincoln, and certain other individuals, who wish to remain anonymous; the comments of all helped to make for a stronger book. We appreciate the help of Tara Miller of Brookings Foreign Policy Studies in coordinating this project and the first-rate editing job done by Eileen Hughes. Mikuni extends his appreciation to the staff of Mikuni & Company, specifically to Arai Atsuko and Shiraishi Miyuki. Murphy thanks the College of International Relations and Graduate School of International Political Economy at Tsukuba University for providing him with a base in Japan from which to work on this book as well as the intellectual stimulation from interactions with colleagues and students. Murphy also wishes to note the indispensable personal loyalty and support of Kawada Osamu during the completion of this project. While our debts are many, we are solely responsible for any errors. Our opinions and conclusions are our own.

In this book, we have followed the Japanese practice of putting the family names of Japanese people first—for example, Koizumi Junichiro, rather than Junichiro Koizumi—except in two cases where the individual has previously been published in the Western order: Akio Mikuni and Hideo Sato.

Akio Mikuni
R. Taggart Murphy

*Tokyo*
*June 2002*

# Japan's Policy Trap

# 1

# *The Policy Trap*

As Japan enters its twelfth consecutive year of economic stagnation, it has begun to dawn on the world that something peculiar is going on. The term "recession" is often trotted out, but whatever may be happening in Japan, it does not seem to be a garden-variety recession. "Recession" suggests a sharp, severe economic decline lasting a few quarters; the word carries the connotation of a common disease like the measles or mumps, with a clear-cut cause and an approved course of treatment. But while Japan's authorities appear to have administered the standard recession therapy—interest-rate cuts, easy money, and fiscal pump priming—they have little to show for it other than a staggering level of government debt.

More frightening terms are sometimes heard—depression, liquidity trap—with their deliberate echoes of the 1930s. Those words came into use back then, when economists realized that the world had fallen into something far more intractable than a recession. But except for the intractable part, they manifestly do not fit contemporary Japan. Unemployment rates and bankruptcies may have

1

risen to historical highs, but the country does not look or feel like a country anywhere close to a depression. There are no bread lines, no signs of widespread destitution, no angry, radicalized mobs to provide easy prey for populist demagogues.

"Stagnation" comes closer, since Japan's economy has neither seen much growth in the past ten years nor really shrunk. But while the label works well enough, it does not help us to get a grip on the situation, partly because there is no useful precedent. No one has ever really thought about what it means to muddle along year after year with no improvement and no crash. True, much of the world was in the grip of stagnation twenty-five years ago—"stagflation" they called it, since it combined anemic growth with high inflation. It bothered economists at the time because they had never seen anything quite like it. But again, Japan's problems today do not seem to resemble at all the difficulties faced by the developed world in the mid 1970s. Inflation is nowhere to be seen, the currency is reasonably strong, and the country continues to run high trade and current account surpluses—an economic picture that is the opposite of that in the United States and much of Europe back then.

This is not the first time, of course, that Japan has puzzled the world. Indeed, the country has been something of an enigma ever since the "little land of topsy-turvy" emerged out of a rosy mist of geishas and cherry blossoms to crush the Russian navy in 1905. In more recent times the country posted the most phenomenal record of economic growth in history while violating virtually every single tenet of Western economic orthodoxy. Policy analysts sputtered helplessly about "fairness" and "free rides" while defensive neoclassical economists were reduced to remarking that Japan could have recorded even higher levels of growth if only its government had gotten "out of the way."

The onset of Japan's economic difficulties has led, naturally, to a good deal of "I told you so" crowing from such quarters as well as more reasoned attempts to analyze the "souring" of policy ingredients that are said to have once worked well enough but no longer do. The *schadenfreude* is, however, more muted than one might expect given the threat to conventional economic wisdom that Japan seemed to pose a decade ago. For if the West could not understand how a war-devastated Japan could build the world's premiere industrial machine from scratch in less than twenty years, the onset of Japan's difficulties did not clear up the myriad enigmas enveloping economic and political reality there. There is talk of policy errors by the central bank and grumbling over a succession of weak prime ministers. But those "explanations" do not go very far in helping us grasp how a country can stagger along year after year at close to zero growth with its banking system in a shambles and all the while avoid anything that looks like a real recessionary shakeout.

## The Goals of Policymaking

Much of the difficulty in analyzing Japan in both its high-growth and its stagnation phases can be traced to mistaken assumptions about the nature of policymaking in Japan and the objectives of Tokyo's policymakers. Western observers tend, understandably, to assume that these men—they are all men—want prosperity for Japan and that they measure prosperity by the usual yardsticks: employment rates, living standards, per capita gross domestic product (GDP), corporate earnings, productivity growth, and the vibrancy of the markets for money, equities, real estate, and goods. Now, Japan's policymakers have nothing against prosperity as the West defines it, provided that it does not undermine their control of economic and political outcomes. And they understand that the world expects them to discuss their achievements and shortcomings with reference to the commonly employed yardsticks. But they have goals that transcend prosperity.

Japan's decisionmakers have run their country for well over a century now with three objectives: independence, survival, and control—the independence of their country from foreign domination, their own survival as a ruling elite, and their continued control of key economic and political levers. Their historical memory taught them to secure those goals by maximizing production capacity and mastering and controlling important upstream industrial technologies. And they did, but their aim was not to purchase prosperity for Japanese citizens; it was to buy protection in what they saw as a hostile world. They believed that the only sure route to the control of production and technology lay in aggressive, centrally directed capital spending, and they measured their success by the technological and manufacturing prowess of Japanese companies and the size of Japan's trade and current account surpluses.[1]

That remains true to this day. Perhaps nothing more astonishes educated opinion in the West than Japan's obsession with its trade and current account surpluses. There is no doubt that the obsession exists; a decline in the current account surplus that began in the spring of 2001 gave rise to a veritable orgy of doomsday pieces in Japan's media in which commentators went to the extreme of making off-the-wall comparisons of Japan with Indonesia.[2] Agitation of that kind seems to betray basic economic illiteracy, and comments such as that by Ito Takatoshi, a former official of the Ministry of Finance (MOF)—"If nothing is done [about the deterioration of Japan's trade surplus], the yen will eventually drop and Japanese won't be wealthy anymore"—suggests that Japanese educated opinion is still in thrall to the crassest sort of mercantilism.[3] For not only does Japan enjoy the world's largest pile of claims on foreigners—claims that can be used to buy all the imports Japan could possibly need for years to come—it still boasts a panoply of world-beating industries and companies. Real wealth, as economists since the days of Adam Smith and David Hume have understood, comes not from piles of gold or their modern equivalent—a huge and unnecessary buildup of international reserves produced by an unbroken string of current account surpluses—but from the skills and productivity of a country's citizens, with which Japan is exceptionally well endowed.

For the current account is simply that—an accounting entry that captures current cash flows (trade settlements, dividends, interest, transfers) to and from the outside world while plugging the gap between savings and investment in an economy.[4] A poor developing country without a convertible currency might need to monitor its current account to ensure that it has adequate foreign exchange to purchase needed imports. But Japan is one of the world's richest, most highly developed countries. For policymakers in such a place to concern themselves with the ups and downs of the current account can remind economically literate Westerners of grownups still haunted by childhood fears of being picked on in the sandbox.

But this comparison ignores Japan's single-minded concern with the maximization of production capacity and exports. For those charged with carrying out the policies, the current account serves as *the* most critical indicator of economic well-being. To them, a current account deficit flashes dire distress signals: of excessive imports, of poor export performance, and, above all, of savings inadequate to finance investments in production capacity without dangerous reliance on foreigners. Meanwhile, a constant string of surpluses reassures policymakers that they are following the right course: that savings and exports are sufficient to provide Japan with a protective cocoon of claims on other countries. The importance of the current account surplus is so embedded in the thinking of Japan's decisionmakers that to secure it they have been willing to sacrifice much of the prosperity that could otherwise have been theirs. They have seen to it that the surplus was not consumed domestically; instead, they have invested it overseas, where it finances the deficits of trading partners. But unlike King Midas, gloating over gold he would not spend, the Japanese have accepted payment for their export earnings and returns from their investments abroad not in precious metals or their own currency but in dollars—the fiat currency of another country, a currency that has lost two-thirds of its purchasing power over the past three decades.

Part of Japan's obsession with its current account and the level of its exports reflects the inordinate sway of the bureaucracy over political and economic life in Japan, a matter we will consider more closely in chapter 2. Free of any requirement for political accountability, the Japanese bureaucracy, like bureaucracies everywhere, operates on a kind of inherited autopilot, fighting, in a manner of speaking, the last war. The bureaucracy assumed untrammeled control of economic policymaking in Japan during the late 1940s, a time when officials had to be concerned about the hoarding and rationing of precious foreign exchange. With nothing to change it, that mentality has persisted to this day. But it also reflects the underlying bureaucratic drive to retain control of economic outcomes rather than ceding control to markets or to foreigners. That, in turn, spells maximization of production capacity financed by domestic savings. Unlike other industrialized nations, Japan has built and maintained an industrial capacity that far exceeds its domestic requirements, a capacity that takes financial form as a current account surplus.

To induce and sustain a current account surplus, Japan's policymakers have allocated purchasing power preferentially, to manufacturers on the one hand and to exporters of financial capital on the other. They chose a centralized banking system as the most effective way of doing this. Manufacturers and exporters of capital were given to understand that their task in the system was to play their respective roles in maximizing production capacity. Profits, the sine qua non of viability in market economies, were incidental. Manufacturers and banks were never expected to pay attention to profits; Japan's governing bureaucracy did that for them. The bureaucrats ensured the viability of important players by controlling key prices in the economy and by socializing risks that in market economies are borne by individual enterprises. Banks lent without credit risk; major companies produced without market and supply risks. Both were thereby made responsive to bureaucratic directive, not to the greed of profit-seeking shareholders. Western analysts often wonder at the lack of corporate governance in Japan, but the absence of outside investors to bring pressure for profit and return has enabled Japan's governing bureaucracy to allocate managerial resources to targeted industries without any distractions.

By their own lights, Japan's policymakers have been successful. They have run current account surpluses now for more than thirty years (figure 1-1 shows these surpluses as a percentage of GDP). The surpluses have accumulated to the point that Japan's claims on other countries have made Japan far and away the world's number-one net creditor nation; in other words, the net claims of Japanese institutions on foreigners—the bonds and equity that they hold, the loans that they have made, and the factories, buildings, and companies that they own abroad, less foreign ownership of Japanese domestic assets—far exceed those of any other country. Meanwhile, Japanese companies dominate a wide range of industrial processes, upstream components, and key technologies, enabling Japan to rack up current account surpluses for as far into the future as the eye can see.

The rest of the world, of course, views things in a different light. Japan's huge surpluses seem less a mark of industrial strength than a system-straining imbalance, a sign that both the Japanese economy and global trade and financial systems are out of kilter. For example, C. Fred Bergsten, the head of a prominent Washington think tank, doubted as far back as 1986 whether "the world will sustain external surpluses on the part of Japan on the order of $50 billion or so for the rest of the decade."[5] Japan's surpluses, which are now more than twice that size, are being sustained into their second decade beyond the one in which Bergsten made his prediction, but his comment was not in the least exceptional. For Japan's imbalances—and their counterparts, the swollen current account deficits of the United States—were not supposed to be possible in today's world. The floating exchange rate system, heralded at its birth in 1973 as an automatic adjustment mechanism that would prevent the accumulation of such payment imbalances, has seen the opposite happen. Payment imbalances reached levels never witnessed

**Figure 1-1.** *Japan's Current Account Surplus (Deficit) as a Percentage of Nominal GDP*

Percentage

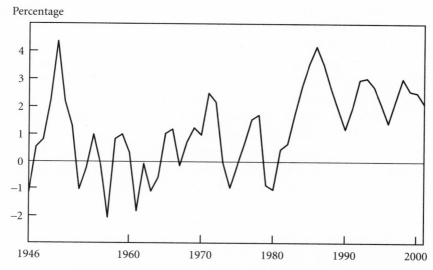

Sources: *Balance of Payments,* Ministry of Finance and Bank of Japan; *Annual Report on National Accounts,* Cabinet Office; and *Estimates of Long-Term Economic Statistics of Japan Since 1868,* Toyo Keizai Shinposha. Calculated, arranged, and estimated by Mikuni & Co. © 2002 Mikuni & Co., Ltd.

under a fixed-rate system, a matter that monetarist cheerleaders for floating rates have never satisfactorily explained.

Theoretically, an imbalanced current account should, at some point, correct itself. Current account surpluses ultimately derive from sales made by a country's companies in foreign markets, sales that then are translated into cash within the country and thus into credit in its own currency. That credit should in the normal course of things find its way into consumption and housing investments, stimulating economic activity and bringing on rising prices. Economic activity creates additional demand for credit. Banks, seeing more profits, raise their interest rates. Eventually, rising prices and rising interest rates erode the competitiveness of the country's exports while making imports cheaper. The current account surplus falls, and equilibrium is restored to the country's balance of payments.

But Japan's governing bureaucracy has long had both the desire and the means to suppress consumption by ordinary citizens while maximizing the savings of the wealthy, who—having been traditionally discouraged by both social pressure and the fear of tax audits from too much conspicuous consumption—have a high propensity to save. Exorbitant land prices helped accomplish those objectives by pushing up both housing and general living costs while transferring income from the working population to well-to-do landowners. Responding to bureaucratic rather than market imperatives, the banking system extended credit to exporters by exchanging the dollars they earned for the yen they needed, yen that went to finance capital rather than consumer spending and thereby tended to increase the current account surplus. Meanwhile, the dollars were left inside the U.S. banking system, where they helped finance demand for Japanese goods. That policy regime blocked any tendency toward achieving the equilibrium in international payments advertised by the proponents of floating rates. Production capacity, built without consideration for profitability and without the financial discipline imposed by a market economy, grew far beyond the needs of the domestic economy. But rather than permit market forces to reduce excess capacity, Japan's decisionmakers sought to keep it humming. The waves of exports necessary for this required proactive policies to suppress the exchange rate—policies that we will examine in detail. Those policies ultimately gave rise to the deflationary trap that Japan finds itself in today.

We have written this book in order to describe that trap. We hope to demonstrate that the institutions put in place to perpetuate the current account surplus have distorted monetary policy in a deflationary direction and that the effects can no longer be easily corrected by other policy measures. Not that Japan's governing bureaucracy has not repeatedly tried, by deliberately blowing bubbles in asset markets—principally land and equities—and then, once the bubbles burst, by giving the economy periodic doses of fiscal stimulus. The cash thrown off first by the bubbles and then by the deficit spending went mostly to banks and the post office savings system in the form of deposits, where it helped counteract the deflationary effects of the policies necessary to support the accumulated current account surplus. But the days when such tactics worked are coming to an end, for reasons that we will explain. And they have left Japan with a crushing burden of bad loans that continues to hobble the country's banking system and a public sector debt that is the largest among developed countries.

Partly as a result, the Bank of Japan (BOJ) is running out of policy options. A number of analysts have called on the BOJ to flood the economy with money in order to counteract deflation; they urge the government to issue new bonds and the BOJ to buy them. The BOJ would, in the course of things, pay for or back up the bonds ("fund" them, as bankers say) with new money.

But that new money would have to consist mostly of currency in circulation plus deposits maintained by banks with the BOJ. Together they form what the BOJ defines as its "monetary base." Economists often use the term "high-powered money" for such monies because the central bank can, in normal circumstances, use them both to create other forms of money and to accelerate the movement of money through the economy (increase the so-called velocity of money).[6] In most countries, currency in circulation rises in tandem with economic activity and the expansion of bank credit. But in Japan, that connection has broken down. Currency in circulation has in fact been rising faster than GDP as worries over the soundness of Japan's banks plus the negligible interest rates on offer have triggered large withdrawals of cash from the banking system. Meanwhile, the BOJ has been purchasing Japanese government bonds (JGBs) from the banks and other financial intermediaries that hold them. (In Japan, government securities typically are held not by individuals or any other end-investor but by deposit-taking institutions, a point of great significance to which we will return.) The BOJ has done that for precisely the same reasons that so many analysts are calling for the government to issue a flood of new bonds that the BOJ would buy: to lower interest rates and stimulate economic activity with new money. But there has been no measurable impact except on the growth of the liabilities of the BOJ and the Japanese government. GDP growth remains flat, prices continue to fall, and other forms of monetary aggregates stagnate while high-powered money increases—see figure 1-2, which portrays the growth of the money supply broadly defined (that is, M2 plus CDs) over that of high-powered money. For the banks, facing no demand for loans, are simply placing the money coming into their coffers from the BOJ's purchases of JGBs back into the BOJ, creating an endless loop.

Some have called for the BOJ to range farther afield—to buy equity, land, problem loans. But if the BOJ has not been doing that directly, the government as a whole most certainly has, with funding ultimately provided by the BOJ. The postal savings system and the government's pension funds have been buying equity. Today, the government is the largest net buyer of land. The BOJ has lent money to insolvent financial institutions. Problem loans have been moved into the Deposit Insurance System, which either borrows

**Figure 1-2.** *M2 + CDs as a Multiple of High-Powered Money*

Multiple

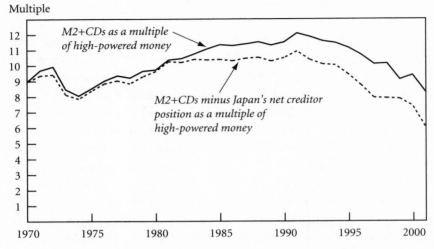

Sources: *Financial and Economic Statistics Monthly,* Bank of Japan; *International Investment Position of Japan,* Ministry of Finance. Calculated, arranged, and estimated by Mikuni & Co. © 2002 Mikuni & Co., Ltd.

money from the BOJ or from private lenders under government guarantee. None of those measures have stimulated the economy.

The BOJ thus finds itself today trapped in a deadly impasse—forced against its will, as we shall examine in more detail, to do things that defeat its very attempts to increase the broader money supply and thus boost the economy. Meanwhile, the dead weight of excess capacity has accelerated the deflationary impact of monetary policy on the domestic economy, dampening capital spending and slowing economic activity.

## Escaping the Policy Trap

Like a fat man stuffing himself with rich food, Japan has continued to gorge on current account surpluses denominated largely in dollars, and its economy is now being adversely affected. Because exports and foreign currency earnings are essential to a country's economic health, just as protein and carbohydrates are to the physical well-being of a person, that may not be intuitively obvious. But just as someone who eats too much for too many years ends up burdened with layers of extra fat that strain vital organs and promote lethargy and disease, the Japanese economy is sinking under piles of dollars that far exceed the country's needs, and it must work overtime to support them.

Telling fat people to lose weight is easy. Getting them to make the comprehensive changes in their diet and lifestyle that they must in order to lose weight is hard and often impossible. The same is true for Japan and its rich, fatty, dollar-denominated current account surpluses. Even if the will and ability to overhaul the Japanese economy existed, it could not be done without triggering economic and political upheaval both in Japan and around the world. For a half-century of ruthless pursuit of technological and industrial superiority at the expense of all other goals—including profits and domestic living standards—has given Japan a comprehensive, vertically and horizontally integrated industrial structure that far exceeds its domestic needs. That costly structure must be supported by high levels of demand— that is, by a robust global economy—at a time when developing nations such as China have set their sights on meeting that very demand in order to realize their own economic visions.

Nor can shifting operations out of Japan spring the trap. That, in fact, has been the primary response of Japanese industry to the dilemma in which it finds itself. But while such tactics may, for example, insulate to some extent Toyota's or Matsushita's North American profits from sudden shifts in the yen/dollar rate, they do not begin to solve Japan's overall problem—indeed, they worsen it. The Japanese media have, in recent years, been given to hand wringing over the supposed "hollowing out" of the Japanese economy. Much of that is exaggerated—despite the relocation of many operations abroad, the highest value-added and most technologically advanced manufacturing continues to be done at home. But it does point to the depressing effects on the domestic economy of the tactics adopted by Japanese industry to escape the policy trap.

## The Current Account and the Yen/Dollar Rate

The rise of the Japanese currency is illustrated in figure 1-3, which shows movement in the yen/dollar rate since 1971, when the yen first floated against the dollar. Despite a good deal of seesawing, most of the climb in the value of the yen occurred between 1971 and 1987. Periodic surges in the

**Figure 1-3.** *Yen/Dollar Rate Since 1955*[a]

Yen/Dollar

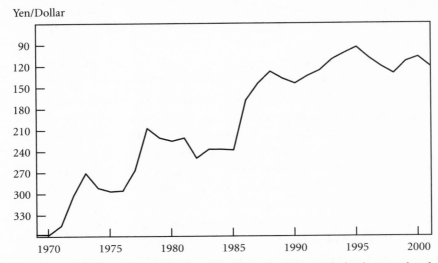

Source: *Financial and Economic Statistics Monthly,* Bank of Japan. Calculated, arranged, and estimated by Mikuni & Co. © 2002 Mikuni & Co., Ltd.

a. For every year after 1969, the rate given is an average for the year.

yen's dollar value have, of course, occurred since then, most dramatically in the spring of 1995. But as of this writing, the yen is not even 20 percent stronger in dollar terms than it was in 1987. That is so remarkable, given that Japan racked up annual current account surpluses of more than 2 percent of GDP during most of the same period, that it cries out for explanation. And the most obvious explanation is that Japan's monetary policymakers have been attempting to peg the yen at a given exchange rate. For if Japan were earning dollars simply to fulfill domestic economic needs, the dollars would at some point have been converted into yen or spent on imports. But Japan is earning dollars not to satisfy wants but to build up a form of political capital.

Some may argue that we are approaching the issue incorrectly. Perhaps it is not so much that the yen has been weaker than Japan's trade numbers would lead one to expect, but that the dollar has been far stronger than U.S. trade numbers would suggest. As of this writing, the dollar is strong not just vis-à-vis the yen but all the currencies (save pounds sterling) of the major

U.S. trading partners. Might not the dollar's worldwide strength suggest that it is the American rather than the Japanese anomaly that ought to be the focus of attention? After all, U.S. current account deficits are even larger in both absolute numbers and as percentages of GDP than Japan's surpluses. Since 2000, China has outstripped Japan as the country running the largest trade surplus with the United States. Surely one has to look beyond Japan for an explanation of the dollar's strength in the face of record American external deficits.

We argue in this book that in fact the Japanese policy regime itself is the key element in understanding the dollar's persistent strength. But before we start to build that case, we need to reiterate that it is not just the present softness of the Japanese yen that is remarkable—the persistence of that softness over fifteen years in the face of relentless current account surpluses demands explanation. In the wake of its debut, the euro may have dropped to levels that no one expected, but that drop may well have been simple birthpangs. And it bears remembering that several of the euro's predecessor currencies—notably the mark—had long been bywords for strong currency. Europe's external accounts have, by and large, provided a reasonable indicator of the relative strength of its currencies.

Not so Japan's. Perhaps the puzzle of endless current account surpluses joined to a softish currency may seem to be resolved by the growth of Japan's claims on other countries, or gross external assets, documented in figure 1-4. Given Japan's current account, there is nothing particularly remarkable about that growth; indeed, it is inevitable. If you earn surpluses in your trade with other countries and do not spend those surpluses on imports—in other words, if you keep running surpluses—you will accumulate claims on other countries. And those claims—the foreign bonds, stocks, and companies you buy, the factories and resorts you build abroad, the loans you make—eventually pose problems. For, like fat that is never transformed by the body into energy through physical activity but is simply stored, claims on foreign countries that are never converted into products or services that the Japanese will use end up creating economic problems.

Therein lies the significance of the information in figure 1-4—for otherwise, this information is little more than a tautology. The great majority of Japan's claims on the rest of the world are denominated in U.S. dollars, mostly because Japan's external trade is conducted largely in dollars. Japan

## *Figure 1-4. Japan's Gross External Assets and Liabilities*

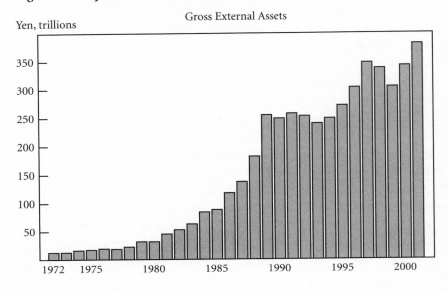

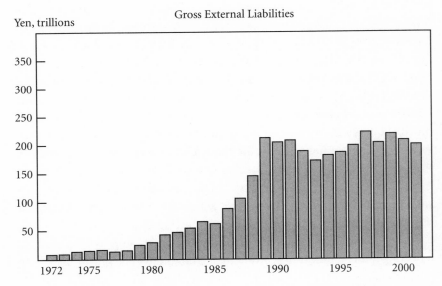

Source: *International Investment Position of Japan,* Ministry of Finance. Calculated, arranged, and estimated by Mikuni & Co. © 2002 Mikuni & Co., Ltd.

runs surpluses not just with the United States but with the entire rest of the world, except for a handful of commodity exporters—mostly, members of the Organization of the Petroleum Exporting Countries (OPEC) and, in recent years, China. Japanese companies bill their overseas customers largely in dollars rather than yen.[7] That helps explain the persistence of an undervalued yen in the face of record current account surpluses. The Japanese economy as a whole retains many of the dollars earned by Japanese exporters; if it converted all of them into goods and services, Japan would not, of course, be running surpluses. It could theoretically convert the dollars into a third currency, such as euros or pounds sterling, but it has not done so, perhaps because the issuers of those currencies are not as hospitable to Japanese exports as is the United States. And then, until the coming of the euro, the dollar was the only currency that circulated in sufficient quantities to accommodate the bulk of Japan's claims. Nor could Japan easily convert those claims into yen without driving the yen up. For large pools of yen to circulate outside Japan not only would Japan have to import more, Japanese importers would have to pay foreign exporters in yen, which they typically do not do.[8]

Many have asked why Japan does not take the intuitively obvious step and print more yen, then exchange its dollars for those yen. But we contend in this book that the authorities have in fact "printed" more yen than real economic activity would warrant, by creating bubbles in asset prices, prodding banks to lend beyond the real credit needs of the economy, and spending large amounts on unnecessary public works. The "printing" of all those yen has, as we hope to demonstrate, been required to support Japan's accumulated dollar position.

But while the relentless growth of Japan's dollar-denominated claims on the rest of the world may seem to answer the question of how Japan can continue to pile up current account surpluses without triggering surges in the yen's value, those claims point to a far more complex puzzle than simply the failure of the yen to strengthen to the point that Japan's surpluses would decline.

## Japan's Creditor Position and the Money Supply

Since 1980, when Japan recovered from what is known there as the "second oil shock," brought on by the Iranian revolution, Japan's gross external assets as a percentage of GDP have steadily climbed to the point that they now exceed 70 percent of GDP, as illustrated in figure 1-5. With no end to Japan's current account surpluses in sight, that number promises to rise ever higher.

From the immediate postwar years through the early 1980s, Japan's accumulated current account surplus rose roughly in tandem with both foreign exchange reserves and currency in circulation (see figure 1-6). Currency in circulation throughout that period was backed by foreign exchange reserves—overwhelmingly denominated in U.S. dollars—with the ratio of currency in circulation to foreign exchange holdings remaining roughly constant at 3 to 1.

Since enactment of the Bank of Japan Act in 1942, Japan has had a monetary system nominally based on fiat money—theoretically, the yen has been backed only by the government's promise to pay in its own currency. But from 1949 to 1973, Japan in fact pegged its currency to the U.S. dollar. As the economist Ichinose Atsushi pointed out, "From the immediate postwar period through the mid-1960s, it was widely understood that the BOJ determined monetary policy according to the balance of international payments."[9] In other words, as figure 1-6 demonstrates, during that period Japan ran what was essentially a dollar exchange standard—that is, the most important variable determining Japan's domestic money supply was the level of its dollar holdings.

To some extent, of course, that was true of every country in the Bretton Woods system except the United States. That system, which prevailed from 1944 to 1971, institutionalized the U.S. dollar as the foundation of the global financial order. Dollars served as the monetary backing for the national currency of all participants, except that of the United States itself, which was backed by gold. Therefore, each country had to keep a close eye on its dollar reserves.

The Japanese authorities were, however, unusually zealous in exercising control of the country's dollar holdings. In the 1950s and early 1960s, all foreign currency earned by Japanese companies had to be turned over to the government, which carefully rationed the precious commodity in order to maintain a 3 to 1 ratio between domestic currency and the official foreign reserves, a ratio viewed as essential for the credibility of monetary management. Meanwhile, control over foreign exchange constituted perhaps the most important tool in the government's implementation of industrial policy.[10] To preserve precious foreign exchange, the authorities did all they

**Figure 1-5.** *Japan's Gross External Assets and Liabilities as Percentages of Nominal GDP*

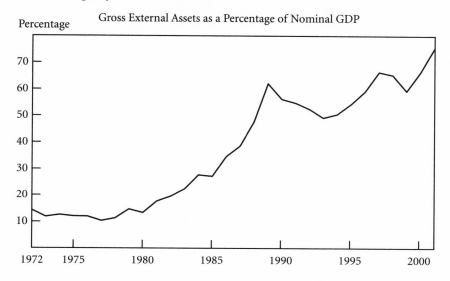

Percentage    Gross External Assets as a Percentage of Nominal GDP

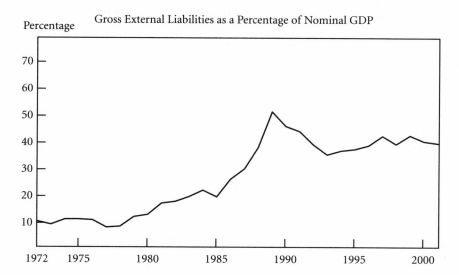

Percentage    Gross External Liabilities as a Percentage of Nominal GDP

Sources: *International Investment Position of Japan,* Ministry of Finance; *Annual Report on National Accounts,* Cabinet Office. Calculated, arranged, and estimated by Mikuni & Co. © 2002 Mikuni & Co., Ltd.

**Figure 1-6.** *Japan's Accumulated Current Account Surpluses, Official Foreign Exchange Reserves, and Currency in Circulation as Percentages of Nominal GDP during the Postwar Period*

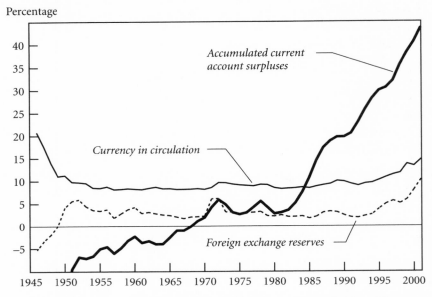

Sources: *Financial and Economic Statistics Monthly,* Bank of Japan; *Balance of Payments,* Ministry of Finance and Bank of Japan; *Annual Report on National Accounts,* Cabinet Office; and *Estimates of Long-Term Economic Statistics of Japan Since 1868,* Toyo Keizai Shinposha. Calculated, arranged, and estimated by Mikuni & Co. © 2002 Mikuni & Co., Ltd.

could to hold down the current account deficits that automatically drained reserves.

Accordingly, the monetary authorities tightened credit immediately whenever Japan's trade balance went into the red. Thus trade deficits were automatically associated with tight money, while trade surpluses initially triggered easy money—as in the case of the Korean War, which saw Japan earning temporary trade surpluses as it filled the demands of an insatiable American military. The BOJ carried out monetary policy through what was euphemistically termed "guidance" to banks but what in fact amounted to direct control of credit availability and thus control of real economic activity. The BOJ and the MOF worked assiduously to head off any pressure on the fixed yen/dollar rate by ensuring that monetary policy automatically followed the vicissitudes of Japan's balance of payments. To all intents and purposes, then, Japan ran what is known as a currency board system, although that was not what it was called, something we will consider in more detail in chapter 4.

But when Japan began to run chronic trade surpluses in the late 1960s, the relationship between Japan's dollar holdings and its domestic money supply began to diverge drastically from what it had been, as dollars accumulated in the coffers of both banks and the government. The exponential growth of Japanese business made it impractical for businessmen to wait for bureaucrats to scrutinize each application for foreign exchange. Banks were given more latitude to hold dollars, and eventually official foreign exchange reserves no longer served as a useful indicator of either Japan's export earnings or its money supply. In 1970, the country emerged as a net creditor—its claims on other countries for the first time exceeded foreign claims on Japan. Both official and unofficial reserves started to rise rapidly.

At first, Japan reveled in the freedom from balance of payment constraints. In earlier years, whenever growth had accelerated, the trade deficit had increased, because growth fueled demand for capital goods. The BOJ had had to cut back credit availability, and thereby growth, to preserve Japan's dollar holdings. But as Japan became self-sufficient in capital goods production, imports of capital goods, which had formed a substantial portion of the country's imports, largely disappeared and a *structural* current account surplus started to emerge. The BOJ no longer needed to tighten credit; reserves climbed as the current account surplus rose. The BOJ could increase currency in circulation without constraint to accommodate the accelerated activity in the real economy of production and trade.

As long as that state of affairs prevailed, the rapid increase in reserves posed no problem for Japan. But when reserves started to rise even more rapidly than the needs of the real economy for currency in circulation, the authorities faced a new and vexing challenge. The excess reserves threatened inflation, for if the BOJ created yen currency in equivalent amounts—"monetized" the excess dollar holdings, as economists would say—the additional unneeded currency might boost the prices of goods and services, as "too much money" usually does. Had Japan continued the practice of the 1960s and allowed currency in circulation to run at three times the level of Japan's total dollar holdings, today currency in circulation would stand at more than 1 quadrillion yen, rather than the current 70 trillion yen— that is, fourteen times the present level. No country could possibly accommodate that kind of money without horrendous inflation. Of course those numbers are absurd, but they give some inkling of the policy challenge posed by Japan's swollen dollar reserves.

To prevent the onset of inflation, the authorities were forced, in the language of monetary economists, to "sterilize" the reserves—that is, to counteract their impact on the domestic money supply. As we will see in chapter 4, Japan had faced similar dilemmas in the past, as far back as World War I. And in the early 1970s, when confronted by an inflation-threatening surge of dollars pouring into the country, the authorities turned to a special account first set up during the Korean War to cope with the influx of dollars stemming from American special procurements for the war effort. That account, known as the Foreign Exchange Special Account (FESA), gave authorities a place to park excess dollars. The dollars were removed from the BOJ's balance sheet, permitting the BOJ to keep a lid on currency in circulation. But the FESA had to be funded out of taxes. To ensure that the entire burden of sterilization did not fall on the government, the MOF also began to allow private institutions to buy and hold foreign currency. But that really only shifted the burden. For the MOF exercised its extraordinary level of informal controls—"guidance," again—to ensure that the banks and other institutions did not sell their dollar holdings lest the exchange rate soar.

Just as Japan's accumulating reserves were becoming, in the early 1970s, the monetary equivalent of an excessively rich diet, the postwar Bretton Woods system of fixed exchange rates collapsed. The wreck of the system shocked Japan's economic establishment to its core; indeed, the very word *shokku*, derived from the English "shock," entered the Japanese language at that point. No Japanese word seemed to convey quite the stunned horror that fell on Japan's officials as they grappled with the destruction of an external economic framework that had for them been so comfortable. In retrospect, they might have seen it coming. For by the mid 1960s, restiveness at what many viewed as willful exploitation by the Americans of their own central position in the system had already led a number of countries—most notably France—to exercise their right under the system to convert dollar holdings to gold. But Japan never did. Jacques Rueff, a prominent French economist and adviser to French president Charles de Gaulle, cited two reasons why Japan (and West Germany) did not follow France's lead: security and market access.[11] By maintaining their foreign reserves in depreciating dollars, Japan and Germany were effectively transferring purchasing power to the United States and thus indirectly subsidizing American military spending in their respective countries. And as long as the dollars held by Japan and Germany were not converted to gold or another currency, American imports from the two countries did not result in any deflationary impact on the United States, because the dollars used to pay for those imports remained in the U.S. banking system—why Rueff would speak famously of the U.S. "deficit without tears."

But once the Bretton Woods system crumbled, the Japanese found that the increasing piles of dollars began to pose all kinds of problems. They could not sell their dollars for German marks or Swiss francs. There was not enough of those currencies to begin with, and the German and Swiss governments would have reacted with outrage to such a move—but then, of course, Germany and Switzerland were not, unlike the United States, markets that had to be kept open to Japanese products at all costs. Nor could the dollars be sold for yen. That would strengthen the yen to such an extent that Japan's exports would be curtailed, menacing an economic structure deliberately built around export-led growth. And a strong yen could wash away the carefully constructed series of dikes that played such a crucial role in the Japanese system by keeping imports at bay, imports that could drown politically sensitive or "strategic" parts of the economy. Of course, that was the whole point of floating exchange rates—to create an international monetary framework that would automatically, or so its proponents hoped, reduce external imbalances without provoking global system-shaking crises. In Japan's case, that would mean lowering its exports and increasing its imports until its external accounts were back in balance.

But Japan's administrative elite never accepted that logic. With the coming of floating exchange rates, officials believed with overwhelming urgency that come what may, they had to retain some kind of de facto peg, suppressing the yen in order to permit the Japanese export machine to continue humming and to forestall waves of unwanted imports. That meant that the dollars Japan earned could not be exchanged for yen; they had to be retained and recycled as dollars.

Japan's policy of keeping its trade and current account surpluses intact helped the United States to run counterbalancing deficits. For the policy apparatus put in place by the Japanese authorities involved, by necessity, a series of measures to acquire and retain dollars. Had the Japanese not implemented those measures but sold their dollars, the yen would have climbed much faster than it did, reducing both the Japanese surplus and the American deficit. The United States, like any normal country suffering chronic deficits in its external accounts, would have been forced to curb its appetite for imports as its currency weakened to the point that it could no longer finance external deficits. The United States escaped that discipline thanks in large part to Japan, which is why, periodic bluster about the Japanese surplus notwithstanding, Washington has sooner or later always come around to supporting Japan's strong dollar/weak yen policy.

But Japan has paid a price. In the early postwar years, as we have seen, dollars formed the base for Japan's monetary creation and thus the more dollars, the more domestic credit. But once Japan had more dollars than it needed, the dollars paradoxically began to decrease domestic credit availability since money, as we will see, had to be drained off in taxes to support them. A credit squeeze imposes a deflationary drag on an economy. To counteract that drag, the Japanese authorities employed various means, eventually resorting to the creation of the greatest bubble in history.

## Deflation and Claims on the Outside World

The notion that holding large piles of dollars is deflationary may seem counterintuitive. How can more money be deflationary? Certainly, there can be little doubt that Japan has, in the past decade, experienced the first significant deflation to be seen anywhere since the 1930s; figure 1-7, which depicts the movements of the wholesale price index, demonstrates that. We argue that deflation is rooted in Japan's snowballing external assets, which represent claims on foreigners that Japan cannot really use. Japan cannot exchange enough of them for either imports or yen. They far exceed Japan's import needs and, as we have seen, if they were exchanged for yen, the yen would become so strong that many if not most export-dependent Japanese companies would be ruined.

The dilemma that those claims pose for Japan and why they are ultimately deflationary can be understood by moving from the rarefied world of statistics and charts to the reality of production, sales, and cash flows that those statistics reflect. When a Japanese manufacturer like Sony sells a product abroad, it receives dollars. Sony can do one of four things with those dollars:

**Figure 1-7.** *Movement of the Wholesale Price Index and the Consumer Price Index in the Postwar Period (Base Year 1970)*

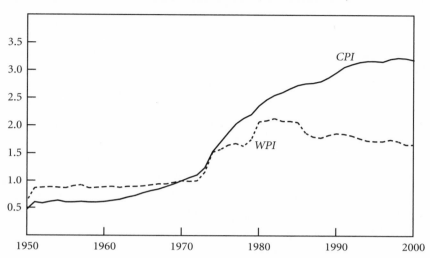

Sources: *Financial and Economic Statistics Monthly,* Bank of Japan. Calculated, arranged, and estimated by Mikuni & Co. © 2002 Mikuni & Co., Ltd.

—immediately exchange the dollars for yen held overseas by foreigners.

—use the dollars to import capital goods or other products manufactured outside Japan whose manufacture was financed in dollars (that is, the necessary labor and supplies were paid for in dollars).

—retain the dollars to finance its own investments abroad.

—sell the dollars for yen to a Japanese bank and use the yen it receives to pay wages and suppliers in Japan.

The first two alternatives create no financing problem. But Japanese manufacturers have not much followed them. If they had followed them, Japan would not have accumulated the surpluses it has; either imports would have risen sharply or the yen would have gone through the roof, braking Japan's export drive. The third alternative—retaining dollars—requires borrowing yen from banks to pay wages in Japan. In the 1980s, many Japanese companies did begin to do that. For the most part, however, companies have sold their dollars to Japanese banks for yen.

But the Japanese bank where Sony exchanges its dollars for yen can no more use those dollars in Japan than Sony can. The bank must usually lend to its Japanese clients in yen, not in dollars. (The bank can, of course, exchange or lend the dollars to Japanese companies importing foreign goods. But since Japan runs trade surpluses, the country has obviously been earning more dollars than it needs for imports, and each year, it earns more and more.) So the bank in turns sells most of its dollars to the BOJ, which then turns them over to the FESA.

Before Japan's dollar earnings outstripped the country's need for international reserves to finance imports, the Bank of Japan could match the banks' dollar holdings with yen credit creation. That yen credit creation went, in a manner of speaking, to pay the Japanese manufacturers who made the exports in the first place. But once the holdings of dollars grew too large for Japan's needs for additional credit, something had to be done with them.

One alternative would have been to sell the dollars for yen. But, as we have seen, there are simply too few yen circulating outside Japan. If Japanese banks had begun to sell dollars in large quantities, the yen would have strengthened, damaging exporters' competitiveness as Japanese goods became more expensive in foreign markets. Instead, public and private sector Japanese financial institutions deployed the dollars overseas. Many of them ended up in the form of U.S. government and agency securities owned by Japanese government entities including the BOJ, forming a major part of the $700 billion plus held at the Federal Reserve Bank of New York on behalf of foreign central banks. The rest took the form of loans, bonds, or equity investments that financed economic activity abroad. Some of that economic activity resulted in increased demand for Japanese exports. But by the early 1970s Japan's dollar holdings already were rising faster than its exports. After the OPEC oil price hikes of 1973, Japan again could profitably use all the dollars it earned since it needed so many of them to pay its oil bills. But beginning in the mid 1970s and particularly after 1980, Japan's accumulated dollars rose far in excess of its exports. That is illustrated in figure 1-8, which shows Japan's exports as a percentage of the country's external assets (all the loans, bonds, equities, companies, factories, and so forth it owns abroad). As the figure demonstrates, those assets now outstrip annual exports by the order of five to one.

The dollars earned by Japan's excess of exports over imports stem from production outstripping domestic consumption, which in turn derives from production capacity greater than that required by Japan's domestic needs. In fact, Japan's production capacity not only exceeds the country's

**Figure 1-8.** *Exports as a Percentage of Japan's Gross External Assets*

Percentage

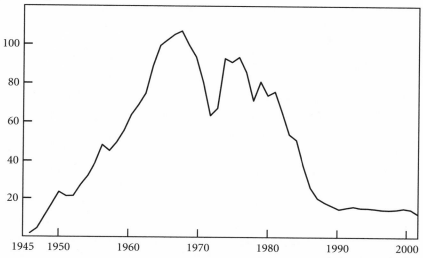

Sources: *International Investment Position of Japan,* Ministry of Finance; *Balance of Payments,* Ministry of Finance and Bank of Japan; and *Estimates of Long-Term Economic Statistics of Japan Since 1868,* Toyo Keizai Shinposha. Calculated, arranged, and estimated by Mikuni & Co. © 2002 Mikuni & Co., Ltd.

domestic requirements, but since the early 1980s it has exceeded what Japan can export as well. Excess capacity of such magnitude is inherently defla-tionary. To counteract that deflation, Japanese authorities have resorted to creating yen liabilities unrelated to production, in two ways: by creating asset bubbles and by spending on useless public works.[12]

Yet they were necessary to maintain a current account surplus, which requires production to exceed consumption and savings to exceed invest-ment. In order to ensure that the surplus continued, Japan had to be willing to accept payment in dollars. But because the extra production, the wages and supplies, that went into making that surplus had to be paid for in yen—because the excess of domestic savings over investment that resulted in that surplus had to be denominated in yen—the authorities were forced to fund Japan's accumulating dollars with yen liabilities.

That portion of Japan's total production that represents the excess of exports over imports is not available for consumption in Japan. Yet wages were paid out to produce it. As long as Japan's surpluses continue to accumulate, as long as Japan continues to hold its surpluses in dollars, all of Japan's economic activities have to be paid for by the total sales proceeds *minus what is exported*. Therefore those who are paid to produce cannot be allowed to spend everything that they earn; ways must be found of reducing their income, and the difference must go to support the excess of production over consumption.

Japan's governing bureaucracy first encountered that dilemma at the time of World War I; in chapter 4, we will examine what happened. Since that time, they have learned to cope with it by deliberately reducing the income of those who actually produce goods and services. First, high land prices helped transfer income away from Japan's working producers through high rents and land sales at stratospheric prices. The land bubble of the 1980s worked exceptionally well in transferring income away from producers and in creating deposits independent of real economic activity. But with the collapse of the bubble, a combination of hikes in regressive consumption taxes and reductions in progressive income and capital gains taxes had to do much of the work of transferring income away from working people and to well-to-do Japanese with a low propensity to consume. Second, wasteful spending on useless public works—what Alex Kerr describes as "the Business of Monuments"—has also reduced the income available to actual wealth producers while putting it in the hands, as we will see, of those who place it on deposit and do not spend it. And as land prices have declined, despite the best efforts of bureaucrats, fiscal spending has had to increase in order to keep pace with the current account surplus.

The problems stemming from Japan's accumulated dollar hoard can also be understood through the prism of accounting. A fundamental rule of financial accounting requires that assets be matched with liabilities. The dollars that Japan holds are, in accounting terms, assets. Those assets require liabilities to match them—to "fund them," as bankers would say. And it is in the way that Japan's monetary authorities have had to find and create those liabilities that the story of Japan's deflationary dilemma unfolds.

Overwhelmingly, in Japan those liabilities take the form of yen deposits. When the deposits are not put to work inside the Japanese economy through loans or equity investments but instead go to support a pool of idle dollars (idle at least as far as Japan is concerned), they remove money from

**Figure 1-9.** *Money Supply Less Accumulated Current Account Surplus*

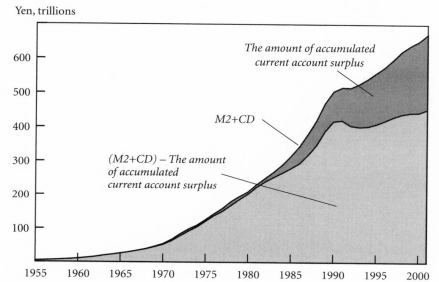

Yen, trillions

Sources: *Financial and Economic Statistics Monthly,* Bank of Japan; *Balance of Payments,* Ministry of Finance and Bank of Japan. Calculated, arranged, and estimated by Mikuni & Co. © 2002 Mikuni & Co., Ltd.

the financial system. The money in those deposits is not being spent on imports, it is not being spent on Japanese goods and services, and it is not being spent on real investments in factories and equipment. It simply supports idle dollars. The drain created by Japan's idle dollars is illustrated in figure 1-9, which shows the money supply (defined as M2 plus CDs) minus those dollars. Domestic credit needs must be met from what remains. When enough money is drained from a financial system, deflation—falling prices—follows and with it economic slowdown.

To put Japan's dilemma in other terms, the workers and suppliers who are paid in yen to earn excess dollars do not produce anything that is ultimately exchanged with other Japanese. They produce things for foreigners. If the foreigners in turn produced things that were bought by Japanese, that would not be a problem. But they do not—that is what it means to have endlessly accumulating trade surpluses. And the deposits that go to pay the

Japanese who have produced things for foreigners without return represent a drain on the Japanese economy.

## U.S. Deficits and Japan's Dollar Surpluses

The dollars held by Japanese entities are claims on the U.S. Federal Reserve System, exercisable directly or indirectly through U.S. banks. It does not matter whether deposit holders at the Federal Reserve are U.S. nationals or foreigners. When American entities pay for imports by wiring dollars to an exporter's account—which they typically do—those dollars never leave the U.S. banking system. A Japanese bank or the FESA may nominally own the dollars, but they continue to function as money in the United States, serving as funding for American economic activity.

By holding its reserves in dollars, Japan has more or less encouraged the United States to spend and import more. The United States does not need to pay for imports—that is, earn foreign exchange through exports or asset sales—as long as exporting countries such as Japan are satisfied to receive claims on the Federal Reserve as payment. If the U.S. currency were still backed by gold, the chronic deficits with Japan would have seen the transfer of American gold holdings into Japanese accounts. But instead, because of the willingness of Japan to receive claims on the Federal Reserve without ever exercising those claims, American deficits with Japan are automatically financed. Japan's exports of goods to the United States come with the exports of capital (that is, the dollar holdings) necessary to pay for them. Indeed, the buildup of "foreign" dollars in the U.S. banking system during the past two decades seems to have had macroeconomic effects comparable with a deliberate easing of monetary policy by the Federal Reserve, and it almost certainly contributed to the run-up in American asset prices (for example, the NASDAQ bubble) of the late 1990s.

These arrangements can be considered a kind of duplication of reserves in the United States and Japan. By continuing to pile up claims inside the U.S. banking system, the BOJ is in essence lending to the Federal Reserve, creating monetary reserves that are theoretically twice as large as the underlying transactions that gave rise to the reserves because the money can be used in both the United States and Japan. But, as noted, Japan cannot monetize its dollar holdings for domestic use without inviting problems once those holdings exceed the need for currency in circulation. That is the financial problem posed, to put it crudely but accurately, when Japanese workers make goods for Americans but are then never paid with American goods or services.

Japan is not the only country in history to have accumulated large net claims on foreigners. But in most cases those claims have been denominated *in the creditor's currency*. Switzerland and Germany, for example, also have run large current account surpluses during much of the last three decades; Switzerland's external assets, like Japan's, far exceed its annual exports. But these countries allowed their currencies to appreciate and did not block imports, with the result that their international balance of payments never became as lopsided as Japan's. Furthermore, German exports typically were paid for in marks; Swiss claims on foreigners typically were denominated in Swiss francs. From a financial point of view, it makes no difference whether claims are accumulated on foreigners or on residents as long as they are denominated in the country's own currency; the money never leaves the domestic banking system. Central bankers can ignore the claims.

But if those claims are denominated in a foreign currency, then they become problematic, because beyond a certain point they cannot be used domestically. In Japan, that point was reached by the late 1960s, when the country's dollar holdings exceeded its need for currency in circulation. Since that time, Japan has been deliberately transferring purchasing power to the United States—a transfer that has taken the financial form of buoyant U.S. money, bond, and equity markets and, increasingly, deflation in Japan.

In the 1970s, when the dollar was finally delinked from gold and the Japanese began to accumulate surpluses denominated in nothing but claims on the central bank of another country, foreign exchange markets reacted with waves of instability, driving down the price of the dollar on the assumption that the situation could not be sustained. And periodically since then—most notably in 1987 and 1995—tremors have shaken global markets at the prospect of an unwinding of Japan's accumulated dollar position. But most of the time—particularly since 1989—markets generally have been reassured that Japan's capital exports to the United States will never be repatriated, that its position will never be unwound.

Japanese officials have worked tirelessly to maintain that reassurance, acting to keep Japan's surplus invested in the United States and to thwart speculation against the dollar. The original rationale for Japan's accumulation of dollars lay in the notion that demographic trends would ultimately lead to a decline in Japanese savings, that Japan would need finally to draw down those dollar holdings. But any sign that that is in fact starting to happen, that Japan is finally beginning to spend its accumulated dollar holdings—that is, that its current surplus is beginning to shrink—has been met with an outpouring of anxiety. And whatever rationale might be on offer, officials have invariably acted to perpetuate existing arrangements.

Japan's dollar surpluses form a nearly unique problem in modern economic history. (We say "nearly unique" because Taiwan, which has comparable levels of dollar-denominated international reserves, suggests some parallels with Japan.) Saudi Arabia and the Gulf emirates have enjoyed surpluses since the 1970s that are comparable in scale to the Japanese surpluses. But while those countries do have their own currencies, in economic terms their currencies are nothing more than accounting entries. They have no serious economic activity other than pumping oil out of the ground and selling it on world markets for ten to twenty times what it costs them to extract it. They are little more than dollar-based *rentier* economies, and their economic significance would disappear overnight if oil were replaced by another energy source.

But Japan is the world's second-largest economy, not because Japan can extract extortionate rents but because over the past half-century the Japanese have built the most wholly integrated industrial structure on earth. Japan still outclasses the rest of the world in cost control, product quality, and technological sophistication in a number of centrally important finished goods—most notably automobiles—as well as a wide range of upstream product segments. Japanese companies have to rely on foreigners only for commodities, aircraft, and cutting-edge computer, information technology (IT), and Internet-related products for which they, in turn, provide components that no one else makes.

This situation has been the implied goal of Japanese economic policy since the late nineteenth century—the building of an industrial structure that would reduce reliance on foreigners to the bare minimum. And while Japan has faltered in the last decade in the IT arena, that should not disguise its overall success in reaching its goal. But that success has landed Japan in a trap. As all the hand wringing over a recent shrinking of the current account surplus demonstrates, the trap itself is not understood, not to mention any realistic means of escape.

## The Public/Private "Divide" and the Policy Trap

We have described Japan's policy trap with the language of accounting—the increasing difficulty faced by the authorities in creating domestic liabilities that can offset Japan's largely useless dollar assets. But those accounting conventions illustrate a larger reality. In Japan, no clear dividing line exists between the public and the private sector. As we will demonstrate, Japan's banks are essentially creatures of its governing bureaucracy. Banks support corporations with credit allocations determined by bureaucratic objectives rather than concerns for profitability. Neither banks nor corporations are expected to provide for their own institutional survival, which is why both can ignore profits. They play their respective roles in the Japanese economy, ensconced in an all-enveloping system of mutual protection, with their viability the ultimate responsibility of the bureaucracy.

Since first invented by Venetian merchants in the late Middle Ages, financial accounting has served as an indispensable tool for those charged with responsibility for the survival and growth of economic entities. Accounts prepared under the rules of double-entry bookkeeping provide a comprehensive picture of financial health and flash immediate warning when things are going wrong. Independent financial institutions in Japan applying proper accounting rules could not have accumulated the dollar positions they have. The mismatch between the dollar assets they hold and the yen liabilities they use to support them would have drawn the attention of any prudent manager, not to mention an outside regulator or investor.

But in Japan, banks and other institutions are allowed and even required to sustain risks that would be regarded as unacceptable elsewhere in order to preserve their place in the Japanese system. For the supposedly independent entities of Japanese finance—banks, securities firms, insurance companies—are not genuinely independent; they function as part of one large integrated system that has served to socialize risk. Mismatches that would have been caught and corrected at the level of the individual bank or company in a Western economy surface only at the national level in Japan—in the current account, the balance sheet of the Bank of Japan, the assets and liabilities of the entire financial system—where they can no longer be disguised or avoided.

For in the last twenty years, Japan's accumulated current account surplus has outstripped both official reserves and currency in circulation, accelerating at a rate higher than the GDP growth rate and bringing on a deflationary build-up of dollars. It is here that the essence of the policy trap in which Japan finds itself is to be found, and we believe that it lies at the heart of the difficulties that Japan has experienced over the past decade.

The Japanese economy has long been described as a bicycle that must be kept moving lest it tip over—when neither borrowers nor their financiers demonstrate significant profits, growth is essential for both to remain solvent. In the 1990s, the bicycle pretty much stopped moving, and while it has not yet tipped over, the stagnation of the last ten years has presented Japan's elite officials with a historically unprecedented challenge that their institutional memory gives them little guidance in coping with.

Considering the dimensions of Japan's policy trap, a growing chorus of economists worldwide has, as noted, urged Japan to print yen in response in order to create inflation. We will argue that the structure of the Japanese financial system, the nation's tax policies, its real estate markets, and a host of other factors have combined to make it far more difficult to create inflation today than most economists realize. That makes the dilemma faced by the Japanese authorities all the more acute because to work properly, the Japanese financial system requires at least nominal GDP to grow. And at the heart of the inability today to boost either real growth or inflation—the components of nominal GDP—lies Japan's mountain of dollar claims, which acts like a huge hole in Japan's monetary bucket.

Hence the policy trap that we intend to describe in this book. We see no way out of the trap short of a reversal in Japan's current account or, in other words, a shift in the fundamental parameters of savings and investment that ultimately determine the current account. But we are not talking exclusively or even primarily about economic measures here; a reversal would both require and cause far-reaching political and institutional changes. And those changes would not stop at Japan's borders. Reducing Japan's surplus cannot occur in isolation; it must be accompanied by a reduction in deficits somewhere else—most obviously through far-reaching shifts in the U.S. economy, which since 1945 has exhibited a bias toward consumption and against saving that has given rise to a current account deficit that is now structurally embedded in the U.S. economy.

Japanese policy officials thus find themselves boxed in, with no choice other than to continue piling up dollar claims. But as the deflationary

**Figure 1-10.** *Year-on-Year Growth Rates of City Bank Loans and Nominal GDP*

Percent

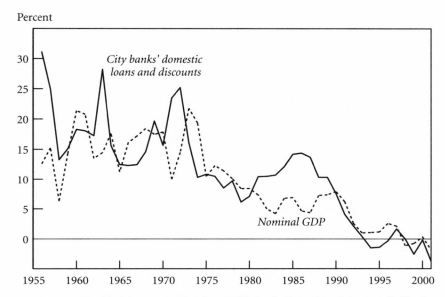

Sources: *Financial and Economic Statistics Monthly,* Bank of Japan; statistics compiled by the Japanese Bankers Association; *Annual Report on National Accounts,* Cabinet Office. Calculated, arranged, and estimated by Mikuni & Co. © 2002 Mikuni & Co., Ltd.

impact of the dollar claims grows ever larger, policymakers in Tokyo are running out of methods to create the matching liabilities needed to fund them. In Japan, those liabilities take the form primarily of deposits. The bubble economy of the late 1980s represented an attempt to break out of the policy trap by rapidly expanding those deposits. As shown in figure 1-10, which documents the excess of bank credit creation over GDP growth, the authorities were successful during the 1980s in fostering an expansion in bank credit that far outstripped the expansion of the real economy. That flood of credit helped foster two of the greatest asset bubbles in history, with the market value of companies listed on the Tokyo stock exchange briefly surpassing that of its equivalent in New York while Japan's real estate prices soared to such heights that, in one widely quoted statistic, the implicit market value of the grounds of the Imperial Palace outstripped that of all the real estate in Canada. The trading in those assets at levels that bore no relation to economic fundamentals brought on a surge in yen deposits—the liabilities needed to fund Japan's dollar assets.

But creating deposits through bank loans became far more problematic following the twin crashes of the Japanese real estate and equity markets in the early 1990s, which brought down with them an avalanche of bad loans that buried much of the nation's banking system. With the collapse of the bubble, the Japanese government has had to turn to massive public works spending in order to create liabilities. Japan's public works "monster" acts to create deposits, to put money in the hands of people who will take it to the bank or the post office rather than spend it, thereby creating the necessary liabilities to support Japan's dollars. But the cost has been an explosion in public sector debt that has begun to threaten the government's continued ability to create those liabilities.

## A Natural Limit?

The day of reckoning for Japanese mercantilism thus has repeatedly been postponed. Commentators talk of the 1990s as a "wasted decade" for Japan, but the country has not collapsed. Japanese industries may no longer bestride the world as visibly as they did in the 1980s. They may take a back seat to the Americans in IT-related industries. But Japanese companies continue to dominate an impressive array of key upstream product segments. And while Japan's administrators may no longer be able to provide the steadily rising household incomes that characterized the period from 1955 through 1990, Japan's industrial preeminence guarantees that for the foreseeable future the country can make or buy what it needs to feed, clothe, and house its population in reasonable comfort. The situation is far from ideal, but it seems tolerable both to the elite and to the wider populace. The elite certainly has no intention of risking its hold on power by instituting any kind of fundamental structural change, while the wider public displays little appetite for the economic and political upheavals that would be the inevitable price of a real shift in existing power alignments.

That seeming stability is reinforced by the global economic environment in which Japan is embedded. Japan's dollar-support policies helped the United States run eye-popping current account deficits that permitted the country to extend the economic expansion of the 1990s for years beyond the point that domestic capacity and labor market constraints would otherwise have halted it. There are no important parties anywhere in the world—not in Washington, not in Brussels, not in Beijing—that would welcome the long, steep recession necessary to end U.S. current account deficits. Tokyo can thus count on automatic reinforcement from abroad for continuing its present policy regime. Whatever lip service may be given to making "reforms" that ostensibly aim to increase Japanese and decrease American imports, no one seriously wants to risk disturbing the status quo.

While the political forces aligned in favor of continuing the present policy may seem overwhelming, we believe that ultimately it will reach a natural limit—and that the limit will be reached sooner rather than later. Over and over again during the past ten years, the Japanese government has announced that the corner has been turned, that the economy is in an upswing. And over and over again those hopes have proven false. Japan's stagnation has persisted far longer than even the most pessimistic analysts anticipated when the grip of the present stagnation first became clear in the early 1990s. And while those who predicted that the stagnation would end in a "hard landing" rather than a robust recovery have also, to date, been proven wrong, the fact that it has continued far longer than anyone thought possible is no guarantee that it will continue indefinitely. Among other things, we believe that Japan is rapidly running out of ways to support its endlessly growing pile of dollar claims and that when the day comes when those claims can no longer be supported, the world could see a horrific deflationary spiral in Japan, a crash in the global value of the dollar, or both.

Further, in an ironic twist, Japan's continuing economic stagnation has begun to threaten the supremacy of Japanese manufacturing, with visible erosion in the country's competitiveness. Japanese companies have been unable to repeat in the personal computer and mobile phone segments their earlier successes with electronic calculators and VCRs. Since miniaturization has long been a notable strength of Japanese industry, Japan's stumbling in the transition from mainframes to PCs seems particularly ominous. The twin crunch of higher domestic costs and inroads from Korean and Taiwanese competitors copying Japanese manufacturing methods has forced Japanese companies to retreat. Even Japan's greatest success story in the past decade—mobile phones—turns out, on closer examination, to be less than total. Japan's biggest competitors are firms such as Nokia and Ericsson, operating in a Europe that has demonstrated a far greater willingness to fund and support national industrial champions than a United States with its often blind ideological hostility to anything that smacks of industrial policy. Japan's mobile phone makers, long coddled by Nippon Telephone and Telegraph—and the Ministry of Posts and Telecommunications (now part of the Ministry of Public Management, Home Affairs, Posts, and Telecommunications), which stands behind it—are fragmented; while they dominate the domestic market, they have not yet taken their place on the honor roll of Japanese industries that have conquered the world. A formidable line of predecessors in industries ranging from textiles through automobiles, machine tools, televisions, VCRs, and many others followed the characteristic Japanese path of first dominating domestic markets and then proceeding to extend their dominance to the entire world. But mobile phone makers have not yet joined their ranks. Indeed, it has been more than a decade since the Japanese have made a global conquest of an important industry.

Japan's large manufacturers have in the past decade chosen instead to concentrate on upstream components whose sales are assured rather than risk venturing into new product segments, leaving the battle for supremacy in new markets and new arenas to their Western competitors. And while Japanese companies continue to enjoy great strength, as noted, across a wide range of product segments, the success of the Koreans in such areas as D-RAM chips has shown that even a component-focused strategy is not without its pitfalls. Korean companies such as Samsung have taken a leaf from Japan's book, pouring vast amounts of investment into production facilities in order to capture market share. Caught between innovative Western firms that, as much as any firms can, control the direction of the most important new markets and new industries, and Korean, Chinese, and other Asian competitors with far lower costs, even Japan's dearly purchased and heretofore seemingly impregnable industrial supremacy is now threatened. Since that supremacy and the construction of a vast production apparatus to support it has long been the ultimate goal of Japanese economic policy, the end of that supremacy could finally force Japan's policy elite into the political and structural overhaul necessary to cope with a rapidly changing world.

## A Political Dilemma Masked as an Economic Problem

At the beginning of this chapter, we noted that mistaken assumptions were clouding proper analysis of Japan's dilemma. The biggest of those mistakes lies in the way the dilemma is understood. It is described as an economic problem, and to be sure it manifests itself in a variety of economic phenomena. Monetary and fiscal policies, corporate strategy and governance, structural drags on efficiency—all have accordingly drawn the attention of analysts. But Japan's dilemma is ultimately political. Japan's economic system is the product of political arrangements. Calls can be heard everywhere for reform—for more competition, for allowing markets to determine corporate control, for ending bureaucratic "interference." But as long as those exhortations ignore the underlying political reality, they are no more useful than utopian demands for world peace and universal prosperity that do not confront the roles of war and poverty in perpetuating existing power alignments.

Tokyo's policy regime today may seem to outsiders to be hopelessly malfunctioning and outdated. But it is not the outcome of a few recent cabinets trying to cling to power or of the jockeying among political parties to cultivate votes. Its roots lie far back in Japanese history, well before Japan's construction of the political facade of a constitutional democracy—one governed, with one brief hiatus since 1955, by the stable, conservative Liberal Democratic Party (LDP). That facade has been useful in providing Japan with an acceptable face to the outside world and in neutralizing any potential for disorder from leftist or other dissatisfied groups with the capacity to make trouble. But the facade is little more than a distraction in trying to get a handle on the reality of the policymaking that has now landed Japan in a trap whose grip seems even stronger, if—for the moment—less painful, than the notorious liquidity trap diagnosed in the 1930s as the cause of the Great Depression. To understand how Japan fell into this trap and how its jaws might conceivably be sprung, we must first turn to the deep-rooted political arrangements that determine policy.

# 2

# *The Preservation of Bureaucratic Power*

Power in Japan is masked. For upward of a thousand years now, the country's ruling elite has understood and employed the key to maintaining an unbroken hold on power: disguising and diffusing the sources of that power. The aristocratic families that dominated early Japan learned to ensnare the organs of government in labyrinthine marital alliances with emperors and ex-emperors. During the era of the shoguns, it was common to find chamberlains ruling through child shoguns who exercised "authority" in the name of cloistered and powerless "sovereigns." Today, shadowy rings of retired officials and Liberal Democratic Party puppet masters determine the tenure and staffing of senior bureaucratic and political positions. The Japanese elite has learned to deflect challenges to its control by making it impossible to determine precisely where that control originates or how it is administered.

That has become a fairly commonplace observation in discussions of the difficulties faced by Japanese politicians and voters in their attempts to exercise political control over the bureaucracy. But it also poses an unusual challenge to the policy analyst. Alex Kerr has noted that "a lack of reliable data is the single most significant difference between Japan's democracy and the democracies of the West."[1] Scholars of monetary policy in the United States or bank regulation in Britain, for example, can rely on a comprehensive written record of debates, legislative hearings, court cases, and memorandums. No such resource is available to the scholar or analyst seeking to understand the implementation of a Japanese policy regime designed to suppress the value of the yen. In fact, at the time of the regime's birth back in the early 1970s, attempts to discuss its merits were, as we shall see, deliberately suppressed by the Bank of Japan and the Ministry of Finance.

Journalists and external analysts are not the only ones who have difficulty obtaining accurate data on bureaucratic policymaking. Japanese politicians themselves cannot easily secure data from the bureaucrats who nominally work for them. Kan Naoto, now a major figure in Japan's leading opposition party, the Democratic Party of Japan, encountered bureaucratic stonewalling when he served in Hashimoto Ryutaro's coalition government as minister of health and welfare in 1996. Kan was attempting to get to the roots of the ministry's complicity in the distribution to Japanese hemophiliacs of untreated blood products that had infected scores of them with HIV some ten years earlier. As he explained in a book he later wrote about his experience as minister, bureaucrats revealed some of the relevant data to him under duress but told him that under no circumstances should he go public with it.[2] To the astonishment of observers, Kan ignored their advice, but the flow of information from the ministry ceased the moment he left office. And no one has been able to obtain any information on the subject since.

In order, therefore, to understand contemporary patterns of bureaucratic policymaking, we have had to discern precedent more on the basis of what was done than what was said; that, in turn, has required paying close attention to history. It is not our intention here to write a history of foreign exchange and monetary policy in Japan; it is to describe Japan's current policy trap. But because in Japan policymaking occurs without formal scrutiny of legislative mandate, executive implementation, and judicial review, we have had to rely heavily on the circumstantial evidence of history in understanding the decisionmaking of monetary authorities. The link between the American victory in the Spanish-American War and the Federal Reserve's monetary policy today is, for example, tenuous at best; conversely, Japan's policy response to the reparations paid by China in the wake of Japan's victory in the Sino-Japanese War of 1895 set a precedent of the utmost contemporary relevance. That precedent gives valuable insight into the conduct today of the Ministry of Finance as it tries to cope with the monetary effects of thirty years of accumulated current account surpluses. We accordingly intend to try our readers' patience with a rather detailed look at how Japan's governing bureaucracy adopted and refined over the past century a strategy that would bend monetary and foreign exchange policies to the service of bureaucratic power.

Indeed, it is the nature of that power—the extralegal power of the Japanese bureaucracy—that looms as perhaps the greatest conceptual block that Westerners face in grasping the full nature of policymaking in Japan. Coming from a world where institutions charged with the conduct of public policy derive their legitimacy from an explicit legal foundation, Western observers find it almost incomprehensible that policymaking bodies can function—and function brilliantly—on this kind of extralegal basis.[3]

## *The Japanese Government as Confederation*

But grasping the institutional reality of the Japanese system—unaccountable bureaucratic power without judicial or political oversight; the lack of any meaningful distinction between the public and private sectors—is necessary to understanding the formulation and execution of policy. This is particularly true in areas as complex as monetary and foreign exchange policies, with their central roles in the wider economy. Westerners are used to thinking, for example, of monetary policy as being driven by central banks that carefully attempt to determine the appropriate supply and price of money in order to meet market-driven demand. The demand for money itself is the end result of a myriad of interactions among financial institutions, corporations, and households responding to market signals. But banks in Japan are not independent profit-driven entities filling consumers' demand for funds by balancing risk and return. They are creatures of a bureaucracy that sets monetary goals to achieve bureaucratic imperatives: security, control, freedom of decisionmaking, and determination of economic outcomes. The banks serve to carry out those goals.

Japan's central government itself is little more than a weak confederation of ministries, each of which within its own bailiwick is essentially a sovereign entity. The control enjoyed by the governing institutions of the European Union (EU) over money and industrial standardization gives them more power over member countries such as France or Germany than the Japanese cabinet and Diet have over the Ministry of Finance and the Ministry of Construction (recently renamed the Ministry of Land, Infrastructure, and Transport—MLIT—following the absorption of the former Ministry of Transportation). Because each of those ministries oversees and represents segments of Japanese society that—unlike American states, Canadian provinces, or EU countries—are not demarcated by territory, observers frequently fail to grasp that Japan's governing setup resembles a federation such as the United States or Australia, although Japan is more properly termed a confederation because the central government has so little real power. Hirose Michisada, a political journalist and editor at the *Asahi Shimbun*, has described the Japanese governing setup as a federation of ministries, even citing a 1964 government report to support his contention.[4] Cabinet ministers up to and including the prime minister are completely dependent on the bureaucracy not just for policy decisions but also for electoral success; as Hirose describes, the bureaucracy assists the election campaigns of ministers who do what they are told. Hirose notes that the bureaucracy purchases political protection from the LDP with a flow of subsidies for LDP voters; those subsidies represent some 30 percent of the national budget.[5] Voters have no realistic present alternative to this system and have resigned themselves to the bureaucracy's de facto hijacking of Japan's constitution because, at least until recently, the system has delivered a rising level of economic prosperity.

To be sure, MOF, MITI (recently rechristened METI—Ministry of Economy, Trade, and Industry), and the other ministries theoretically derive their power from legislation, and administrative decisions are supposed to be consistent with the law. It is important to understand, however, that in reality Japan's bureaucratic mandarins enjoy almost unlimited freedom to interpret laws in whatever way they deem appropriate. Further, legislation itself is driven by bureaucratic initiative and typically enacted with little more than pro forma discussion in the Diet. Much policy "debate" consists of questions written by bureaucrats—although read aloud by Diet members—met with responses written by the same bureaucrats, albeit read aloud by different Diet members.[6] Meanwhile, neither the enactment nor the interpretation of legislation is subject to any meaningful judicial review.

The judiciary itself is part of the bureaucracy, and it respects the principle of noninterference in the internal affairs of the various ministries.

Provided that policymaking within a given ministry does not conflict with the policy agenda of any other ministry, it can pretty much do what it likes. Igarashi Takayoshi, a lawyer and prolific author, collaborated a few years ago with Ogawa Akio, a reporter for the *Asahi Shimbun*, on a book that discusses the overwhelming power that the bureaucracy enjoys over the formulation of national policy vis-à-vis the Diet, Japan's nominally preeminent legislature.[7] The Diet had been established in the prewar period under the Meiji constitution as part of an elaborate effort by Japan's real leaders to create the facade of a modern state. The Diet also helped give ordinary people the sense that they had a voice in politics, making it easier to govern them. But the Diet had no actual control or oversight of the bureaucracy; each ministry was theoretically responsible solely to the Emperor. The Emperor was not a despot but a divinity; therefore the Emperor was held to be infallible. Since each ministry went through the ritual of seeking imperial approval for its policies, ministerial decisions were likewise deemed infallible. During the buildup to World War II, there was some recognition that the weakness of the central government's institutions could give rise to endless ministerial conflicts (the most famous being the failure of the Imperial Army and the Imperial Navy—both ministries in the pre-1945 governments—to achieve any kind of strategic coordination) and the inability to set priorities. Attempts were made to strengthen the power of the cabinet and the prime minister.[8] But it could not be done; even in the face of defeat and the imminent destruction of Japan, no central decisionmaking organ could be imposed over the quarrelling ministries. The Imperial Army had dragged Japan into war essentially on its own initiative, without any central state apparatus that could call a halt to what amounted to national suicide.

## Bureaucratic Power and Japan's Ruling Elite

The status of bureaucrats vis-à-vis elected politicians and their freedom from judicial or political oversight may not on the surface seem to have a great deal to do with exchange rates and the money supply. But, in fact, grasping the nature of policymaking in Japan is essential to understanding the country's economic predicament. Alas, the existence of a postwar constitution modeled on the U.S. Constitution (and, indeed, largely written by

Americans) and the democratic facade it provides of a prime minister, a cabinet, and elections clouds proper analysis of Japanese political—and thus economic—reality. Readers of the day-to-day commentary on Japan in the international media would have a hard time understanding that the role of Japan's elected politicians in the formulation of policy scarcely extends beyond power broking or that the electorate has never had any real opportunity to choose among competing visions of Japan's future. Manifest and fundamental differences between Japan and the Western democracies are explained away with such mischievous terms as "consensus democracy" and irrelevant comparisons to French *dirigisme*, as if French voters had not on several occasions in the last century forced sharp changes in the country's direction and as if the supremacy of an elected president in the Fifth Republic over the French bureaucracy was not immediately obvious. And similarly, the notion that the endless jockeying for the upper hand among the semi-independent fiefdoms that comprise the inner core of Japan's power elite represents any kind of search for "consensus" simply gets in the way of understanding the world in which those who actually determine and carry out public policy in Japan operate.

Confronted with evidence of the myriad undemocratic and market-stifling features of Japanese economic and political life, many point to the survival in the postwar world of institutions that trace their roots far back before 1945. To be sure, the pervasive presence of those institutions is now much more widely understood than was true even ten years ago.[9] But that does not help in analyzing public policy in Japan unless one grasps how those prewar institutions themselves actually functioned. The underlying political purpose of both Japan's pre- and post-1945 regimes has been to protect the privileges and position of a ruling elite that is the institutional descendant of Japan's premodern ruling class. Today's powerholders are the direct heirs of their feudal predecessors, not so much through birth lines—although family plays a much larger role in the composition of Japan's governing elite than is usually recognized—as in the continuous monopoly they hold on both the first claim on the nation's economic resources and the political privilege of determining policy without accounting to outsiders.

The Meiji Restoration of 1868 did not represent the overturning of one class by another—the classical Marxist definition of revolution. If anything, it was a counterrevolution, as the most provincial and militarized elements of the ruling elite—distraught at the erosion of samurai privilege and what they deemed the pusillanimous response of the shogunate to the sudden appearance of demanding foreigners in Japanese waters—mounted a coup d'état. They succeeded in reversing the gradual, centuries-long shift of economic power away from the samurai and toward an Osaka-centered merchant class that in retrospect appears to have been a genuine bourgeoisie in embryo, with the result that the bourgeoisie was stillborn. While the feudal prerogatives of the samurai were ostensibly ended, merchants were bankrupted and ownership of the country's fledgling industries and banks was handed by the Meiji government largely to members of the former samurai class at what amounted to giveaway prices. Meanwhile, meaningless elections were instituted that gave ordinary citizens no real say in how they were governed.

While membership in the shogunal ruling class had been explicit—one was either born into a family that enjoyed feudal entitlements or not—and membership in its contemporary descendent is more fluid, the continuous transfer of power and privilege from one generation to another has never been seriously disrupted by either political upheaval or economic change. A handful of wealthy entrepreneurs such as Honda's Honda Soichiro or Sony's Morita Akio notwithstanding, no rising *class* grown rich on new technologies, no Japanese equivalent of Detroit or Silicon Valley has forced the Tokyo-centered elite to share either economic or political power. Membership in today's ruling elite comes not through the commercialization of important new technologies or the mobilization of disaffected voters, but through the gates of Japan's most prestigious universities—in particular, the law faculty of Tokyo University. And while admission to those universities is determined by examinations ostensibly open to all, passing the exams requires a sustained effort that to all intents and purposes can be mustered only by privileged families that understand how to prep their sons and have the resources to do it. (Girls can, and do, pass those examinations too, but women play at best a supporting role as wives and mothers within the highest circles of Japan's governing elite.)

The preservation of class privilege has guided Japan's policymaking since the late nineteenth century. At a minimum, that meant preserving national autonomy, which in turn required the forced industrialization of the Japanese economy in order to modernize and equip the Japanese military sufficiently to deter the threat of colonization by the Western powers.

Industrialization demanded the socialization of the masses of ordinary Japanese to meet the needs of industry and the military. After 1945, a ruling class that had nearly destroyed itself by its inability to bridle its own rogue elements managed to retain its grip on power by skillfully manipulating Occupation officials—most notably, General Douglas MacArthur—and by being willing to accept the de facto status of a protectorate in the global anticommunist alliance being built by the United States.[10] When the Occupation ended, Japan's power holders turned over control of the country's foreign policy and national security to Washington—or, more precisely, they tacitly agreed that they would not attempt to regain that control—in return for the implicit right to manage domestic affairs in a way that ran counter to the publicly trumpeted governing principles of the American-led alliance: democratic capitalism.

## Control of Dollar Earnings

The privilege of managing domestic affairs without American supervision did not, however, extend to controlling the country's export earnings. As we noted in the previous chapter, Japan has maintained what amounts to a dollar exchange standard since 1949, when the Japanese government regained the nominal right to dispose of its foreign currency earnings as it saw fit. Like virtually every other country in the noncommunist world, Japan initially chose to retain those earnings in dollars, the currency of the country that at the time accounted for nearly half the output of the planet. But with the relative decline of American economic preeminence over subsequent decades, Japan did not join other countries such as France in attempting to force the United States to preserve the purchasing power of the dollar or face the loss of the currency's hegemony over global finance. By the mid 1960s, France had begun to exercise its rights under the Bretton Woods system to begin moving its reserves from dollars to gold. Later Paris mounted a joint effort with other European governments to construct, with the euro, an alternative to the dollar in the global monetary order.

Japan never did anything like that; its control over its own foreign exchange earnings therefore has never really been tested. Several European nations had also accumulated substantial surpluses, but for the most part they did not leave their surpluses in dollars. Understanding that retaining their export earnings in dollars could give the United States a quasi-colonial leverage over them, they exercised their rights under the Bretton Woods system to convert their holdings into gold or, later, into their own currencies.

But when the United States severed the gold link in 1971, Japan—joined subsequently by the other economies of East Asia—continued to accept American paper in return for its exports. All the East Asian countries evidenced low absorption of imports (particularly finished consumer goods) and were to organize their economies around the rapid buildup of production capacity. One might even conclude that Japan and its East Asian neighbors have been allowed to run substantial surpluses with the United States precisely because they denominate the proceeds of those surpluses in U.S. dollars. Since the surpluses are kept within the American banking system— as is automatic if you denominate trade and investment earnings in dollars—the United States has done little more than mount ritual objections to East Asian trading practices.

Claims on another country denominated in the fiat currency of that country are, at least theoretically, subject to a number of different risks: devaluation, convertibility (the inability for whatever reason to convert the foreign currency into one's own), blocking (the deliberate suspension of an outflow of payments on debts denominated in the debtor's currency), and default. The risk of default is minimal since American debts are denominated in U.S. currency; the U.S. government can always simply print more of it. But Japan has endured a great decline in the value of its dollar holdings, both against the yen per se—the dollar today only buys a third as many yen as it did thirty years ago—and in general terms, because the purchasing power of the dollar is now one-sixth what it was in the mid 1960s. Further, as we noted in the previous chapter, most of Japan's dollar holdings cannot effectively be converted into yen since so few yen circulate outside Japan. And while it is not easy to imagine a scenario in which the United States would actually block repayment of American debts, a sudden panicked attempt by Japanese investors to repatriate their dollar holdings simultaneously might provoke the American authorities into at least a temporary suspension of payments.

Why would Japan expose itself to such risks without making any attempt to forestall them? The United States has had at best a sporadic record in reassuring foreign holders of dollars about those risks. In 1944, during the negotiations at the Bretton Woods resort that gave its name to the postwar monetary order, John Maynard Keynes—that order's principal architect—had tried to construct institutional arrangements that would require countries running current account surpluses as well as those running deficits to undertake policy adjustments to restore global equilibrium. He had been overruled by an American delegation that did not want to be stuck with the bill for the profligacy of others. But when the United States emerged twenty-five years later as the leading deficit country, it chose to break the Bretton Woods system rather than submit to the necessary policy discipline.

Thanks in large measure to Japan's unwillingness or inability to denominate its earnings in any currency other than dollars, however, the United States has escaped the discipline typically imposed willy-nilly on countries running large current account deficits: a forced slowdown in growth to bring those deficits back into balance. Japan's elite officials can presumably recite textbook explanations on the theoretical workings of today's floating rate system, but in practice they have acted as if they were willfully blind to its origins and logic. For the international division of labor implicit in floating rates, with foreign exchange markets theoretically serving as the principal mechanism to adjust international imbalances, presupposes that economies are organized around the concepts of efficiency and profitability. Such concepts have never taken root in Japan. The Japanese economy has been built on different principles: the maximization of production capacity and, by extension, external surpluses. Japan's tenacious resistance to the implications of an international monetary regime based on floating rates—its determination to resist any weakening of its ability to accumulate surpluses—was matched by the American need to finance a yawning gap between consumption and production with the export of paper dollars. The buildup of Japanese production capacity far beyond its domestic needs followed by copycat developments in neighboring economies stemmed directly from this subversion of the logic of floating rates.

The Japanese elite seems to view the twin imbalances of the global financial order—the Japanese surplus and the American deficit—as exclusively an American problem since it is the United States that runs the deficit. But it has turned out to be Japan's freedom of action that has been constrained, not America's; in the current global financial order, theory notwithstanding, the burden of adjusting to international payment imbalances has fallen not on the world's largest debtor but on its largest creditor. That was demonstrated as recently as July 23, 1997, when then Prime Minister Hashimoto

Ryutaro, presumably briefed by the MOF, mentioned at a symposium at Columbia University that unless Washington was forthcoming with help in stabilizing the yen/dollar rate, Japan might sell some of its vast holdings of U.S. Treasury securities.[11] The remarks produced a brief frisson in the markets, but they were soon shrugged off. Market players understood that Hashimoto was making an empty threat; Japan had accumulated such a huge position in dollars that any attempt to reduce that position would destroy its value, in the process further damaging Japanese exporters already hurting from the slowdown of the 1990s. Japan has endured the devaluation of the dollar without much to show for it; industrial production today is where it was ten years ago. To see why Japan's administrators would remain committed to such a seemingly fruitless policy requires us to probe its role in the preservation of bureaucratic power.

## The Supremacy of Administrative Law

Any external legal authority that could hold the institutions of the ruling elite accountable for their actions is obviously incompatible with the elite's monopoly of policy. Of course, Japan has laws and a legal apparatus of courts, police, and prosecutors. But the rule of law is applied selectively. The great majority of ordinary Japanese—like people anywhere—voluntarily comply with the law. In practical terms, however, they have no redress, no access to courts, when they themselves are subject to arbitrary exercises of power. That explains the mystifying spectacle—mystifying to foreigners, in any case—of groups of Japanese demonstrating for years and even decades against such high-handed bureaucratic actions as the expropriation of land in the late 1960s to build Narita Airport or the erection of hundreds of useless dams that have destroyed every last free-flowing river in the country. The Japanese people have essentially no recourse other than their ability to make endless, embarrassing noise. The ruling elite has systematically squelched the growth of any institutional setup, most notably a functioning legal system, that might allow ordinary people to hold their rulers to account.[12] The truncated legal system that does exist is effectively under the control of the General Secretariat of the Supreme Court, itself staffed by bureaucrats. Japan's power holders largely restrict judicial functions to the maintaining of order among the wider population.

It is helpful to keep in mind here the distinction between civil and administrative law. Japan abounds in administrative rulings, issued by each of the ministries respectively and backed by legislation written by the ministries' bureaucrats, albeit rubber-stamped in the Diet. Ordinary people and companies that depend on the ministries must obey those laws. But absent from the Japanese setup is civil law—a set of universal legal standards to which anyone can appeal that forms the basis of judgments that impartially bind every person and entity from the Imperial Household Agency and the Ministry of Finance down to the corner fruit shop owner and the sushi delivery boy. Within its area of competence, each ministry acts as a sovereign power, enacting, interpreting, and enforcing what amounts to administrative law, whether one calls it "administrative guidance" or regulation.

Thus the much-touted new "independence" of the Bank of Japan turns out, on closer inspection, to be exaggerated. The new law governing the BOJ, enacted in 1998, remains a piece of administrative law. The supposed independence of the BOJ cannot be tested in court. The law itself reveals that the BOJ budgets are still determined by the MOF.[13] Even Thomas Cargill and his coauthors, who seem in their recent book on Japanese monetary policy to accept at face value the claims of the BOJ's new independence, concede that "the Ministry of Finance may retain de facto approval power over the entire Bank of Japan budget."[14] Further, an examination of the laws governing the MOF and the newly established Financial Supervisory Agency (FSA) reveals clauses that directly contradict any assertion of the BOJ's independence.[15] Ikeda Hayato, prime minister in the early 1960s and author of the famous "income doubling plan," had written that the BOJ's function is to serve as an agent of the MOF, which in turn controls foreign exchange and monetary and fiscal policies in one cohesive system.[16] Nothing so far suggests that there has been any real change since Ikeda wrote his book. The real reason for the BOJ's supposed "independence" is to create a plausible scapegoat for the failure of monetary policy to spring Japan's policy trap, to shift blame away from the MOF, which cannot, in the Japanese system, acknowledge the possibility of error. Unlike the MOF, the BOJ is not a sovereign power; it is not part of the "sovereignty of the ministries" and can be instructed to fall on its institutional sword at the appropriate moment.

In Japan, civil law ends up playing little more than a ceremonial role whenever it conflicts with bureaucratic imperative. In 1996, for example, when the MOF needed to wind up the affairs of the seven leading housing loan companies, or *jusen*, which together had accumulated ¥6.4 trillion in uncollectable loans, the disposition of this largest series of financial failures in Japanese history was handled entirely by administrative procedures. MOF officials assumed that they were naturally free to determine how the various claims and obligations of the *jusen* were to be settled without considering the rules that ordinary citizens are expected to follow. No official disclosure of the results of the *jusen* failures has ever been made public, other than that ¥685 billion was allocated to agriculture cooperatives out of tax revenues to compensate them for their losses on loans they extended to the *jusen*. The courts were completely bypassed without any official explanation whatsoever. Since the *jusen* and their lenders had been performing economic functions assigned by bureaucratic fiat, all parties to the *jusen* failures assumed, evidently without even giving the matter a moment's consideration, that the legal procedures governing transactions among private parties were moot. We will discuss the *jusen* affairs in detail, but for now we note that they provide evidence, if any were needed, that Japan's bureaucratic elite holds itself above any notion of accountability to judicial institutions rooted in the rule of law.

The supremacy of what amounts to administrative law has its roots in the prewar Meiji system, in which military law and bureaucratic precedence provided the explicit legal foundations for governance. As Igarashi and Ogawa point out, Meiji administrative law survived the Occupation in unwritten form.[17] In the prewar period, law books featured not just general legal principles but also applications; postwar law books are generally written on a purely theoretical level and tend to lack any discussion of application.[18] But examination of actual bureaucratic practice demonstrates that the principles of the Meiji era continue to guide policy, not the idealistic notions found in Japan's postwar constitution. Bureaucrats act on the belief that qualified administrators should be free to determine policy in whatever manner they deem fit. Since this notion conflicts with the ostensible governing principles of postwar Japan—democracy and popular sovereignty—the bureaucracy no longer issues written regulations. Instead, in the postwar world, it has resorted to unwritten *gyosei shido*, literally administrative guidance, one reason that it is so difficult to analyze the policy process in Japan—it is deliberately not written down. *Gyosei shido* technically lacks the force of law, but in practice it is followed as if it did. The absence of legislation giving legal force to *gyosei shido* allows Japan to pose as a market democracy governed by the rule of law. In reality, Japan is largely administered in an extralegal manner without any basis in the constitution that supposedly forms the supreme law of the land.

Ministries continue to control policy and personnel at all levels, right up to the top policy positions, without legislative oversight or judicial review. Ministries display the natural tendency of bureaucracies anywhere to enhance their own power and reach, but in Japan they are subject to no restraint other than the ambitions of other ministries. As a result, meetings of the Japanese cabinet resemble ceremonial encounters among figurehead monarchs, which is why they typically last no more than twenty minutes. The meetings certainly do not serve to determine the relative importance of each ministry's agenda by any criterion of the national interest. To be sure, initiatives have risen from time to time to increase the number of appointments to top-level policymaking positions made by the Diet rather than the ministries themselves, but to date they have had no real impact on the ability of at least the more powerful ministries to set policy free of outside interference, despite the publicity given to recent name changes and the absorption of some of the weaker ministries by the stronger.

Meanwhile, the most important responsibility of the prime minister is the visible and well-timed resignation, even though he typically has little knowledge of and less input into the policies that may have brought on his downfall. A prime minister who knows his place and resigns at the proper moment to absorb resentment will be rewarded by the bureaucracy with lucrative construction spending or other subsidies that benefit his district. Mori Yoshiro, for example, who directly preceded Koizumi Junichiro as prime minister, was regarded both in and out of Japan as a buffoon, but that was largely an act. In fact, he is a canny politician and was actually very well suited to the role he was supposed to play. His pose of ignorance and "incompetence" served as a useful lightning rod for widespread fear at Japan's loss of direction and the palpable sense that the Japanese policy elite no longer knew what to do. His inevitable "fall" from "power" in April 2001 happened when exasperation reached a politically dangerous point, and it served to give the policy elite a brief breathing space. And in fact, as head of one of the LDP's major factions, he is at least as powerful now as he was while he was prime minister.

Similarly, the emergence of Koizumi Junichiro as prime minister in the wake of Mori's resignation convinced many that finally Japan had a prime minister with both the will and the ability to address Japan's myriad problems. Koizumi seemed to come out of nowhere when he defeated Hashimoto Ryutaro for the position of LDP president and thus prime minister. Koizumi's victory over a man deemed the establishment candidate and his immense initial popularity with the public gave the early days of his prime ministership an almost revolutionary aura. But whatever ideas Koizumi may have entertained about the need for reform, the institutional weakness of his office makes implemention of any reform program dependent on the approval and cooperation of a critical mass of bureaucrats and LDP leaders. Meanwhile, he provides a perfect foil if, as seems likely, the reform efforts fail and the grip of Japan's policy trap tightens further.

## Credit Flows and the Ministerial Balance of Power

The MOF typically is regarded as the most powerful of the ministries, and the MOF's reputation as first among equals derives from its central role in both raising money and distributing purchasing power. Its *shukei kyoku,* or budget bureau, enjoys the reputation of the most powerful bureau in the most powerful ministry; the bureau's directors usually go on to assume the post of MOF administrative vice minister (*jimu jikan*), widely seen as the single most influential position in the Japanese bureaucracy. The right to determine the distribution of the country's budget would seem naturally to be the base of the MOF's power were it not for the fact that the percentage of funds going to each of the other ministries in any given year never changes. For the secret of the MOF's power does not rest in its pro forma ability to grant or withhold rewards. Rather, it lies in the MOF's role as the ultimate guarantor of the bureaucracy's freedom from political interference. The pressure for political discussion over the allocation of money—the very stuff of democratic politics—does not arise in Japan because the MOF acts to maintain the existing financial balance of power among the various ministries. The national budget therefore has far less to do with the needs of the Japanese economy at any particular point in the business cycle than it does with the distribution of income: the reallocation of money from Japan's productive sectors to those essential to the perpetuation of the existing balance of power.

The harvesting of income from the productive sectors of society and the distribution of that income to the ruling elite and its dependents has its roots in Japan's feudal past. The shogunal bureaucracy mostly concerned itself with confiscating wealth generated by Japan's agricultural sector—held by economic thinkers in premodern Japan to be the sole source of genuine wealth—and distributing that wealth among the samurai class. The parameters have shifted from peasants in rice paddies and a parasitical urban warrior class on one hand to factory workers and a subsidy-dependent countryside on the other. But the essence of the system has remained intact. The bureaucracy still acts primarily to redistribute income from the productive sectors of society to the parasitical, thereby buying off groups—for example, farmers and other small landowners—that can disrupt social peace and threaten bureaucratic rule. Since the late nineteenth century, however, export-led manufacturing has replaced agriculture as the source of wealth. And it is factory workers, "salary men," and entrepreneurs rather than peasants whose earnings today are confiscated, through high and rigged prices for many essential consumer goods. Meanwhile, the contemporary beneficiaries of income distribution are primarily a parasitical network of well-to-do rural farmers and construction companies rather than a class of idle warriors.

Similarly, credit has replaced feudal-era units of rice production as the basis for reallocating purchasing power. Under explicit if unwritten bureaucratic directive, in the postwar era banks lent money to corporations far in excess of the needs of industry. The recipients could not turn the money down; instead, they had essentially no choice but to buy land and equities at prices far above those that any market-driven system would conceivably have generated. The farmers who sold the land realized steep capital gains and tended largely to keep the proceeds of their sales on deposit with banks, where they helped fund Japan's hoard of claims on foreign countries. Credit creation became income creation for farmers and the bloated construction sector, while the asset bubbles blown off by the process effectively reduced the purchasing power of the income left to Japan's ultimate wealth creators.[19] During the asset bubble of the late 1980s, for example, owning a home became an unrealizable dream for ordinary Japanese working families.

Through lending directed by the MOF and the BOJ, banks have played a crucial role in the income transfer arrangements of the modern era. Bank assets are tools of MOF's macroeconomic policy implementation, and like the retainers of old, who trailed behind Japan's ruling elite of daimyo and samurai wherever they went, banks follow the MOF's lead. Meanwhile, wages and other key prices in Japan are not set by market forces. Prices are manipulated to give more income to the farming and construction sectors. Land prices were used to transfer income from landless urban workers to farmers—many of whom did little actual farming and were in fact urban residents—and owners of small stores and factories, a phenomenon that became particularly notable in the 1980s.

Public construction spending likewise is used to allocate money and income to favored construction firms and their owners, who do not actually do much work but put the funds they receive on deposit. Japan's mountains, for example, are honeycombed with tunnels, many—even most—of which are unnecessary because they do no more than save a handful of cars a few minutes of driving. When tunnels are built, the orders are divided among several local construction firms, but those firms typically lack the ability to do the work specified. They "upcontract" (*uenage*) or "toss on" (*marunage*) business to firms that can actually complete the tunnels. Some of the middlemen are local firms with strong Liberal Democratic Party connections; others are agencies tied to particular ministries, such as the New Development Materials Company, which is affiliated with the Ministry of Public Management, Home Affairs, Posts, and Telecommunications (formerly the Ministry of Posts and Telecommunications). Any materials ordered in the construction of a new post office must go through this agency, which "simply channels orders to the suppliers that the builder would have used anyway."[20] In any case, the entities rake off money without sweat, like their samurai predecessors. The *Yomiuri Shimbun* ran a report of a recent example of this practice. The winning bid on a tunnel construction project in Ehime Prefecture was submitted by a local construction company, Hotta Kensetsu, for ¥1.9 billion. The work was upcontracted at ¥1.64 billion to another local firm, which then "tossed on" the project to a large nationwide construction firm that could actually complete the work for ¥1.26 billion. Hotta Kensetsu is owned by an LDP Diet member and the firm received ¥380 million simply to send an engineer to the tunnel site to "supervise" the project.[21] The incident reported in the *Yomiuri* was exceptional only in that it saw the light of day; the press does not report most such incidents.

Indeed, LDP politicians serve primarily as the organized voice of income receivers and carry out the final disposition of money collected and allocated by the bureaucracy—a vote for the LDP in a particular district means a vote for more public spending in that district. Japan theoretically has a representative democracy, but with the failure to reallocate representation to reflect demographic shifts in the past half-century, the votes of up to five wealth producers in Osaka or Tokyo are needed to outweigh that of one wealth consumer in the countryside.[22] Because the bureaucracy is in charge of allocating income and wealth, the fundamentals of economic policy are rarely discussed openly in the Diet.

Japan's administrative system thus functions to allocate money without cause and without accountability. Growing up in such a world, few Japanese—particularly in policy or political circles—can understand or accept the notion of an invisible hand producing desirable economic outcomes guided only by the individual decisions of millions of consumers and producers. It is accordingly not possible in Japan to separate economic analysis or forecasting from a review of bureaucratic policy. The notion that an economy can run free of bureaucratic oversight has never really dawned on power holders in Japan. Talk of an end to bureaucratic power therefore seems completely irresponsible, equivalent to talk of economic ruin. No alternative to bureaucratic rule, whether market- or voter-driven, has ever been taken seriously.

Which does not mean that the bureaucracy always speaks with one voice. Ministries can and do compete among themselves, but such competition is never allowed to reach the point that it threatens the stability of bureaucratic rule. The Ministry of Agriculture, Forestry, and Fisheries (MAFF) and the MLIT often build two parallel roads even though the region may not need two roads. Without a disinterested means of deciding on one instead of the other and with separate sets of constituencies and dependents each ministry must satisfy, it is far easier for the ministries to build two roads than engage in a serious dispute. For a dispute could threaten their mutual interest in a system that preserves mutual noninterference in and control over their respective bailiwicks. Besides, roads are constructed not to serve the people who will use them but to serve construction companies and their employees, who vote for the LDP and thus, by extension, the perpetuation of the Japanese system.

## *The Protection of Protégés*

As part of the de facto sovereignty of the ministries, each ministry is expected to control and underwrite the viability of its protégés. Banks in Japan, for example, owe their existence not to legal charters granted by legally constituted regulatory entities, but to licenses granted by the MOF or, in recent years, by the Financial Supervisory Agency, which ostensibly was set up to curb the power of the MOF. But the FSA is quite obviously a MOF offshoot; widely trumpeted realignments such as this should be taken with a very large helping of salt. If dramatic postwar reforms did not change actual bureaucratic practice, it is silly to expect recent label changes, institutional offshoots, and modest personnel shifts among the various ministries to be much more than public relations exercises. And as Diet member Shiozaki Yasuhisa has noted in an article calling for the establishment of a U.S.-type securities and exchange commission, "By and large, the structure of financial administration has reverted to the old '*okura-sho*' [the pre-reform Japanese name for the MOF] style. Most of the administrative staffers [of the FSA] have been transferred from the MOF."[23] Meanwhile, the banks licensed by the MOF and "supervised" by the FSA are ultimately part of the MOF/FSA bailiwick and are subject not to laws that apply impartially to all but rather to administrative fiat.

Further, no identifiable distinction can be found between a "private sector" composed of financial institutions operating in response to market forces and within a transparent legal framework on one hand and a "public sector" of central banks and finance ministries charged with monetary policy and regulatory functions on the other. Indeed, using the very terms "private" and "public" to distinguish sectors in Japan is problematic because they imply the existence of the institutions that in the West accompany the division of the two sectors—a functioning legal system, for example, to which private sector institutions can appeal.

The banking system in Japan is a case in point. Since 1927, banks have essentially been creatures of the MOF and have existed to carry out MOF policies. Retired MOF officials pepper the senior executive ranks of Japan's financial institutions.[24] This phenomenon of *amakudari* (literally, "descent from heaven"), whereby retired bureaucrats take up positions on the boards of the firms they used to supervise while retired executives in those firms go on to occupy positions in the firms' subsidiaries and affiliates, is now rather well known. What may be less well known, however, is that the personnel department of the ministry—not of the bank or company where the retiree ostensibly works—still manages the affairs of the retiree, thereby guaranteeing that in any potential conflict of interest, the retiree will put the ministry's interest first.

Banks have no legal recourse in civil law against MOF decisions, and MOF and FSA officials can at will deprive them of their privileges—and even shut them down or order them to merge with each other. Nor are such decisions made by any identifiable set of objective criteria. Banking authorities in many countries will, for example, act to prop up an institution whose lending and payments infrastructure plays an indispensable role in a regional economy. Yet the MOF allowed the Hokkaido Takushoku Bank ("Takugin," as it was known by its Japanese acronym) to fail. Takugin played just such a role in Japan's northernmost island of Hokkaido, and its collapse has brought regional depression in its wake. By Western standards of prudential accounting, Takugin was undoubtedly a failing institution, but that is true of virtually all major Japanese banks. It has never been publicly revealed why Takugin was allowed to fail while others continue to be propped up.

Meanwhile, the wave of mergers that has swept over the Japanese banking sector in the past decade may have been driven by the same underlying forces, information technology and computerization, that have given rise to comparable mergers in the United States and Europe. But unlike in the United States, in Japan the decisionmakers in those deals were not easily identifiable shareholders, market players, and boards of directors. The mergers were decided behind closed doors by unidentified officials acting in response to bureaucratic rather than market pressure and with the close knowledge and support of the MOF, which would be expected to underwrite the viability of the newly merged entities. The attempted merger of the Kita Nihon, Shokusan, and Tokuyo banks in 1994 is a case in point. Executives of Tokuyo discovered that the MOF had plans to merge them when they read about it in the newspapers.[25]

Foreigners seeing opportunity in the restructuring of the Japanese banking industry can be rudely surprised by the extralegal nature of the "guidance" administered by Japan's banking authorities. An example is the American group Ripplewood Holdings, which in 2000 purchased the Long-Term Credit Bank of Japan (LTCB) from the Japanese government, which had nationalized it after its collapse. The bank, rechristened Shinsei ("rebirth") Bank, has been the recipient of unwanted "guidance" from the FSA. In most countries, regulators might advise bankers to apply stringent lending standards. But the FSA has been pressuring the bank to do just the reverse—to keep the funds flowing to borrowers the bank's own credit department regards as dodgy. The FSA commissioner is quoted as having told Shinsei's CEO that "Shinsei should behave in line with other Japanese banks," referring to Shinsei's refusal to roll over loans to four well-connected firms, and threatening that "Shinsei should be concerned about its reputation risk, as anything can happen down the road."[26] Shinsei's powerful connections in the United States may give it some immunity to this kind of pressure (among its advisers are Paul Volcker, former chairman of the Federal Reserve, and Vernon Jordan, a managing director of Lazard Freres and a leading figure in the Democratic Party). But the incident served to remind the global investment community that banking in Japan does not conform to Western practice. Banks have been and are subject to extralegal "guidance"or interference by bureaucrats at any time on any matter, and most have no choice but to comply. The notion that a bank could bring suit and defend itself in court from the kind of pressure the FSA has been applying to Shinsei is simply unthinkable in Japan.

Meanwhile, corporate management in Japan more closely resembles the management of a factory in the West than it does the management of a major Western company. A Western company must constantly fret over access to credit, the threat of takeover, the pleasing of shareholders, and the health of markets for its financing, supplies, and products. In Japan, all those concerns are socialized—ultimately they are the responsibility of the major ministries and the vast unofficial business bureaucracies such as the Keidanren (Federation of Economic Organizations). An individual company in Japan, like a factory in the West, is expected to produce as much as it can of a product of as high a quality as it can manage at as low a cost as possible. Sales, strategy, financing, and market risks are ultimately somebody else's responsibility.

Economic activities carried out by banks and companies protected and fostered by the ministries are, in practice, subject only to administrative, not civil, law. The public prosecutor will not initiate legal proceedings against ministry officials or the protégés of a ministry without the tacit approval of that ministry, notwithstanding the theatrical productions periodically staged for Japanese television of teams of prosecutors descending on ministries caught up in one or another "scandal." Such dramas are usually scripted down to the last detail, with the purported offenders in the bureaucratic ranks quietly reassigned to ministry affiliates after media attention has shifted elsewhere and journalists and prosecutors have abandoned their assigned poses.

Periodic displays of prosecutorial zeal notwithstanding, outside investors cannot sue managers for fiduciary negligence unless the MOF and the other economic ministries give the green light. Victims of corporate malpractice cannot expect legal redress and can hope to obtain satisfaction only if a corporation steps on so many toes that the miscreant provokes one of the "scandals" that periodically blow through Japan, when it suddenly becomes open season on a previously untouchable entity. We will return to the crucial role scandals play in the Japanese political and economic order, but for now it is sufficient to note that the sheer inadequacy of Japan's legal infrastructure renders courts impractical for settling economic disputes. Such disputes among large players are resolved away from public scrutiny by the relevant bureaucracies; smaller fry rely on intimidation and frequently employ criminal organizations to recover lost funds. "Private out-of-court settlement of business failure is the dominant practice in Japan," write two scholars of Japan's bankruptcy procedures, who go on to refer to the "pervasive role that organized crime plays in the handling of corporate financial distress in Japan."[27]

With an economic system that lacks an adequate framework of legal institutions and market forces that have been deliberately enfeebled, bureaucratic imperative determines the winners and losers, the successful and the less successful, in economic competition. The major Japanese ministries and other bureaucracies that dominate Japanese economic life—the large corporate and banking clusters, the ostensibly "private sector" or *zaikai* bureaucracies such as the Keidanren, and the myriad of industrial associations that serve to set prices and other competitive conditions within each industry—operate in a manner familiar to students of bureaucracy anywhere: they constantly attempt to expand their influence and area of control. The only real check on bureaucratic power in Japan is other bureaucracies.

Ostensibly private sector institutions in Japan are almost always locked into relations with other entities that are more feudal than contractual in character. A large company or bank does business under the protection of a major ministry. It complies with ministerial "guidance" while relying on the ministry to ensure its continued viability. In turn, the major company controls what its principal subsidiaries and suppliers do (even when the pro forma equity stake may be rather small), and it is expected to protect them. Such relations extend down into the second and third tier of the Japanese economy.

To retain and expand its influence, a ministry or other major bureaucratic organization must demonstrate that it can protect its protégés; in Japan, the inability to do that is the clearest sign of trouble. Japanese insiders understood that Nippon Credit Bank (NCB) had been fatally weakened when its affiliate Crown Leasing collapsed. And in turn, NCB's failure—coupled with those of LTCB, Takugin, and Yamaichi Securities—led directly to open season on the Ministry of Finance in the media and among public prosecutors. Contrary to the impression given in the Western press, the MOF's troubles did not spell the end of its sway over Japanese economic life and its position of primacy among the ministries. If anything, in fact, its relative power has increased as its dependents—which include all of Japan's financial institutions as well as every sector of the economy that depends on the flow of public money—now understand acutely that their continued viability depends more than ever, in this era of straitened economic circumstances, on the MOF. But the MOF's inability to live up to the tacit guarantee that it had extended to all institutions under its purview led its legion of resentful enemies to crawl out of the woodwork, as it were, and indulge in a spasm of MOF-bashing.

Few bureaucratic entities in Japan, however, can boast the resilience and sheer reach of the MOF. In the end, the free-for-all that annoyed and troubled the MOF for some months in 1999 resulted in little more than the temporary derailing of some individual careers; the intense pressure to reduce the MOF's sway over Japanese economic life was ultimately deflected by its allies and dependents in the LDP and the business community. As we noted above, the ostensibly independent FSA, set up to relieve the MOF of key functions, is now widely understood to be an institutional outgrowth of the MOF. But no other entity, with the exception of the Imperial Household, enjoys the kind of insulation that protects the MOF from the consequences of the policy trap that it helped bring about. The characteristic Japanese free-for-all—spates of indignant articles in the press, teams of public prosecutors rounding up "evidence" from hapless bureaucrats or businessmen, press conferences where contrite leaders bow deeply, resignations by figure-head CEOs or ministers—can, when directed at an institution with less heft than the MOF, prove fatal. And the usual signal for the onset of a free-for-all—as in the case of the major bank failures—is the collapse of protégés.

A case in point is the most spectacular of recent bankruptcies—that of the Sogo department store, which ended up contributing to the loss of independence by its "main bank," the Industrial Bank of Japan (IBJ). Not only had IBJ provided working capital financing and organized syndicates of other lenders to finance new stores for Sogo, but Sogo's president was an IBJ "graduate." IBJ president Nishimura Masao testified before the Diet that IBJ had known since 1994 that Sogo was insolvent but continued to prop the company up. Sogo was so closely identified with IBJ that not doing so would have been tantamount to a public admission that IBJ itself was in trouble, and that is a major reason why IBJ continued to pour money down the black hole of Sogo's balance sheets. Protégés in Japan are not expected to act as if they might be at risk. Now IBJ itself—long regarded as Japan's premiere financial institution—is being folded into the new Mizuho Group, along with the Dai-Ichi Kangyo Bank and the Fuji Bank.

Japanese organizations typically will do everything in their power to pro-tect their protégés and will allow them to fail only when all other measures have been exhausted. The remarkable feature of the Sogo case was not that for years IBJ bailed out a company that was beyond rescue, but that the bankruptcy happened after all. For both Sogo and IBJ had so many power-ful connections that until the last minute it appeared that Sogo would in fact be rescued with injections of what amounted to public funds. It was deemed so remarkable in Japan that the bankruptcy in fact proceeded that on the morning after the announcement, the *Asahi Shimbun*—Japan's premiere general circulation newspaper—ran an enormous black-bordered headline of the type normally reserved for declarations of war or earthquakes that lay waste to whole cities.

## The "Sovereignty of the Ministries" and the Current Account

By now, the significance for macroeconomic policy should be obvious. It is extraordinarily difficult in Japan to retire production capacity because it involves the open admission of failure, the political implications of which can be traumatic. Mothballing a factory, not to mention firing people or going bankrupt, puts not only the viability of the company involved in doubt but also that of the ministry, bank, or larger company charged with its protection. The "creative destruction" that economist Joseph Schumpeter discussed as the sine qua non of capitalist transformation thus happens in Japan in only a highly attenuated form, if at all. Neither the tangible capacity of production facilities nor the intangible capacity of companies and employees can easily be shut down. Nothing resembling the American mergers and acquisitions market exists. Except in very rare cases, companies with low or nonexistent profitability cannot be taken over by outsiders or have their people fired and poorly performing business units cannot be shut down or spun off. Nor can firms on their own reduce employment except through gradual attrition; the protection of protégés very much includes the protection of core male employees.

That is particularly true in manufacturing. Manufacturing capacity continues to be treated as the seed corn of Japan's future prosperity, and shutting down manufacturing capacity remains almost unthinkable, which is why bankruptcy rates among manufacturers are so much lower than among other businesses (see figure 2-1). Despite Japan's straitened economic circumstances, it is still essentially impossible to drive manufacturers with elite connections into bankruptcy. They will be sustained by their banks and the banks in turn supported by the Ministry of Finance: the Japanese term is *gososendan*, or convoy, referring to a convoy of companies protected by a bank or a convoy of banks guarded by the MOF. The banks and trading companies (the *sogo shosha*, as they are known in Japan) that provide such a high percentage of working capital finance in Japan informally divide their borrowers into two groups: those sufficiently protected in the Japanese system to make bankruptcy unthinkable (the term used is *yoshingendo shoryaku saki* or, literally, "entities outside credit limits"), and other firms. Only in the world of small entrepreneurs, third- and fourth-tier subcontractors, and single proprietorships that serve as the shock absorbers for the larger firms has bankruptcy been a common phenomenon.

And what is true for individual companies is naturally true for whole industries. The notion common to development economics of a nation marching steadily into higher and higher value-added industries as the country accumulates capital and know-how only captures half the picture in Japan. For while over the past half-century Japan has, to be sure, steadily added progressively more technologically sophisticated industries to its eco-

**Figure 2-1.** *Total Liabilities of Japanese Companies in Bankruptcy, Manufacturing versus Nonmanufacturing Sectors*

Yen, trillion

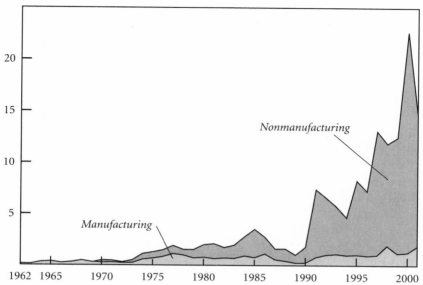

Sources: *Monthly and Annual Report,* Tokyo Shoko Research. Calculated, arranged, and estimated by Mikuni & Co. © 2002 Mikuni & Co., Ltd.

nomic base, it has not exited older industries or turned them over to other countries. The Japanese economy resembles a palimpsest continuously being written over—peering through the latest additions reveals layers of earlier writing. Still functioning beneath the turn-of-the-millennium economy of cellular phones and advanced materials is an early 1980s economy of commodity-type semiconductors and VCRs, a 1970s economy of automobiles and machine tools, a 1960s economy of shipbuilding and rolled steel, and a 1950s economy of textiles. In the countryside, one can go back farther still and find agricultural plots of a size suitable only for eighteenth-century production techniques and cottage craft industries still operating the way they did in medieval times. Once an industry is established in Japan, once the network of suppliers and factories that sustain the industry is in place, it is never abandoned. Even the forced shutdown of Japan's collieries in the late 1950s, often cited as an example of MITI's sway over the Japanese economy, was not total. Coal mines remained in production for decades, subsidized by utilities with payments that were far in excess of world market prices. At worst, Japanese companies under extreme cost pressure will transfer production abroad to facilities they themselves own. The notion that Japan should go back to depending on foreigners on any significant scale for a product that the country had learned to make for itself flies in the face of what the Japanese call common sense.

True, the huge price gaps between many Japanese and foreign-made goods have, over the past decade, finally brought a surge of imports into Japan in a number of product segments, and we will discuss its very great significance. But for the time being, we will note that imports typically wash away the dikes of cartels and corporate ties that protect a given Japanese product segment only when the Japanese product is orders of magnitude more expensive than its foreign counterpart. And even then, Japanese manufacturers are usually kept alive by transfusions of bank credit and subsidies arranged by the bureaucracy, which is why executives in more successful firms are known to grumble that they are competing against banks. Figure 2-2, showing the declining ratio over time of sales turnover to fixed assets over the entire universe of Japanese corporations (excluding financial institutions), demonstrates that production capacity, once in place, becomes what amounts to a permanent part of the Japanese economic base.

And that production capacity is constantly being expanded. Since the early Meiji period, Japan's ruling elite has had two overriding goals for economic policy: to make Japan's military prowess and industrial infrastructure equal to that of the Western powers and to finance the economic transformation involved without relying on foreign capital. And while the emphasis on military prowess per se was, for the time being, pushed aside in 1945, the drive for industrial supremacy never slackened, necessitating, of course, constant additions to the nation's productive base.

A structural current account surplus is the inevitable outcome in an economy whose driving force is the constant expansion of production capacity without regard for profits, capacity made possible by financial, tax, and compensation systems designed to pump out limitless savings without regard for return. And when no mechanism exists to phase out profitless capacity, when the retention of internationally uncompetitive industries such as agriculture and pharmaceuticals forms an indispensable part of the

**Figure 2-2.** *Ratio of Sales to Net Property, Plant and Equipment* [a]

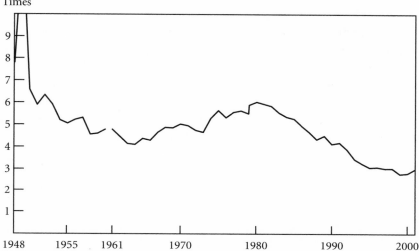

Times

Sources: *Financial Statements Statistics of Corporations by Industry,* Ministry of Finance. Calculated, arranged, and estimated by Mikuni & Co. © 2002 Mikuni & Co., Ltd.

a. All industries, excluding financial institutions. In 1949 the ratio soared to 13.6 times. The period 1948–59 shows the calendar year; 1960–2001 shows the fiscal year ending March 31 of the subsequent year.

political stability that undergirds Japanese economic life, it should come as no surprise that the current account surplus has expanded to historically unprecedented levels. For businesses that can be and are run without regard for profits, that churn out production regardless of market demand, will flood international markets with goods priced at whatever it takes to move them, not to cover costs and generate profits. That predilection, when combined with a financial system that enables Japanese corporate managers to make investment decisions as if the cost and availability of capital hardly mattered, results in a structural current account surplus. With the purposeful suppression of market forces that would otherwise bring exports and imports into some balance, the current account surplus will probably keep expanding until the world collectively cannot run the compensating deficits that as a matter of simple arithmetic must exist. Or else until the surplus buries the Japanese economy under an avalanche of deflationary dollar claims that can neither be exchanged nor redeemed. For the goal of Japan's modern economic policy since it began in the 1870s has, in essence, been to achieve a current account surplus. And a national policy to grow wealthy not in order to buy comfort for a population but to accumulate claims on foreign countries—claims that can never realistically be exercised—is a contemporary version of mercantilism.

But a huge difference exists between contemporary Japan and the classically mercantilist regime of Colbert and Richelieu. The latter sought to build up a treasure chest in the universal currency of gold. Japan overwhelmingly denominates its claims on foreigners in the fiat currency of the world's leading net debtor nation. How this situation came to pass and what it means for the economic future of Japan and the world will occupy our attention for the rest of this book.

# 3

# *Monetary Policy and Mercantilism*

I n the late 1990s, Japan's financial authorities found themselves the audience at a concert of advice given by a worldwide chorus of economists, pundits, and central bankers. Instructing Japanese officials on how they should run their country is not, of course, a new phenomenon; it has been a favorite sport among a certain class of *gaijin* at least since the days of Commodore Perry. And the onset of the country's long and seemingly intractable economic malaise a decade earlier had seen fresh waves of foreign exhortations as the Japanese were scolded for their failure to clean up the "bad loan problem," retire excess capacity, give free rein to market forces, and so forth. But the advice that emerged in the late 1990s from such eminent economists as Paul Krugman had a new twist to it. The underlying analysis went something like this: the Japanese government's repeated doses of fiscal stimulus had failed to do anything more than prevent the economy from tipping over into a depression. Structural reforms—while perhaps ultimately necessary—had, for the time being, become part of the problem. Widespread talk of corporate restructuring and

**Figure 3-1.** *Household Savings as a Percentage of Disposable Income*[a]

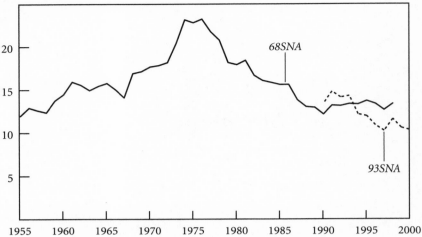

Percentage

Source: *Annual Report on National Accounts*, Cabinet Office. Calculated, arranged, and estimated by Mikuni & Co. © 2002 Mikuni & Co., Ltd.

a. 68SNA and 93SNA refer to System of National Accounts with base years 1968 and 1993, respectively.

the end of lifetime employment had generated understandable fears among Japanese households of loss of jobs and income. The result: Japan's households were spending as little and saving as much as ever—precisely the opposite of what the economy needed.

As figure 3-1 demonstrates, after declining from their peak in the mid 1970s, savings ratios stabilized somewhat late in the 1980s and have remained roughly constant ever since, despite the aging of Japan's population. Under ordinary circumstances, a population with Japan's demographic profile would see savings rates fall as retired people draw down cash to finance living costs. But scared by the relentless bad news about the economy, Japanese households have continued to squirrel away money—a problem for an economy that suffers from such anemic demand. The new thinking from abroad therefore saw monetary policy as the only solution to Japan's problems: the authorities needed to flood the economy with cheap money, inducing banks to lend, businesses to invest, and consumers to spend. Krugman recommended that the Bank of Japan deliberately create inflationary expectations, thereby forcing households to transform their liquid assets into real goods or see the value of those assets melt down.[1] Adam Posen went so far as to call for an explicit 3 percent annual inflation target.[2] That policy prescription seemed so obvious to those urging it that they could ascribe Tokyo's failure to take their advice only to the stubbornness of the Bank of Japan's leaders, who they assumed were determined to hang on to their much touted new independence and wedded to the stubborn, retrograde view that inflation was always and everywhere public enemy number one.

But much of their advice rested on the assumption that Japan's monetary authorities in the MOF and the BOJ had not in fact already tried it, that they had not for some years been deliberately attempting to inflate Japan's way out of its problems. We contend that the authorities have been doing precisely that—attempting to pump up nominal GDP (real GDP plus the inflation rate) by whatever means they can. They have not been successful, but they have tried. But alas for these attempts, structural elements that historically imparted an inflationary bias to the Japanese economy now work to lock in deflation. Those elements include highly leveraged financial institutions and corporations, lock-step wage increases, a system of taxation that encourages households to sell land and equity while inducing corporations to buy and hold those assets, industrial associations that suppress price competition, and a fully intermediated financial system. Inflation cannot, in current circumstances, be easily sparked without fundamental structural overhaul. Japan's authorities may have hesitated to take the final step recommended by so many foreign economists—flooding the economy with money by having the MOF issue bonds and the BOJ buy them—precisely because they have good reason to fear that the measures would not generate the inflation necessary to lift nominal GDP. And their armory of policy tools would then stand revealed as empty.

To see why the recommended policy steps could very well backfire, to grasp the policy dilemma that faces Japan's monetary officials, observers need to remind themselves that the Japanese authorities go about creating money rather differently from their counterparts in the West, particularly in the United States. Of course, it is widely understood that Japan's authorities rely much more heavily on bank loans than on open market operations to get money out into the economy than does the Federal Reserve. The issue is more complex, however, than simply choosing between policy tools. In the West, government bonds typically end up being purchased by final investors, including individuals. When central banks in Western countries buy bonds from the market, they increase purchasing power by putting money into the hands of households. But in Japan, some four-fifths of all bonds are held in the accounts of deposit-taking institutions. Purchasing power has thus *already* been transmitted to households; buying more bonds from banks, in the absence of other measures, will not serve to increase it. There really is no bond market per se independent of the banking system, and banks are in fact lending to the government through their purchases of JGBs.

## The Japanese Banking System

To grasp how the BOJ supplies the Japanese economy with money, we need to review in the context of overall policy goals several features of Japan's banking system as it evolved in the postwar era. Those features are, of course, well known to those with even the most superficial acquaintance with Japanese finance. But often their significance for monetary policy is overlooked.

The first feature is the separation until very recently of Japan's banks into classes: city bank, long-term credit bank, trust bank, local bank, and credit association. The classes were differentiated by their funding powers, type of lending, geographic spread, and customer base. But what really mattered— especially in the realm of monetary policy—was whether a given bank was more a generator or a collector of deposits. That may sound puzzling because by definition what a bank does is assemble money—that is, collect deposits—and then lend it. And many of Japan's banks—particularly the *chiho ginko* (local banks) and their smaller brethren among the *shinyo kinko*, *shinyo kumi-ai* (types of credit association), and the like— did just that. They collected deposits and lent out the proceeds. The larger, more prominent banks did this too, of course, but their real significance extended beyond the role of simple deposit collector. For they actively generated— one might even say "created"—deposits.

What does it mean for a bank to generate or create deposits? Is it not in the real world of production and trade that deposit creation is said to take place? Of course, whenever a bank lends money, by simply entering the loan on its books the bank automatically creates a countervailing deposit by crediting funds to the account of the borrower. The bank has a loan outstanding, while the company borrowing now has money on deposit at the bank. Deposits will flow out into other banks as the company uses the money it has borrowed to pay the workers and suppliers needed in the production process. Those banks then can use those deposits to make new loans. Each time the money is redeposited and as long as the money stays within the banking system, banks can make yet more loans funded by the new deposits. This "multiplier" phenomenon is a commonplace of monetary economics familiar everywhere.

In the West, this cycle of credit creation ends when the original loan is paid back out of the cash from the sale of the finished goods financed at some point by the loan. The level of deposits thus generally tracks the level of economic activity. Meanwhile, the bond issues and other long-term vehicles that finance capital investments are expected to be retired over the course of several years by the cash flow generated from those investments. But things have not necessarily worked that way in Japan. Until very recently Japanese banks typically did not plan for their loans to be retired; they provided what amounted to evergreen credit that was rarely extinguished, credit that financed both the inventory cycle and the great majority of capital investments undertaken by Japanese corporations. Only in the last few years have the banks been forced to demand repayment, a matter we will take up in considerable detail. Through most of the postwar period, by lending without expectation of being repaid, the banks created deposits and thus income for deposit holders without any causal connection with the real economy of production and trade. Profitability—the capacity of a company to generate the cash necessary to service and repay loans—did not, in the Japanese economy, determine creditworthiness. Instead, the banks allocated credit—literally creating deposits in the accounts of favored entities—according to other criteria.

Positioned at the center of galaxies of manufacturing and trading firms to which they were linked by complex networks of both cross-shareholdings and other ties, Japan's banks functioned as a combination of venture capitalist and investment, merchant, and commercial banker to Japanese industry. That is to say that they provided seed money for new businesses (venture capital); financed plant and equipment and other big-ticket projects with long pay-back horizons (investment banking); took what amounted to equity stakes in companies, financing every aspect of corporate activity (merchant banking); and provided the day-to-day financing of production and trade (commercial banking). These financing functions—functions that are spread among several classes of institutions in at least the United States and Britain, if not France and Germany—were all performed by the same group of banks in Japan. Those banks provided the overwhelming preponderance of external finance (that is, financing above and beyond retained earnings) of whatever form to Japanese corporations. Indeed, until the mid 1980s, when the Tokyo stock market began to play a significant role in corporate finance after a thirty-five-year hiatus, banks provided virtually all of it.[3] If the financing did not take the form of loans, then it took the form of the bonds and equity issued by corporations and bought mostly by the banks, thus ending up also as deposits. In fact, virtually all financing in Japan takes the form, at one point or another, of bank deposits.

At the top of the roster of prominent institutions central to Japanese finance stood the leading "city" banks (*toshi ginko*), as they were known in Japan —Mitsubishi, Sumitomo, Mitsui, Fuji, Sanwa, Dai-Ichi Kangyo— with their central role in deposit creation. But the roster also included the long-term banks (IBJ, LTCB, and NCB); the bigger trust banks (Mitsubishi Trust and Sumitomo Trust in particular); specialized banks such as the Bank of Tokyo; and the very top three or four local banks (for example, the Bank of Yokohama).

The involvement by Japanese banks in every aspect of their customers' businesses has properly drawn attention from scholars of Japanese finance and often is contrasted to the more limited roles usually played by their American counterparts. Most observers correctly noted that Japanese banks resembled more closely what are known as the "universal" banks of continental Europe (for example, Deutsche Bank) than they did their nominal American peers. But a much more critical contrast between Japan's most important banks and their American and European counterparts lay in the way they raised money to fund their assets. A bank's assets consist mostly of loans it has made, and it must raise the money to back those loans—"fund its assets" in bankerspeak. That is most typically done by taking in deposits, although it is not limited to that. And it is the funding practices of Japan's banks—the way they went about providing backing for their loans—that leads us to label them deposit creators.

Western banks are constrained in their lending activities by the funding available to them through their deposit bases and through the interbank and capital markets, where they can go to raise additional funds. Japan's core banks, however, booked loans and financed the purchase of equity stakes in their most important customers independent of their funding activities. A Western bank that cannot raise enough deposits from the market cannot make loans. But a Japanese bank could go to the BOJ. The BOJ bridged what bankers call the asset/liability gap—the gap between the amount of loans and the amount available to back those loans—either by lending to the bank directly or through the "call loans" it arranged through a group of specialist market makers known as *tanshi gaisha*, literally "short-term capital companies," which move money among sectors of the banking system at the BOJ's direction.[4] Direct BOJ lending usually consisted of new money injected into the banking system, while the call money market operated by the *tanshi gaisha* steered the excess deposits collected by the 120-odd local banks, the seven trust banks, and the myriad of credit associations into the accounts of the core city banks.[5]

It was not a bank's market-driven ability to raise deposits or issue securities that determined the amount of lending the bank could do. Instead, banks provided money to well-connected Japanese companies independent of both their own funding powers and any assessment of the companies' credit risk. Credit risk was, in any case, a meaningless concept in Japan, where bankruptcy did not happen to well-connected companies that played by the rules. It was up to the bureaucracy to guarantee the viability of both banks and their major corporate borrowers. Western bankers will say about themselves that they are "exposed" to their borrowers—that is, that their borrowers place them at risk—and a well-managed bank carefully monitors and limits its exposure by keeping a close eye on both a borrower's creditworthiness and the value of collateral for its loans. Japanese banks were technically exposed to their major customers in numerous ways: through secured and unsecured loans, equity investments, long-term capital and revolving credit facilities. But the concept of exposure made little sense in an environment in which risk as it is understood in the West had no meaning, so Japanese banks did not worry about it. Nor did they fret over their reputation or acceptability in the call money or bank debenture markets, as their Western counterparts would. After all, call money lenders and the buyers of bank debentures did not even bother to specify the name of the bank when they bought bank paper—a situation that persisted until well into the 1990s, when it first began to dawn on market participants that the authorities were not going to be able to keep every bank afloat.[6]

## *"Window Guidance" and Gososendan*

Unlike their Western counterparts, who were concerned with their institution's reputation in the financial markets, Japan's banks were instead acutely sensitive to the *madoguchi shido* (literally, window guidance) of the Bank of Japan. *Madoguchi shido* started originally as limits imposed by the BOJ on each city bank on its net additional lending for a given period. *Madoguchi shido* has been pervasive throughout the postwar period, although the first public announcement of bank lending limits was not made until 1957. The BOJ's explanation for the policy cited the ostensible need to restrain the lending of Japanese banks eager to expand market share without any concern for profitability.

In the 1960s, the BOJ widened the ambit of window guidance to include the long-term credit, trust, and bigger regional banks; otherwise, those institutions plausibly could have taken business away from the city banks. From that time forward, the BOJ specified for each bank the net additional amount of lending it could do in each quarter. In 1973, smaller regional banks and the larger credit unions were added to the list of those subject to window guidance, and the BOJ began to give "guidance" to all institutions on securities investments as well. In 1982, banks were granted the ostensible freedom to draw up their own lending plans, but they usually continued to follow the BOJ's instructions given for the ultimate purpose of reaching overall money supply targets.[7] Window guidance lasted until June 1991, when supposedly it was abolished. In the past, the BOJ had suspended it several times, only to revive it later. But in the wake of the bursting of the late-1980s bubble, it had become difficult, if not impossible, for banks to increase loans; therefore, there was no need to control additional net lending per quarter. The potential for revival nonetheless remains omnipresent, and the spirit of window guidance remains. When public money was distributed to the larger banks in 1998, for example, the newly constituted Financial Supervisory Agency worked with each bank to determine a set amount of new loans to be made to small and medium-sized firms.

Toyooka Tomiei, an outspoken economist and former editor of *Toyo Keizai*, perhaps Japan's premier journal devoted to economic affairs, notes in his book *Jisho Kinyuron*[8] that the BOJ's window guidance was followed quite obediently because the BOJ has, by the very nature of the arrangement, so much leverage over the banks. Window guidance was not legally binding, but it was followed as if it were. The banks needed access to the BOJ's discount window to fund what came to be known in Japan as "over-loan" (the practice of lending in excess of the deposit base); flouting the BOJ's wishes was therefore inconceivable. Banks accepted window guidance as essential for maintaining market share and as quid pro quo for the protection provided by the BOJ and the MOF. The Japanese called it *gososendan*, or convoy, with all the banks moving together under the protection of the warships, the BOJ and the MOF. That partly explains why retail banking products such as term deposit interest rates and transfer fees—even ATM hours—were essentially identical from bank to bank. The banks were permitted, indeed required, to operate what amounted to a cartel.

*Gososendan* has its origin in the war years, but the singular nature of Japanese banking has roots farther back in the past. Most of Japan's city banks trace their origins to the late nineteenth century, when they were established by the ruling elite in order to raise money for companies owned, in most cases, by the same people who owned the banks. The owners, the great *zaibatsu* families (the Sumitomo, the Mitsui, the Iwasaki of Mitsubishi, the Yasuda, the Asano) did not trust securities markets they could not control. The term *zaibatsu*, literally "financial clique," describes groups of corporations and banks owned by holding companies that were in turn controlled by the *zaibatsu* families. After World War II, the families were stripped of their control and the *zaibatsu* were reconstituted as *keiretsu* or *guruppu gaisha*— literally, "group companies"—with member companies and banks holding controlling shares in each other. *Zaibatsu* corporations thus financed most of their operations with bank borrowing rather than equity or bond issues and did not come under pressure from either *zaibatsu* banks or their shareholders to repay the money they borrowed.

During the buildup to the war, the government stepped in to redirect the flow of bank lending, primarily to the munitions industry. The borrowers sold goods to the government, and bankers deemed loans to those borrowers to be secure—that is to say, requiring no set-aside or provisions for loan losses—although the loans could not be justified by either the collateral holdings of borrowers or any conceivable cash flow. Borrowers could not, however, turn down government orders to expand production, nor could banks disobey orders to provide the necessary financing. The financial authorities and the banks started to rely on inflation to retire loans to companies in war-related industries. And with the government underwriting both borrowers and lenders, they had become de facto public institutions.

The situation continued after the war with companies in MITI-designated "strategic" industries and other well-connected firms taking the place of the munitions makers (in many cases—for example, Mitsubishi Heavy Industries, Hitachi, Nissan, and Toshiba—they were the same companies). The banks kept right on lending just as they had during the war years under the assumption that the loans were backed by an implicit government guarantee. Even the periodic use of inflation to retire bank debt persisted to a lesser extent, a matter we will consider in more detail in chapter 5. And the purpose of Japan's monetary regime remained essentially the same: to ensure that Japan's key manufacturers, whether munitions firms in the early 1940s or companies in designated strategic and export industries after the war, never need worry about money. Unlimited low-cost financing served as an essential ingredient in industrial Japan's ability to wrest global market leadership from Western companies in a succession of industries.

## Aggregate Controls: Interest Rates and Quotas

In market economies, interest rates typically act as the ultimate restraint on bank lending. When interest rates rise above a certain level, corporate demand for funds slackens. But in Japan, interest rates were held by bureaucratic fiat at deliberately low levels regardless of credit risk or macroeconomic conditions in order to improve the export competitiveness of Japanese industry by reducing the cost of financing, a key cost component. Corporations would use all the borrowing made available to them to invest in production facilities, in research and development (R&D) labs, and in furnishing suppliers' credit to foreign customers at correspondingly low rates.

In the past, Western regulators also used reserve requirements to restrain aggregate bank lending if they believed interest rates were doing an inadequate job. Those requirements have become less common in recent years, but Japanese authorities rarely used them. Other things being equal, raising requirements boosts interest rates. Rather than raise the cost of financing to Japanese industry, the authorities used window guidance and the quota system both to control the aggregate level of credit in the economy and to allocate credit to favored sectors.

Bank quotas thus came to be the principal macroeconomic policy tool of the Japanese authorities. The BOJ used window guidance to control the level of inflation in the Japanese economy, as we will see in chapter 5, and, first in the early 1970s and again in the 1980s, the BOJ used window guidance in an attempt to inflate both asset and general prices. Seeing to it that there was enough money to fund each bank's quota was the responsibility of the BOJ. The BOJ could not expect to manage the quantity and disposition of bank assets without simultaneously arranging for the necessary liabilities to fund the assets; that is why one could argue that the BOJ functioned as the "funds provider of first resort" as far as the city banks were concerned. The same could be said of the MOF with respect to the long-term banks. The long-term banks relied mostly on bank debentures rather than deposits to fund their loans, and it was up to the MOF to ensure that the debentures were purchased in sufficient quantities.

Since the MOF and the BOJ determined the quantity and, to a very large extent, the recipients of credit extended by Japan's core banks, both the banks themselves and the loans they made came to be regarded in the Japanese system as falling effectively under government guarantee. Bankers did not do the rigorous, numbers-based credit analysis familiar to generations of fledgling Western bankers; funds were not set aside to cover loan losses, and loans were not priced with any concern for bank capital ratios. Major Japanese companies in good standing did not go bankrupt, so credit analysis was simply a matter of ascertaining that potential borrowers were indeed in good standing. Scrutiny of corporate use of bank loans was hardly necessary since it was the responsibility of the bureaucracy to ensure the viability of leading corporate borrowers.

Loans to smaller, less well connected entities were almost invariably secured by collateral—most commonly land—and bankers typically retained the right to require collateral even when lending to the large, established companies. Banks had full confidence in the ability of bureaucrats to control land prices and therefore believed that they had eliminated risk from domestic lending. Collateral, which forms backup security in case a company fails to generate sufficient cash to pay back a loan, is considered useful in Western countries in the event of default, but it is called on only when a company has in fact defaulted. But in Japan, collateral just as often served to *prevent* defaults. Large companies that held land with huge unrealized capital gains—capital gains that grew with each passing year—could always find lenders. Neither the banks nor their borrowers paid much attention to the purported health of the loans that formed the principal vehicle of Japanese corporate finance since they both believed that land prices had no place to go but up. In any case, most loans were continually renewed; with interest obligations so easily met while principal was simply rolled over, there was no real way of testing the soundness of lending. And no one worried about capital cushions when funding arrangements and the pricing of loans were set to all intents and purposes by the MOF and the BOJ. Japan's banks lived, in a manner of speaking, on the spread between funding costs arranged by the MOF and returns arranged by MITI.

## Banks, Land, and Monetary Policy

In Western countries, banks and other financial institutions determine the aggregate level of credit in an economy through their responses to interest rates, central bank reserve requirements, and market demand for funds. Japanese banks obviously did not make that determination, nor was aggregate credit set inside the BOJ. True, the BOJ provided credit that backed the currency in circulation demanded by a given level of economic activity. It did not, however, carry out monetary policy in the manner of its American counterpart. The Federal Reserve influences the supply of money largely through purchasing government securities for newly created money— thereby adding to the money supply—or selling securities, thereby shrinking it. In Japan's case, however, the authorities carried out monetary policy through the direct management of bank assets, which included not just bank loans but security investments made by the banks. Bank securities portfolios included the equity and debt securities of their major customers plus government securities. Indeed, Japan's government securities were bought almost entirely by syndicates of financial institutions arranged by the MOF, making it easy for the MOF to mesh Japan's monetary and fiscal policies.

Ultimate responsibility for Japan's monetary policy lay with the institution that determined the level of total financial assets in the economy—both loans and security investments—and that institution was the Ministry of Finance. Ikeda Hayato makes that clear in his memoirs. As a senior MOF bureaucrat, finance minister, and then prime minister, Ikeda was involved at the core of Japanese finance from the immediate postwar years through his death in

1964. He was the first member of the postwar generation to rise to great political prominence and could, as much as anyone, be plausibly called the "father of the Japanese economic miracle." He notes in his book that "foreign exchange control policy had to be operated in concert with monetary and fiscal policy"; that overall responsibility for currency values and trade policies "should not be ambivalent"; and that the "MOF and the BOJ had overall control" of all important monetary policy levers with "foreign exchange policy determined by the MOF with operations carried out by the BOJ."[9]

The MOF had the last word in supervisory control of all financial institutions, including not just banks, but the life and non–life insurance companies and securities firms as well. And while the huge postal savings system was managed by the Ministry of Posts and Telecommunications, the assets of the postal savings system were turned over to the Trust Fund Bureau of the MOF to use as it saw fit. As for the banks, the MOF micromanaged them down to branch openings and senior personnel appointments. MOF officials were consulted regularly by bank management on the direction and quantity of credit extended. To be sure, the BOJ directly managed bank assets through the quota system. And on the liability side, it ensured adequate bank funding by its own lending to banks, its supervision of the call money market, and the interest rates it decreed on bank deposits. But the BOJ ultimately was a participant—a very essential participant—in a system supervised in total by the MOF.

If the authorities wanted to tighten money, the BOJ could easily order reductions in loan growth at each bank. But money tightening was the exception during the so-called "miracle," or high-growth, years (1955–1973). As figure 3-2 indicates, those years were characterized by rapid monetary growth, which provided the financial fuel for Japan's unprecedented industrial expansion.

Neoclassical economic theory teaches that rapid gunning of the money supply ahead of market demand for credit may lead to a short and temporary increase in real economic activity but that it will mostly dissipate as inflation. But while prices in Japan did creep up during those years, most of the monetary growth was in fact translated into real assets. A combination of three factors made that possible. First, household income was systematically suppressed. Company (as opposed to trade) unions, together with the lifetime employment protocol and the seniority system, operated to prevent the emergence of a genuine labor market and upward pressure on wages.

**Figure 3-2.** *Year-on-Year Growth Rates of the Money Supply (M2 + CDs) and Nominal GDP*

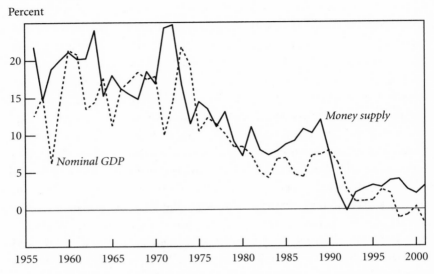

Sources: *Financial and Economic Statistics Monthly,* Bank of Japan; *Annual Report on National Accounts,* Cabinet Office. Calculated, arranged, and estimated by Mikuni & Co. © 2002 Mikuni & Co., Ltd.

Second, while Japan never quite went as far as places such as Singapore in requiring automatic deductions from income to boost savings, Japanese households were essentially subject to a forced savings regime. A panoply of social, tax, and financial controls ensured that Japanese households would save large portions of their disposable income at low rates of interest. Those controls included the bonus system (Japanese employees typically receive more than one-third of their annual compensation in the form of semi-annual bonuses), the deliberate suppression of consumer credit, punitively high marginal income tax rates coupled with what amounted to tax exemptions for any income steered into deposits, low or nonexistent taxes on interest income, no deductibility for interest expenses, and the walling off of Japan's financial system from the outside world to prevent household funds from fleeing offshore in pursuit of higher returns. The savings at the disposal of the financial authorities were enhanced by the heavy reliance of the Japanese economy on cash, cash in modern economies being after all a direct liability of the central bank.[10]

Finally, the savings channeled through Japan's centrally directed banking system were augmented by public works spending aimed at boosting land prices that in turn resulted in yet higher levels of savings. In the prewar years, public construction spending in various areas of the country had naturally been welcomed and encouraged by Diet members, who could claim credit for it with their constituents. During the buildup to the war, however, Japan's bureaucrats—particularly the *kakushin kanryo* (literally, "reform bureaucrats"), as they were known—influenced by what seemed to be the success of central planning in countries such as the USSR and Nazi Germany, tried to systematize and centralize plans for national land development. They were initially frustrated in their plans by Japan's slide toward defeat.

After the war, however, the reform bureaucrats and their heirs formed the core of the governing bureaucracy and proceeded to implement national land development. In 1962, under Ikeda's leadership, the *Zenkoku Sogo Kaihatsu Keikaku* (National Comprehensive Development Plan) was launched. LDP Diet members gave their total support to the plan, since they understood that the public construction spending that formed its heart had two major, politically valuable impacts: first, it diverted household earnings from the productive, urban areas of the country to the increasingly unproductive rural districts that formed the heart of the LDP's power base. Second, it triggered land price increases that enabled indebted farmers to sell land and pay back their loans. High land prices provided farmers both capital and income.

In 1969, the *Chika Koji Hou* (Land Price Disclosure Law) was enacted. Under the law, land prices were announced by the *Kokudo cho* (National Land Office, now part of MLIT) in given areas, and all land transactions connected with public works had to take place at those prices—a typical example of the Japanese government's use of decrees rather than markets to determine politically important prices. The decreed prices provided benchmarks for smaller, private deals. The MOF did not mind other transactions consummated at higher prices, but any private transaction done at a price significantly lower than the publicly announced price invited a tax audit. It was, in any case, difficult to find out the prices of other deals. Land transaction prices are generally available in the United States, for example, by consulting the registrar's office at the town hall. But in Japan, only the tax bureau of the MOF kept a complete record of transactions, which it did not disclose. This Official Public Land Price Quotation System (*Chika Koji*

*Kakaku Seido*) thus helped cement the notion of ever-rising land prices and the key importance of land both as collateral in the Japanese banking system and as a generator of deposits. And ever-increasing government purchases of land, indicated in figure 3-3, helped to push up land prices yet further.

A new national comprehensive development plan was formed in the late 1960s and implemented shortly thereafter. In 1972, Tanaka Kakuei was elected prime minister, partly on the strength of his best seller published that year, *Nippon Retto Kaizo Ron* (*Plan for Remodeling the Japanese Archipelago*). Many of the book's recommendations were followed, bringing on a sharp increase in farmland prices.[11] We will consider this early 1970s bubble in greater detail in chapter 5, but it should be noted that while Tanaka was often blamed for the inflationary results of the *Nippon Retto Kaizo Ron*, he was in fact carrying out the original plan formed under the second Ikeda cabinet. A third iteration relying heavily on public spending was implemented in the late 1970s, then a fourth plan in 1987. The last plan played a key role in bringing forth the late 1980s bubble.

All these plans, however, were financed and made possible by the availability of bank credit, which, in turn, they helped create. The plans resulted in capital gains for land sellers—gains closely monitored by the MOF. The rise in land prices can be seen in figure 3-4, which shows land prices in the Tokyo metropolitan area, Kansai, and the rest of Japan during the past thirty years. Land sellers tended to fall into three categories: farmers in rural areas who sold land to the government for public construction projects; landholders on the outskirts of urban areas who sold agricultural plots for housing development; and small store and factory owners in urban cores who sold their holdings at stratospheric prices for redevelopment (this last group was particularly important during the bubble years of the late 1980s). Meanwhile, the developers of the land—the rural construction firms that received orders for public works spending, the housing and golf course developers flush with bank loans—likewise put much of the proceeds of the spending on deposit. That was particularly true of public works spending, because, as pointed out in the previous chapter, so much public works funding is siphoned off in the practice of *uenage* (up-contracting) to pay well-connected rural fixers.

The deliberate efforts of the authorities to drive up land prices produced extra funds that supplemented Japan's highly effective system of forced savings. During the high-growth years before the emergence of structural current account surpluses in the late 1960s, export proceeds were allocated to

**Figure 3-3.** *Net Sales/Purchases of Land by Enterprises, Governments, and Households (Absolute Amounts and as Percentages of Nominal GDP)*

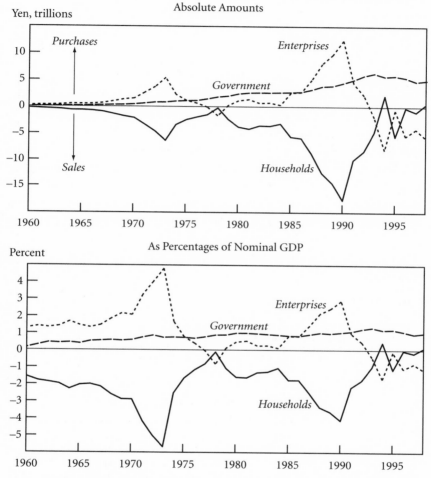

Source: *Annual Report on National Accounts,* Cabinet Office. Calculated, arranged, and estimated by Mikuni & Co. © 2002 Mikuni & Co., Ltd.

manufacturers for the import of capital goods. But the emergence of surpluses indicated a surfeit of savings, because by definition the current account plugs the savings/investment gap in an economy. To sustain that level of savings—or to sustain Japan's current account surpluses, which amounts to the same thing—the savings could not be dissipated. The funds were intermediated through a tightly controlled and centrally administered

**Figure 3-4.** *Total Market Value of Land in the Tokyo Metropolitan Area,*[a] *Kansai Area,*[b] *and the Rest of Japan, 1969–99*

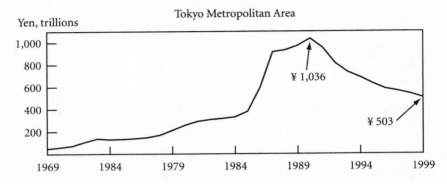

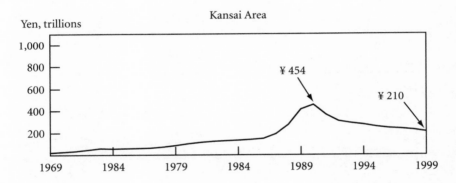

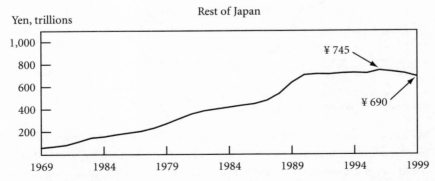

Sources: *Annual Report on National Accounts,* Cabinet Office. Calculated, arranged, and estimated by Mikuni & Co. © 2002 Mikuni & Co., Ltd.

a. Metropolis of Tokyo plus Kanagawa, Chiba, and Saitama Prefectures.

b. Osaka, Kyoto, and Hyogo Prefectures.

banking system that steered them into assets whose values were underwritten by the bureaucracy.

In order to prop up the value of the assets financed by Japan's savings pool, bureaucrats used every means at their command—most important, cartels that both controlled input prices and ensured high domestic profits, captive suppliers subject to relentless and intense cost pressure, and protectionist measures to prevent disruptive foreign competition. Overseas, the tactic of flooding key foreign markets with the production generated by those assets in storms of "torrential rain–type exports," to quote a widely used bureaucratic term, kept the assets in use. Prices were set below the amount that foreign competition could meet thanks to the high, rigged revenues obtained from domestic sales, low financing costs, and the absence of any pressure from shareholders for returns. Wages also were controlled, as noted, through a network of government-supervised employer associations and associations of company unions. Because wage increases could be held below the growth of bank credit (illustrated in figure 3-5, which plots the growth of labor wages compared with that of bank loans), purchasing power could be suppressed in order to help avoid dissipating monetary growth as inflation.

During the high-growth years of 1955 through 1973, monetary policy essentially involved the MOF and the BOJ encouraging Japan's core banks to lend money for the purpose of expanding production capacity. Given the heavy reliance of the Japanese economy on cash in circulation, the expansion of economic activity—virtually synonymous in the Japanese case with the expansion of production capacity—required high levels of currency. Japanese monetary policy could therefore be described as precisely the reverse of that in the West, where bank loans are the final product of monetary creation. In Japan, bank loans came first. To expand liquidity in Japan, the monetary authorities ordered bank loans to expand.

Banks also created credit by buying securities that were under what amounted to central control. Bond issues, which account for a small percentage to begin with of corporate indebtedness, were sold to *kisaikai*, or bond underwriting syndicates, composed largely of major banks that were formed under the watchful eyes of the MOF. New equity issues were controlled by Japan's Big Four securities firms—Nomura, Nikko, Daiwa, and Yamaichi—which brought the securities to market in close consultation with the MOF.

**Figure 3-5.** *Year-on-Year Growth Rates of Wages and City Bank Loans*

Percent

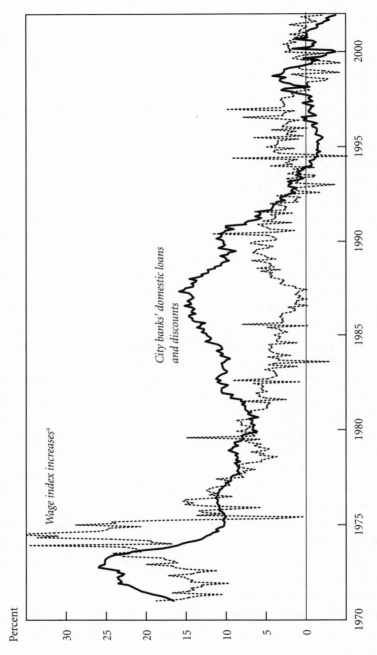

Sources: *Financial and Economic Statistics Monthly*, Bank of Japan; statistics compiled by the Japanese Bankers Association. Calculated, arranged, and estimated by Mikuni & Co. © 2002 Mikuni & Co., Ltd.

a. Manufacturing, thirty employees or more.

## The Wartime Parallel

The ability to control inflation despite rapid monetary growth had its roots in the war years. Official thinking about wartime economic management can be found in a book written by Nakayama Ichiro, a professor at Hitotsubashi University and a frequent chair of various *shingikai* (government-sponsored committees of experts to study problems).[12] As Nakayama noted, weapons and ammunition cannot be bought with the wages paid to workers by munitions manufacturers. To finance production, the government issued bonds and out of the proceeds paid the manufacturers.

Money released into the economy without things to spend it on results in inflation. To head that off, Nakayama wrote, consumption must be proactively reduced or, in other words, savings must rise. The government ensured the growth of savings by seeing to it that the payments made by the government for munitions found their way back to the government, and the simplest way of doing that involved the government itself buying the bonds it issued. That was done by forcing all savings into deposit-taking institutions that had become instruments of government policy; those institutions then bought bonds.

That approach was repeated with minor modifications during the postwar high-growth years. Exports replaced munitions as the central goal of economic policy. Both were subsidized through the deliberate suppression of consumption, including the cartelization of labor markets to hold down wages. The proceeds of munitions sales had been mopped up through bank deposits that funded holdings of government bonds. In the postwar years, export proceeds were maintained largely in dollars and kept on deposit in the U.S. banking system, funded by yen deposits in Japanese banks—a matter we will consider more closely in the next two chapters.

Under ordinary circumstances, a surge in exports without a concomitant surge in imports can lead to inflation as production rises, putting pressure on labor markets and other capacity constraints. The authorities kept inflation under control during Japan's high-growth years, however, by redeploying the forced savings/consumption-suppression tactics that had evolved during the war in favor of an export-led economy after 1945. Credit was created at a blistering pace, but it went largely into the coffers of export producers. Japan's policy officials had learned to keep inflationary leakage to a minimum.

## *Signs of Strain*

In the 1980s, the system began to show clear signs of excess. Urged on by the
BOJ's window guidance, Japan's major banks lent very aggressively despite
a slowdown in real investment spending by Japanese companies and the
consequent departure of many of the banks' key customers, who needed
the banks much less than they had during the high-growth years. Much of
the money went instead to finance the likes of splashy office towers and
leisure facilities. When bank lending had gone primarily into financing the
buildup of Japan's plant and equipment, the bureaucracy had, with its
panoply of industrial policy tools, been able to create conditions that ensured that those assets could generate sufficient cash at least to service debt,
if not to retire it. But with the new generation of assets, the bureaucracy
found itself unable to repeat its performance. That became clear in the
1990s in the wake of the collapse of Japan's bubble economy—the name
given to the explosion of bank credit in the 1980s deliberately fostered by
the authorities and the resulting run up in asset prices. In chapter 6, we will
discuss why the authorities were unable to maintain the value and the cash
flow of the assets the banks had financed during the bubble years. For now,
it is sufficient to note that once it became impossible to prop up asset values, the government had to walk away from the implicit blanket guarantee
it had given to all financial institutions. Banks such as Takugin, LTCB, and
NCB collapsed. Savers responded to growing fears over the viability of the
banks and the government's ability to prop up the financial system by with-
drawing yet more cash from the banking system and storing it under the
proverbial mattress. Cash in circulation thus grew at an even faster rate.

At the beginning of this chapter, we noted that foreign economists such
as Paul Krugman and Adam Posen have been loudly advising the Japanese
government to inflate its way out of its difficulties. Alas, as noted, many of
the structural features embedded in the Japanese economy during the war
and high-growth years—particularly the systemic suppression of consumption—now impart a deflationary bias to the economy that cannot be easily
reversed. For example, wage growth is institutionally suppressed, and the
absence of a genuine labor market that would permit highly qualified individuals to sell their services to the highest bidder makes it very difficult to
spark price increases. And there is no easy way of reversing the steady drift
downward in asset prices. During most of the postwar period, large corpo-

rations borrowed money from banks to expand production capacity without any real attempt to assess the cash flow available from the capacity being financed. Lenders and borrowers both believed that rising asset prices served as sufficient security for borrowing and lending. Furthermore, most loans, as we have seen, were not expected to be paid back.

In the last decade, however, asset prices have tumbled and are no longer sufficient to support the level of leverage in the Japanese economy. It is beginning to be understood that the only sure source for debt repayment is the cash flow generated out of investments financed by the debt. But because until recently nobody paid serious attention to cash flow as a source of debt repayment, many borrowers are not generating enough of it to pay back their debt, and as asset prices continue to fall, more nonperforming loans emerge. Since land prices are not expected to rise for the foreseeable future, many borrowers are attempting to sell assets to raise money, further depressing asset prices.

In such an economy—an economy already drowning in liquidity—inducing price increases by yet more liquidity is devilishly hard. But not for lack of trying—as of this writing, the BOJ has again brought interest rates down to zero and, after putting up token resistance, attempted one more time to boost the money supply in the summer of 2001. But the reason banks are not lending today has nothing to do with any dearth of funding—funds are as ubiquitous as sand at a beach. Bankers do not lend because they no longer believe that the bureaucracy can ensure the soundness of their loans. They gaze nervously at the example of LTCB, one of the core institutions of Japanese finance, which supposedly was covered by an implicit guarantee, one that the MOF ultimately could not honor. They see men who once worked there subject to such unheard-of indignities as losing their jobs or taking orders from foreigners younger than they are. They understand now that if their loans are not sound and their banks start to crumble as a result, the MOF may not bail them out. So they freeze.

Had the MOF seen the results it expected, Japan's vast pile of problem loans would not exist. The MOF does not know what to do about it because the policy regime it supervised was understood to contain self-correcting measures that would prevent the emergence of such loans. The very existence of these nonperforming loans demonstrates that the MOF has been stripped of any policy tools that it believes it could use to solve the problem. Japan has landed in a liquidity trap that even Keynes could not have foreseen.

## The Severing of the Dollar Link

The roots of Japan's present dilemma lie in the Achilles' heel, as it were, of the interlocking monetary and industrial policies put in place during the high-growth years. The bureaucracy used the banking system not simply to finance but actually to push the expansion of production capacity without regard for profitability. Banks were prodded into lending by the bureaucracy; the banks in turn prodded their borrowers—if any prodding was needed—into using all available loans. Most of that monetary growth, as we have seen, translated directly into the assets themselves. But at the same time, the regime allowed for controlled and low but steady inflation in the 1950s and the 1960s, which had the very necessary effect of reducing borrowing relative to sales, resulting in de facto repayment of debt. Inflation, however, is very difficult to maintain with a strong currency, yet a strong currency is precisely what Japan's interlocking industrial and monetary policies entailed, for they inevitably, as we saw in the previous chapter, produced trade surpluses. By the late 1960s, those trade surpluses helped bring down the postwar system of fixed exchange rates so important in providing Japan with a predictable market in which it could dispose of its surplus production.

Japan's policy elite thus faced an excruciating dilemma. The industrial and monetary policy regimes required disposing of production in external markets in order to keep capacity utilization rates as high as possible. High capacity utilization brought further investment in capacity; continuous investment in turn drove both the industrial and the monetary sides of the policy regime. But the inevitable trade surpluses threatened the undervalued yen, which served as a key element of the entire apparatus. By the early 1970s, however, officials had become so attached to promoting the maximization of production that they seem to have lost sight of the underlying rationale. The policy had its roots, as we have noted, in Japan's experience as a catch-up developer in the late-nineteenth century and was reinforced by war and the devastation that followed war. But by the early 1970s, Japan's administrators gave the impression that they could no longer conceive, much less implement, any alternative way of running the economy.

Preserving the policy of endless expansion of production capacity required, above all, that Japan maintain its special relationship with the United States, which provided Japan with the all-essential external market to dispose of Japan's production. Tokyo's policy elite understood the importance of that relationship and assiduously avoided taking any action that could deliberately antagonize the United States. When the needs of domestic interest groups reached the point that they visibly annoyed the Americans—as, for example, with the wave of textile exports that so incensed Richard Nixon, who thought he had a commitment from Prime Minister Sato Eisaku to restrain those exports—the government would typically find some arrangement to mollify the Americans while compensating domestic interests. Tanaka Kakuei provided crucial help in assuaging Japan's textile makers, one reason why he was awarded the prime ministership after Sato had had to play the sacrificial lamb by resigning.

In the mid 1960s, it became clear to most policy analysts what economists such as Jacques Rueff and Robert Triffin had long understood: the Bretton Woods system permitted the United States to export inflation. And the United States would do so rather than finance the Vietnam War on a noninflationary basis. But even though the Japanese knew that full well, even though they understood that the principal macroeconomic concern of the United States had become the preservation of its gold reserves, Japan did not follow France's lead in demanding that the United States exchange the growing hoard of dollar holdings outside the United States for gold. Unlike French president Charles de Gaulle, Tokyo had no interest in poking Washington in the eyes to induce policy changes. The combination that Bretton Woods permitted of a dollar that was simultaneously strong and inflationary suited Japan very well, for it helped boost Japan's exports.

Meanwhile, the MOF had long backed up its support for the fixed-rate regime with tight controls on foreign exchange transactions dating back to the prewar years. After the currency crisis of the early 1970s, the MOF admitted that it had been unable to stem the inflow of short-term speculative money that ultimately forced Japan to give up its defense of the fixed exchange rate. Institutions holding foreign exchange were, however, directly subsidized for the losses sustained after the yen was cut loose from the dollar.

The MOF believed that its controls were essential in stabilizing the yen, that they helped discourage unwanted inflows of capital while encouraging outflows useful in financing Japan's economic activities overseas.[13] In any case, alternative views were nowhere to be seen. For Japan's power holders had succeeded in stifling open discussion of the merits of Japan's exchange rate policies in the buildup to the crisis of the early 1970s. As Robert Angel notes, "Expressions of doubt were banned absolutely within the MOF, and serious efforts even were made to prevent public discussion of the issue within the business community."[14] A group of non-Marxist economists did draw up a proposal to institute what is known as a crawling peg, thereby bringing about a gradual revaluation of the yen; they noted the burden to the Japanese economy of the priority given to financing Japan's export manufacturing infrastructure and pointed out that trade deficits need not necessarily always spell bad news for Japan. But the leading newspapers and business interests denounced their work, and revaluation of the yen was otherwise universally opposed in the press, in academia, and in business and political circles.[15] The press played a key role in stifling debate by neglecting to inform its readers that the rest of the world was demanding a revaluation of the yen; the media in any case were so heavily reliant on the MOF for economic news that they could scarcely conceive of independent reporting and analysis.

The ability to suppress discussion demonstrated that wartime controls on the dissemination of information on matters deemed damaging to the implementation of fiscal and economic policy by the prime minister's office—the *Shinbunshito Keisai Seigenrei* (Ordinance to Limit Publications by Newspapers and the Like)—were, at least on a de facto level, still operating. As Makino pointed out, in the midst of what was obviously the greatest global currency crisis since the 1930s, the *1971 Economic White Paper* contained not a single reference to the exchange value of the yen or to exchange rate adjustment.[16]

## Production and the Socialization of Risk

When, twenty years later, Japan was again subject to intense international criticism for the size of its bloated current account surpluses, the MOF and MITI both blithely dismissed that criticism by noting that Japan's surpluses formed a useful pool of capital for the world without acknowledging even the possibility that they might be problematic. Since discussion of the implications of endless surpluses has been stifled for a generation now, the ability to conceive of alternatives or a plan to end the surpluses no longer seems to exist.

Instead, business leaders in important industries acted until well into the 1990s on the assumption that their job was to produce and that the government would take care of the rest. If the government could not protect them against losses—if, for example, the yen appreciated—then it was up to the government to compensate them. They had fulfilled their part of the implicit bargain by producing as much as they could.

Japanese companies appear from the outside to be profit-seeking entities and, of course, they are happy to make money. But they do not particularly care about losing money, because it is up to the government to guarantee their viability. The bureaucracy, in turn, does not want companies to act as if they are at risk because then they would be hard to control. The bureaucracy instead oversees the various "convoy systems"—the term is not limited to the banking industry—and the innumerable cartels and trade associations through which risks are socialized and managed at the national level.

The bureaucracy compensates producers for any losses suffered through implicit or explicit subsidies with loans from MOF-licensed financial institutions and by the actions of the BOJ. No entity in the Japanese power structure is charged with thinking about the long-term viability of Japan's economic framework or about alternatives to that framework if it should prove to be no longer viable. Nor is there any practical way for the Japanese public at large to get a grip on the situation. As we have seen, Japan's elected politicians have little power over the bureaucracy, which in practice represents the interests of the ruling elite.

## Suppressing the Yen

Despite its best efforts, however, the bureaucracy was unable to preserve the fixed exchange rate of the yen amid the worldwide collapse of the Bretton Woods regime and the futile attempts to revive some sort of fixed-rate framework between 1971 and 1973. From that year on, Japan's authorities have had to suppress the yen/dollar rate by recycling Japan's trade and current account surpluses through the purchase of dollar assets by Japan's financial institutions. The BOJ in turn has attempted to monetize the dollar assets held by private financial institutions, that is, to create equivalent yen funds. But as we saw in chapter 1, beginning in the early 1980s, Japan's net creditor position exceeded the size of the BOJ's assets, making it impossible for the BOJ to monetize all of Japan's dollar holdings (figure 3-6 shows the growth of the BOJ's balance sheet compared with Japan's net creditor position). Instead, banks had to make up the difference.

**Figure 3-6.** *Bank of Japan's Assets Compared with Japan's Net Creditor Position*

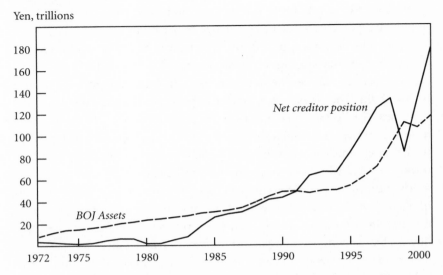

Sources: *Financial and Economic Statistics Monthly,* Bank of Japan; *International Investment Position of Japan,* Ministry of Finance. Calculated, arranged, and estimated by Mikuni & Co. © 2002 Mikuni & Co., Ltd.

The problem ultimately is one of balance sheet dynamics. It is true, of course, that balance sheets are, by definition, balanced, and thus it may at first glance not seem clear why the buildup of Japan's dollar assets on what amounts to Japan's national balance sheet should be a cause for concern. Those assets are supported by liabilities, specifically by the broadest measure of the money supply, M2 plus CDs; the assets would not exist otherwise. But past a certain point, those dollars contribute nothing to domestic economic activities in Japan because they can neither be spent nor exchanged for yen lest the yen soar in value. A portion of Japan's total money supply thus funds dollars that are dead weight as far as Japan is concerned (although they continue, of course, to serve as money inside the U.S. banking system). That created a deflationary dilemma once the BOJ itself could no longer monetize all of Japan's dollar holdings.

The Japanese authorities solved the problem for the time being by engineering bubbles, that is, by fostering conditions that would lead to a buildup in deposits unconnected to real economic activity, thus providing the necessary M2 plus CDs on Japan's national balance sheet to fund the buildup of dollars. Banks monetized or bought dollar assets by creating yen deposits in the accounts of exporters. These operations resulted in the export of capital (in monetary terms, the export of high-powered money) and a resulting shortage of money for domestic bank loans that had to be made up somehow. Rather than finance plant and equipment, the machinery of Japan's financial infrastructure began to divert the steady buildup of deposits into the financing of its dollar holdings. We will consider how that was done in chapters 5 and 6, but for now we will note that the deliberate creation of huge asset bubbles in stocks and land was inevitable, given an overriding policy of suppressing the value of the yen in a system in which credit was created not through market forces but by bureaucratic fiat. The extra liquidity compensated for the siphoning off of money from the Japanese economy by the growing volume of dollar holdings.

That state of affairs happened to be very advantageous for the United States, which embarked, just at that time, on a radical policy shift. Japan's credit-pumping machine was being harnessed to support the dollar, and that allowed the United States to escape the normal consequences of the extraordinary regime that prevailed there in the wake of the so-called Reagan Revolution: very tight money mixed with highly stimulative fiscal deficits.

Coping with a huge influx of foreign exchange, suppressing the value of the yen, and controlling the effects on the domestic economy may appear to have been an unprecedented challenge for the Japanese policy elite. But in fact, there was precedent—stretching back nearly a century. Because Japan's bureaucrats—like bureaucrats anywhere—rely first and foremost on institutional memory in handling policy challenges, it was inevitable that the historical response to the earlier challenges would frame their response when they confronted the task of suppressing the yen in the post–Bretton Woods world. It is now time to consider that background.

# 4

## *Hoarding Gold, Hoarding Dollars*

Mercantilist regimes are thought to carry the seeds of their own destruction. A mercantilist regime may enjoy a period of success as it accumulates specie—or, in today's terms, claims on other countries. But it usually runs into some kind of monetary train wreck. The mercantilist's efforts to convert its claims on others into its own currency drive up the exchange rate because foreigners, whose sales to the mercantilist country are restricted, have few ways of accumulating the mercantilist's currency in the first place, so little of its currency is held outside its borders. The mercantilist's exporters then find that no one can afford to buy their goods. Or the flood of precious metals and other foreign money into the mercantilist country's coffers brings on corrosive inflation—the Spanish Empire is an oft-cited example.

In the last decade, Japan appears to have emerged as today's paradigmatic example of the ultimate bankruptcy of mercantilist policies. Analysts may still be divided on the question of whether the mercantilist methods used in the past were essential to Japan's rapid economic growth, but today there is little disagreement outside Japan that they have outlived their usefulness and now hinder the recovery Japan so badly needs. Richard Katz writes, "It seems clear that Japan's perpetuation of obsolete practices, particularly its import barriers, has exacted a terrible cost,"[1] while Michael Porter and his colleagues note that "self-sufficiency may have made sense 40 years ago, but changes in Japan and the world economy have made such thinking obsolete." They call on "Japan to have the confidence to embrace free trade."[2]

Those observations are surely true. But the tenacity of mercantilist practice in Japan is not simply a matter of head-in-the-sand stubbornness. Persuading officials anywhere to abandon practices that they believe have worked for them in the past is a daunting task. And of course policymakers in many countries, not just Japan, dispute the orthodox neoclassical view that free trade is everywhere and anywhere a good thing; the United States itself developed under a Hamiltonian regime of tariffs and explicit government subsidies to industry. Friedrich List, whose influence on late Meiji thinking on economic policy probably exceeded that of any other single foreign economist, used the United States as his primary example in demonstrating the merits of protectionism and government aid to industry. But the Japanese allergy to free trade transcends the familiar arguments of economic nationalists, for any wholesale implementation of a genuine free trade regime in Japan would undermine bureaucrats' ability to set key prices and allocate credit, disturb the power alignments on which social stability rests, and threaten the livelihood of politically powerful sectors of the population. That is why even today it is still fiercely, if covertly, resisted.

That does not, however, spare Japan from the damage mercantilism does. Nor does it permit Japan to escape the ultimate logic of mercantilism—that it works only so long as the outside world will and can run countervailing trade deficits while absorbing the capital exports that must occur to recycle the mercantilist's current account surpluses. Such logic has led many observers to predict the demise of Japanese mercantilism, regardless of the wishes of the country's policy elite or the political power of the current beneficiaries of protectionism. In chapter 1 we noted C. Fred Bergsten's prediction in 1986 that the world would not accommodate Japan's swollen external surpluses much longer. That Japan's annual surpluses are now more than twice the size they were when Bergsten made his comment and are still, sixteen years later, being accommodated has not dissuaded the legion of commentators who cannot believe that Japan's surpluses will not one day have to shrink. If anything, their number has grown in the face of the manifest woes of the Japanese economy.

We ourselves agree that Japan's mercantilism is ultimately doomed. But Japan's ability to maneuver within the mercantilist trap, to put off the day of reckoning, to cope with the collateral damage—particularly the monetary damage—should command the closest attention. If we understand the mechanisms that have enabled the country to sustain such vast current account surpluses for so long, we can better grasp how those mechanisms may ultimately fail.

## Buying Goodwill with Gold

The floating of the yen in 1973 severely complicated the preservation of mercantilist practices in Japan. The end of fixed rates compelled Japanese authorities to adopt policies to suppress the exchange value of the yen or see the country's protectionist dikes washed away in a sea of cheap imports. The means that they have used to suppress the yen involve not just policy maneuvers but also reliance on a unique set of institutions that, on quasi-automatic pilot, help to counteract the strengthening of the yen. Those institutions evolved over the course of a century as Japan's officials learned to cope with the challenge mercantilism poses to monetary policy: rapid buildup of foreign reserves forces officials to navigate between the inflationary Scylla of monetizing the reserves through domestic money creation and the deflationary Charybdis of siphoning them off from the domestic money supply.

That policy challenge might at first review seem to date only from the late 1960s, when Japan's structural current account surpluses emerged. But the dilemma such surpluses posed—the sudden influx of reserves that required monetary offsetting—had in fact confronted Japan's policymakers three times before. Understanding why an influx of reserves—usually seen as an unalloyed good—can be a policy challenge requires a shift in conceptual filters. Westerners have typically regarded an influx of reserves in monetary terms as an increase in high-powered or base money; that is, money that can be used to create money and thereby increase consumption. But Asian authorities, beginning with the Japanese, have long attempted to suppress consumption. Therefore an influx of reserves has required some kind of offsetting, or sterilization, so that it does *not* increase consumption. Over the last hundred years, Japanese monetary authorities have learned to cope with such challenges in a variety of ways.

The first such challenge appeared as far back as 1895, a consequence of Japan's victory in the Sino-Japanese War of that year. Fukai Eigo, governor of the Bank of Japan from 1935 to 1937, offered in his memoirs some fascinating reflections on the monetary challenge that the victory posed.[3] Chinese reparations payments in gold considerably exceeded the amount Japan had spent on imports of arms and equipment related to the war effort, providing concrete evidence to the Japanese elite of just how economically profitable war could be. The gold went directly into the coffers of the Japanese government, making monetary offset considerably easier than it would later become with trade surpluses earned by numerous individual exporters. Indeed, the Chinese reparations meant that for the first time ever, Japan had sufficient gold to maintain a credible gold standard. Japan had repeatedly attempted in the late nineteenth century to adopt the gold standard in order to establish itself as a creditworthy member of the community of advanced nations, but the country's industrial infrastructure was not sufficiently productive to earn the necessary gold. The Chinese gold reparations, however, removed the pressure on Japan's external payments. International confidence in the yen and in Japan's financial management was thus sufficiently established that by 1905 Japan could float substantial loans in London and New York to finance the Russo-Japanese War, which broke out that year. Indeed, the funding of Japan's war efforts, organized by Jacob Schiff, head of the investment banking firm of Kuhn, Loeb, marked the debut of Wall Street, which had been strictly a domestic financial marketplace, as an international financial center.

Beginning with the Chinese reparations and continuing with the proceeds of Japan's war-related borrowings, Japan launched a policy of leaving its gold and sterling assets on deposit in the City of London, where they were managed largely by the Bank of England. Fukai makes the highly significant point that in doing so, Japan was permitting Britain to manage Tokyo's external assets in the same way that Britain managed the assets of its colonies such as India. He cites Keynes's *Indian Currency and Finance* as the best explanation of the way the City of London managed the external assets of British colonies and how those assets became part of the British banking system.[4] Keynes famously noted that as long as Britain's colonies maintained the profits of their trade with the mother country in the City, fears over the strain on the British economy produced by chronic deficits with the colonies were misplaced. Similarly, Japanese assets held in London became for the time being part of the British money supply. That arrangement helped buy tacit British cooperation in Japan's war effort and removed obstacles to British financing of the Japanese war economy. Nearly a century later, Japan would buy off American unease at its bloated trade surpluses by maintaining the proceeds in dollars rather than removing them from the U.S. banking system, thus helping the United States run the "deficit without tears" referred to by Rueff. And maintaining reserves in the banking system of the superpower of the day formed the financial part of a broader relationship. The Anglo-Japanese alliance formalized in 1902 would be reflected in the latter half of the century by the U.S.-Japan Security Treaty.

The gold standard that Japan adopted in the wake of the Sino-Japanese War should therefore really more accurately be termed a "gold exchange" standard because the Chinese gold that Japan received was physically located in London. There, it backed sterling deposits in the accounts that the Bank of Japan maintained with British banks in the City. Since those holdings were listed as liabilities on the books of British financial institutions— primarily the Bank of England (BOE)—they permitted the British banks to use the BOJ holdings to fund assets in Britain. Had Japan insisted that the gold be transferred to Tokyo, Britain would have had to reduce its money supply concomitantly. To be sure, in an era when shipwrecks were a constant danger, simple security considerations helped dictate that the gold be stored in London rather than repatriated to Japan. And since Britain was a prime supplier of capital goods to Japan and the only source for many essential armaments, the physical presence of the gold in London helped facilitate settlement of import payments. But even more important, it helped buy British friendship. As Suzuki Toshio has noted, "the outstanding feature of English gold reserves during the 19th century was their inadequacy . . . even to preserve convertibility of sterling. Japan's specie holdings in London were of great assistance to the Bank of England in adjusting constant fluctuations in the money market."[5]

Meanwhile, the MOF authorized the BOJ to issue domestic yen currency against the holdings in London—the same system, as Fukai noted, used to issue scrip in Britain's colonies, and which, we might add, serves in modified form today: Japan's holdings of U.S. dollars in the American banking system now perform much the same role that the BOJ's holdings with the BOE did a century ago.

The handling of the Chinese gold reparations marked the beginning of a policy that continues to this day and functions as one of Japan's most critical tools of exchange rate management. Japan's policy elite learned that when the country acquired external reserves, it needed to do so in a manner that did not antagonize powerful foreign countries. Whether those reserves came in the form of gold, sterling, or dollars or whether they were the booty of war, the proceeds of bond issues, or the earnings from trade surpluses, Japan carefully deployed them to avoid reducing the purchasing power of the foreign superpower of the day. That was most easily done by leaving the gold, sterling, or dollars inside the foreign banking system, permitting foreigners to enjoy "deficits without tears" while Japan built up production capacity.

Before World War II, the policy actually had a name—*zaigai seika*, literally, "specie kept outside." Indeed, the Japanese government floated bond issues in London to maintain a given level of specie after the reparations from the Sino-Japanese War were run down.[6]

## Profits and Losses from World War I

Japan was able to maintain the gold exchange standard for some two decades, until the onset of World War I, despite trade deficits resulting from the capital goods imported to modernize production. The U.S.-brokered peace agreement that had ended the 1905 war did not include the reparations payments by Russia that the Japanese public had been led to expect, provoking the first outbursts of serious anti-American feeling in Japan. Fukai notes that the outcome taught Japan that despite victory in battle, war could be very costly. It was many years before Japan could pay back what it had borrowed to win the war; the country again found itself heavily indebted to foreign lenders.

But World War I changed Japan's fortunes dramatically. Nominally on the allied side, Japan did little actual fighting beyond sending a few destroyer escorts to the Mediterranean and seizing German holdings in China and the South Pacific. Trade balances moved strongly into the black as Japan exported both to the belligerent nations and to a booming United States, all the while filling the gap in Asian markets left by the Europeans prevented by war from exporting to their colonies. The ruling elite, including such key figures as Yamagata Aritomo, architect of the modern Japanese military; BOJ governor Inoue Junnosuke; and Ookuma Shigenobu, prime minister briefly in 1908 and again in 1914–16, agreed that the time had come to implement a sea change in Japan's economic policy. Wakatsuki Reijiro, minister of finance in the second Ookuma cabinet, announced the shift in a speech given in 1915.[7] In his talk, he condemned past policies as too sensitive to the vicissitudes of world economic conditions. He noted that theretofore Japan had been trapped in a cycle in which the country was dependent on international capital markets because the cycle started with raising funds abroad in order to import capital goods. The capital goods were used to manufacture exports, which stimulated economic growth, providing the wherewithal for more borrowing and thus starting the cycle all over again. Wakatsuki proposed a different policy, one aimed at freeing Japan from its servitude to international capital markets. Instead of borrowing abroad, the export cycle should begin with domestically led export financing. Exporters were then to earn the foreign exchange necessary to finance capital goods imports, while accumulating financial resources independent of the international capital markets. These policies—the independence of Japanese finance from foreign capital markets coupled with export-led growth— would continue to serve as the guiding principles for Japan's economic management until they finally became moot in the 1980s, when Japan emerged as the world's premier net creditor nation.

Wakatsuki's speech did not, in fact, contain much that was really new; rather, it represented an announcement that the time had finally arrived that Japan could free itself from dependence on foreign capital. Leaders of the Meiji period such as Iwakura Tomomi and Matsukata Masayoshi had long dreamed of that day. On a study mission to Germany in the 1870s, Iwakura, perhaps the most important political figure in the first years after the Meiji Restoration, had been personally warned by Germany's "Iron Chancellor," Otto von Bismarck, of the dangers to national independence of excessive reliance on foreign financing. On becoming finance minister in 1881, Matsukata promptly implemented deflationary policies that resulted in a severe recession in order to terminate Japan's borrowings in the City of London. Yet for a country dependent on imported capital equipment, complete freedom from foreign financing could not be realized until Japan could export enough to acquire the necessary foreign exchange without borrowing. World War I gave Japan that opportunity.

On the eve of the war, most of Japan's specie and other international reserves were held by the government-owned Yokohama Specie Bank (YSB), the pre–World War II predecessor of the Bank of Tokyo (now part of Bank of Tokyo–Mitsubishi). To implement Wakatsuki's policies, the BOJ began to fund YSB's external asset holdings at subsidized interest rates. That permitted the YSB to extend cheap hard currency financing to exporters who used the money to import capital goods that resulted in a large buildup of production capacity.

The buildup in capacity served Japan well when Allied demand for Japanese goods grew, resulting in the sudden appearance of trade surpluses. Between 1915 and 1918, Japan's cumulative current account surplus amounted to ¥2.7 billion; by comparison, annual GDP at the beginning of the war stood at ¥4.7 billion. As the war proceeded, however, imports of capital machinery became difficult to obtain and the classical gold standard that had held together global finance and trade in the nineteenth century was finally suspended. Export earnings could not be converted into gold since most of Japan's trading partners had gone off the gold standard, and governments financed their war efforts with fiat money. Japan had no choice but to accept and hold dollars.

The implications were well understood by one of the principal architects of the postwar Japanese economic miracle, Ishibashi Tanzan, who was finance minister in 1946–47, MITI minister in 1955, and prime minister for three months in 1957 before falling ill and having to resign. During the 1920s, Ishibashi had been editor of *Toyo Keizai*, long Japan's leading journal on economic issues. In the March 16, 1929, issue of the magazine, Ishibashi had written of the huge current account surplus Japan ran up during World War I, the embargo of gold exports imposed by the Western powers, and Japan's resulting inability to redeem its current account surplus by importing gold from those countries. Ishibashi noted that net sales of dollars would have invited an unlimited rise in the yen against the dollar and that a rising yen would in turn have reduced exports of goods and services. As Ishibashi pointed out, since export manufacturers had to pay wages and suppliers in yen, they could not simply accumulate dollar deposits or accounts receivable that could never be collected or redeemed in yen.

Ishibashi conceded that banks could buy dollar receivables from exporters for yen but noted that they also had to satisfy loan demand from their usual customers and could not fund those loans out of dollar receivables unless the receivables were in turn redeemed for yen. That created a problem— what to do with the dollars?

In his memoirs, Fukai points out that Japan was forced to sterilize its dollar holdings. The Bank of Japan could not sell them for yen without driving the yen through the roof, and it could not monetize the dollars without eroding the country's international competitiveness through the inflation that would result. Instead, the MOF isolated—"sterilize" is the technical term—those holdings. The funding of these external assets came directly out of the national budget and through the sale of short-term bills.

Meanwhile, demand by the Allies for Japanese goods drove prices up, and poor people could not buy food. Yet Japan's administrators feared that if wages were raised, Japan's international competitiveness could suffer greatly. By 1917, the combination of snowballing temporary surpluses, a rapidly growing economy, and a tight monetary policy implemented by a BOJ that feared uncontrolled inflation led nonetheless to a climb in the value of the yen. The forward market for dollars dried up; that is, no buyers were to be found for future delivery of dollars.[8] Japanese exporters had no place to sell their dollar export proceeds and ran into serious cash flow problems that threatened their viability. As a result, exports started to decline even before the war ended; there was simply no way to fund the accumulated dollar proceeds and reassure exporters that they would ever be paid.[9]

Winning the Russo-Japanese War may have proved an expensive victory for Japan, but Japan's experience in World War I taught that staying out of war could also be very costly. Once the war ended and the key belligerents resumed nonmilitary production, Japanese exporters were hit by both price and volume competition from other nations with nothing in the way of reparations to fall back on. The economy fell into recession. The return of Allied facilities to nonmilitary production naturally exacerbated the situation confronting Japan. Just at the time that Japan sought to export more, it faced both renewed competition and reduced foreign ability and willingness to absorb Japanese exports. But since Japan had joined the rest of the world in abandoning the gold standard, the resulting current account deficits after 1918 did not force the BOJ to reduce currency in circulation. (Had Japan stuck to the gold standard, the postwar deficits would have resulted in an outflow of gold, forcing the BOJ to reduce domestic money). The deficits did, however, result in the depreciation of the yen from the ¥2 per dollar that had prevailed during the war to ¥2.63.

The governing bureaucracy had made a huge mistake in its failure to anticipate what would happen after the war ended. Not realizing that a collapse in demand was inevitable, companies imported capital goods and cranked up production, and banks financed the buildup of inventories—which could not, as it turned out, be sold. But the Japanese government was not about to admit it had made a terrible miscalculation. Japan's system of governance did not then and does not now contain an institutional means of coping with serious bureaucratic error. The legitimacy of the Japanese bureaucracy—of its right to determine policy—lies in its infallibility; it cannot openly acknowledge mistakes without bringing its infallibility into question. The central importance of the Imperial institution lies in the sacred cloak it provides for bureaucratic infallibility; the assassinations and open intimidation that characterized Japanese political life before 1945 and the "scandals" that have erupted regularly since then substitute for an institutional means of changing course.

Therefore the bureaucracy could not admit in 1919 that it had miscalculated in encouraging the buildup of excess capacity or in forecasting demand. Instead, Inoue—still BOJ governor—gave a speech outlining new policies to cope with the end of the war and the onset of recession.[10] Rather than call for a reduction in domestic production capacity—tantamount to an open admission of error—Inoue encouraged full use of that capacity, which had expanded so substantially during the early years of the war. He insisted that production in excess of domestic demand be exported. And for that purpose, the BOJ was permitted to continue extending export financing on very favorable terms to manufacturers.

But the plant and equipment Japan had amassed during the run up to World War I and then again in the war's immediate aftermath had created so much production capacity that the sum of foreign and domestic markets could not begin to absorb its output. The policy announced by Inoue forced Japan into confrontation with other manufacturing nations who were themselves trying to export their way out of the postwar doldrums, and it led to a poisoning of Japan's relations with the Western powers that would help bring on the next war.

## The Birth of Modern Japanese Finance

Notwithstanding the measures instituted to help exporters, a shakeout loomed. Deprived of the cash flow necessary to retire the debt generated by the buildup of capacity and inventory, corporations found themselves trapped by all the excess capacity they had built. With unsold inventories accumulating, companies began to default on their loans.[11] Confidence in the banking system collapsed, and by the end of 1920, twenty-one banks would close their doors.

But the legacy of the Meiji Restoration prevented any resort to a market-driven shakeout. The pre-Meiji ruling class of samurai and daimyo (the lords of Japan's premodern fiefdoms) had been compensated back in the 1870s for the loss of their feudal privileges with government bonds. Many feudal practices, however, survived the end of the shogunate; the first claim on rice production historically enjoyed by the ruling class was replaced with controlling equity stakes in the new banks, railroads, and industrial corporations established in the last decades of the nineteenth century. The owners expected as a matter of course that those holdings would generate profits on the scale of those their ancestors had enjoyed and that it was up to the bureaucracy to arrange things in such a manner as to secure the profits.

The bureaucracy had subsidized the new enterprises with a view to replacing imports with domestic production. Their viability had been supported with public funds whenever necessary; in any case, "public" funds were thought of as belonging to Japan's rulers, not the general public. Even after nominal equity control of the new enterprises was turned over to the descendants of the feudal elites at what amounted to give-away prices in the 1880s, the elites still acted as if it were up to the bureaucracy to take whatever measures necessary to ensure the continued viability of the enterprises. Nomura Kentaro, a prominent economic historian in prewar Japan, noted in a bulletin of the Keio Gijyuko Economic History Society that "the majority of the samurai class spent several centuries without working to clothe and feed themselves." He went on to point out that members of this class did not understand any relationship between cause and effects and that that was still the case among the ruling elite.[12] Therefore, when hit by the severe recession that followed World War I, the bureaucracy never considered allowing market forces to bring on a widespread shakeout.

External events, however, forced their hand. The great earthquake that devastated Tokyo and Yokohama in 1923 drove many industrial and trading companies, already suffering from the post–World War I recession, into insolvency. They could not redeem the notes they had issued to buy goods. The government asked the BOJ to buy those notes at face value with the idea that the government would compensate the BOJ for the losses. The notes were not settled until 1949—a meaningless gesture since by that point the yen was worth a tiny fraction of its prewar value. But the BOJ's efforts were insufficient, leading to a series of bank failures culminating in the banking crisis of 1927, the most severe financial crisis Japan would face—the immediate post–World War II years excepted—between the 1880s and the 1990s. The crisis represented a watershed in the history of MOF's consolidation of control over the financial system.

During the Meiji period, the ruling elite had, as part of its desperate efforts to force-march the pace of Japan's development, transplanted into Japan wholesale the institutional trappings of a modern industrial economy. Imported institutions were permitted—indeed encouraged—to function as they did in Western countries provided that they did not pose any fundamental challenge to existing power alignments and the ability of the elite to control economic and political outcomes. The moment that such a challenge was felt possible, the institution was modified. Banks and bond markets are a case in point. Japan's core banking institutions played a pivotal role both in financing development and in concentrating control of the economy in the hands of the elite.

Banks modeled on contemporary German institutions had been launched in Japan in 1870. But Iwasaki Yataro, the founder of the Mitsubishi empire, introduced an important institutional modification to the imported German model. Peter Drucker notes that Iwasaki's "idea of a bank was as an institution to attract capital for investment in the industries and businesses of the Mitsubishi zaibatsu in such a form that the public would in no way acquire title of ownership or control. The public would come in as 'depositors', and not as 'investors.' In other words, he looked upon a bank not as a means to create a capital market . . . [but] *as a substitute for a capital market.* [emphasis added] . . . . As a result, Japanese industry is financed primarily by what legally are bank loans. Economically, most of this money is equity capital. But it is not invested in the equity form, but in the form of short-term indebtedness."[13] We have already noted and will return to the very significant ramifications of Drucker's observation that short-term bank lending in Japan in fact plays the role of equity capital in a market economy.[14]

For the moment, however, we need to focus on the distinction between *zaibatsu* banks, such as the Mitsubishi Bank, that sat at the core of the Japanese system and the hundreds of smaller banks that had been launched in the late nineteenth and early twentieth centuries as part of the wholesale import of Western institutions. The smaller banks had stayed alive by funding speculators and peripheral industries. The 1921 postwar shakeout had already seen a score of them go under, but the 1927 crisis essentially finished the job. Meanwhile, Japan's market in corporate bonds was also shut down. Those events suited the MOF very well. Bonds and the smaller banks had been competing for household funds by offering higher yields, but in the wake of the 1927 banking crisis and the failure of so many institutions, the MOF could easily suppress interest rates by forcing household savings into core banks that paid low rates. And what the 1927 crisis did not accomplish, the 1936 legally decreed amalgamation of the remaining banks did.[15] Household funds flowed into core banks because they lacked any alternative, and they were used by the banks to fund purchases of the JGBs that the MOF began to force feed the banks. The JGBs in turn were used to finance the huge military buildup already under way by the late 1920s. Pervasive MOF control of interest rates, household savings, and indeed the banking system itself continued, of course, right through the war years and into the postwar period.

The BOJ, for its part, assumed for the first time in 1927 its characteristic role in postwar Japanese finance: specific responsibility for bridging bank asset/liability gaps. The enactment of the *Nichigin Tokubetsu Yuzu Hoshoho* (BOJ Special Lending Compensation Law) gave the BOJ the legal power to keep any bank open by lending the necessary funds. But the BOJ was not, in practice, expected to use its independent judgment in determining which banks—and which of the banks' major clients—survived and which did not; it would defer to the MOF's decisions. The BOJ initially, for example, resisted pressure from Minister of Finance Takahashi Korekiyo to bail out the Jyugo Bank and, by extension, Kawasaki Shipyards, Jyugo's most important client and the predecessor of today's Kawasaki Heavy Industries. Both were owned by members of the nobility. But on May 8, 1928, when the BOJ announced a bank rescue package of ¥688 million, the BOJ had clearly backed down. For the largest chunk of that amount—¥177 million—went to Jyugo. Until the bail-out loan was settled finally on May 8, 1952, in a currency worth a tiny percentage of what it had been in 1928, ¥88 million remained outstanding.

Meanwhile, international confidence in Japan plummeted to the point that the government felt that it had no choice but to attempt to reestablish the gold standard, as all the major Western governments were doing in the 1920s in an attempt to restore the prewar international financial order. And the bonds that had been floated to finance the Russo-Japanese War forced Tokyo's hand. The bonds were coming due; since repaying them was out of the question, they had to be renewed. That necessitated shoring up Japan's creditworthiness in international markets with the move back to the gold standard. As exports could not easily be increased to underscore the credibility of Japan's intention to return to the gold standard, the only alternative was a forced appreciation of the yen to the prewar rate of ¥2 to the dollar on November 21, 1929, the day of the announcement of the return. The Japanese economy promptly plunged into a severe deflationary recession. The consequent impoverishment of an agricultural sector already living a marginal existence provided a fertile breeding ground for demagogues and xenophobes.

But despite all the upheavals—wars, depression, natural disasters, financial panic—investments in production capacity steadily accelerated during the three decades between 1910 and 1940, as demonstrated by figure 4-1. Japan's financial mandarins in the MOF and the BOJ acted at every juncture to keep production afloat and sacrificed every other consideration to that goal.

## Financing War

In 1931, Britain went off the gold standard. That year also saw the outbreak of the Manchurian Incident and intense speculation against the yen by those convinced that Japan would have to follow in Britain's footsteps. Japan did indeed do so, abandoning its brief return to the gold standard and putting in its place the currency system that prevailed until the Occupation. The BOJ announced that it would no longer redeem existing currency with gold. Meanwhile, the BOJ was given essentially carte blanche to issue new currency; Japan's military elites, who by that point were running the country,

**Figure 4-1.** *Japan's Private Capital Spending*[a]

Yen, billions

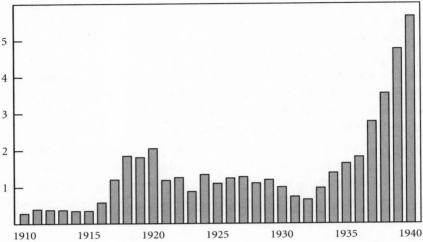

Sources: *Estimates of Long-Term Economic Statistics of Japan Since 1868,* Toyo Keizai Shinposha. Calculated, arranged, and estimated by Mikuni & Co. © 2002 Mikuni & Co., Ltd.

a. Private capital spending = producers' durable equipment + structures other than residential buildings.

certainly did not want the BOJ's external holdings to restrict financing of the war buildup. The BOJ began to issue notes independent of external holdings. The BOJ paid for JGBs issued to finance the buildup with the newly issued currency. The yen/dollar rate naturally plummeted, falling to ¥5 to $1.

The government first disguised what it was doing by changing accounting methods in order to value JGBs at cost rather than market price, in defiance of usual prudential accounting standards that require that securities be "marked to market" to reflect their current value. JGBs generally were financed through postal savings and bank deposits—as they still are—and both the official discount rate and deposit rates were reduced to bolster JGB prices, foreshadowing the zero interest rates that prevailed in the early 2000s. Laws such as the foreign exchange control law, a law whose spirit is still largely in force, were enacted to prevent capital flight.

By the mid 1930s, banks were being ordered to lend money to munitions manufacturers in whatever quantities were deemed necessary, while the government purchased the output. The lack of key components became more and more of a problem once the war widened after Pearl Harbor, with the result that manufacturers piled up unfinished inventory. But the manufacturers did not go bankrupt; they were sustained by bank loans. Secure in the knowledge that inflation would wipe out the value of the mounting piles of uncollectible loans, bankers gave up any pretense of credit analysis. Besides, they had no choice in the matter. Credit analysis would continue to be an irrelevant skill for a Japanese banker until the late 1990s, when the bureaucracy was finally unable to back up the indiscriminate guarantees it had tacitly made to the nation's borrowers.

Indeed, many—even most—of the defining characteristics of postwar Japanese finance can be traced back to the war years, which is why the eminent Tokyo University professor and former MOF official Noguchi Yukio labels Japanese finance "the 1940 system" in a book by that name noted in chapter 2. He played on the term "1955 system," often used to describe the Japanese political setup, but was referring in this case to the measures taken to put the Japanese economy on a war footing.[16]

## Devastation and the Postwar Monetary Regime

In 1941, with the onset of World War II in the Pacific, the government announced arbitrary rates for foreign currencies that would govern all transactions. The stock exchanges were directed to implement similar arrangements for share prices. But by 1945, all such prices had become a joke—Japan's real material wealth had been almost entirely wiped out. The military exchange market between the yen and the dollar was reset at ¥15 to $1 in contrast to the ¥4.25 to $1 that had prevailed on the eve of the war, but with postwar hyperinflation, that rate had to be readjusted to ¥50 to $1 in 1947, ¥270 to $1 in 1948, and, finally, ¥360 to $1 in 1949, where it remained for the next twenty-two years. The challenges of excess capacity, burgeoning current account surpluses, and the disposition of surplus funds all seemed distant memories. In the wake of the ruin visited on Japan by the war, it appeared as if for the foreseeable future Japan would face instead the classic problems of all poor developing countries, living month to month under the implacable pressure of current account deficits, hoarding every precious bit of foreign exchange in order to purchase essential imports.

In the immediate wake of World War II, Japan established what amounted to a currency board. A currency board acts in lieu of a central bank, using only one variable in determining the quantity of domestic money: the foreign exchange rate. If the rate drops, the board automatically decreases the amount of money in circulation until the rate goes back up. If the rate rises, the board does the reverse. Currency boards originally were a feature of colonial regimes and are periodically adopted by countries dependent on foreign financing when confidence in the domestic currency collapses. Indonesia debated instituting such a regime in the aftermath of the 1998 Asian economic crisis.

Japan's decision to adopt what amounted to a currency board was unremarkable, given the state of the Japanese economy at the time. In the immediate postwar years, the yen had become a worthless currency outside Japan, while inside the country it lost virtually all its purchasing power. Japan could not even feed itself, much less afford the imports of capital equipment essential to rebuilding its economy. American aid plus the bit that Japan could earn from exports provided the sole sources of foreign exchange. That foreign exchange was so precious that the bureaucracy naturally took steps to ensure that not a penny of it was wasted; monetary policy, as noted in chapter 1, was inevitably constrained by the overwhelming need to preserve foreign exchange.

Following the end of World War II, GHQ (literally, General Headquarters; GHQ was the most widely used acronym for the American Occupation authorities) controlled all foreign exchange transactions and settlements were done on a case-by-case basis. Beginning in August 1947, however, the Japanese government reasserted a degree of control over foreign exchange, settling accounts with GHQ on a periodic rather than a case-by-case basis. In order to preserve foreign exchange, encourage exports, and discourage imports, businesses were required to apply to the government for foreign exchange and to turn over the foreign exchange proceeds of all sales. The MOF instituted multiple exchange rates at which businesses were compensated for their dollar earnings. An exporter could exchange dollar revenues for yen at up to 600 yen per dollar. But importers would be paid as little as 60 yen per dollar for any imports they sold in Japan.

The fixing of the yen to the dollar at ¥360 to $1 in April 1949 ended the use of multiple rates.[17] Control over foreign exchange passed in totality from GHQ to the Foreign Exchange Control Board, set up by the MOF the previous month, which opened accounts with the Tokyo branches of the handful of foreign banks authorized to open (or reopen) their own branches in Japan. This board functioned in effect as the currency board. In December 1949, the Foreign Exchange and Foreign Administrative Law was enacted, followed a month later by the Foreign Capital Law. Under the two laws, only specific banks were authorized by the MOF to deal in foreign exchange. In 1952, authorized banks were allowed to set up overseas branch offices and to hold foreign exchange assets rather than simply deal in foreign currency. With the signing of the San Francisco Peace Treaty that summer, Japan recovered its sovereignty and became a member of the two major Bretton Woods institutions, the World Bank and the International Monetary Fund (IMF). While those events marked the formal return of Japan to the community of nations, an even bigger event had begun to spur the real recovery of the Japanese economy—and more rapidly than anyone had dreamed possible.

## The Korean War and the FESA

The policy regime in place in the early 1950s, a regime that saw a central government organ monopolize all foreign exchange transactions, is typical of a country in Japan's economic straits in the immediate postwar years. Events soon made those institutional arrangements superfluous, however, as the Korean War, which began in 1950, found Japanese industry scrambling to meet the insatiable demands of the American military. Restrictions on production of items with military potential were quickly lifted; the Japanese were making even napalm bombs and bullets. Special procurements from the U.S. military totaled $2.3 billion (not the yen equivalent thereof; the payments were made in dollars) between 1950 and 1953.[18] Capital allocations were authorized for plant reconstruction, and with Japan selling all it could make, the financing of production and trade soon ceased to be the overwhelming obstacle to recovery that it had been in the late 1940s. A delighted economic bureaucracy saw Japan's current account move into the black years before they had thought it possible; at the height of the Korean War, the current account surplus exceeded 4 percent of GDP.

Pleased as they may have been, however, those developments presented policymakers with the same challenge they faced during World War I—how to cope with an excess of foreign exchange. To solve it, the Japanese authorities took a garden-variety currency board regime and turned it inside out, creating a unique structure that amounted to a reverse currency board, as it were. A typical currency board regime has as its raison d'être a structural scarcity of foreign exchange; the currency board will restrain the growth of the money supply—and thus the nominal growth rate of the economy as a whole—to ensure essential supplies of foreign exchange. But if foreign exchange begins pouring into the nation's coffers, then the simple equation of foreign exchange reserves and monetary growth becomes a problem. Monetization of rapidly growing foreign exchange reserves—in other words, the creation of domestic money equal to that of the reserves—can and will lead to overheating and inflation.

One solution to the dilemma is for the currency board to revalue the currency, setting it at a new and higher peg against the dollar, gold, sterling, or what have you. Exports fall off as the country's goods become more expensive in foreign markets while imports become cheaper and therefore increase. Japan's policy officials never considered such an option, however. They viewed the surge in demand created by the Korean War as a strictly temporary phenomenon, and they were bent on increasing industrial production and exports as fast as possible. Instead, they reached back in their historical memory for guidance and found it in the similar policy challenge posed by the sudden rise in demand for Japanese exports during World War I. As we have seen, the authorities at that time had deliberately held the surge in foreign exchange in limbo.

Ikeda Hayato, finance minister at the time, cited that precedent in explaining why the MOF refused to monetize all the foreign exchange Japan was earning from the Korean War boom.[19] Plant utilization rates had begun to climb, bringing on the risk of inflation if domestic demand could not be curbed. Meanwhile, foreign exchange reserves climbed rapidly. Under ordinary circumstances, foreign exchange was used as a reserve asset against which the Bank of Japan would issue domestic currency. But with reserves climbing rapidly, the added money could—given the high plant utilization rate—have sparked an inflationary conflagration. That gave Japan no choice but to follow the precedent set during World War I and isolate the growing foreign exchange pile from the domestic monetary system.

The dilemma first encountered back in 1917 returned with a vengeance at the time of the Korean War. Recall what happens when Japan's exporters earn dollars. They need to pay their domestic suppliers and employees in yen, so they turn the dollars over to their banks (something that they were required to do in any case in the early 1950s because only authorized foreign exchange banks could legally hold dollars). The dollars become assets of the banks, which create counterbalancing yen deposits in the accounts of exporters. Exporters can then make use of the deposits in the same manner as if they had been earned from domestic sales. Meanwhile, the bank that bought the foreign currency cannot use it in Japan; the dollars—at least with respect to the domestic market—are frozen and the bank's ability to extend loans is reduced concomitantly. To escape this dilemma, the bank will exchange the dollar assets for yen with the Bank of Japan. But if the Bank of Japan purchases the bank's dollars with newly issued yen, then it has added to the overall growth of the money supply—unless it takes a bite somewhere else out of its balance sheet to reduce the money it has created to purchase the exporter's bank's foreign exchange.

MOF officials devised what we have labeled a reverse currency board mechanism that permitted at least the BOJ—if not Japan as a whole—to escape this dilemma. To hold Japan's surplus foreign exchange, they replaced the Foreign Exchange Control Board in July 1952 with the special fund we encountered in chapter 1, the Foreign Exchange Special Account (FESA), run by the MOF's International Finance Bureau. The foreign exchange earned by Japan's exporters ended up in this account rather than on the balance sheet of the Bank of Japan.

The FESA was not a completely isolated case in global economic history. Indeed, it had been specifically modeled on the Exchange Equalization Account that the United Kingdom set up in 1932 after going off the gold standard.[20] But it soon came to play a unique role. The law that established the FESA under the jurisdiction of the minister of finance separated it from the general accounts of the national budget. While funds to support the FESA were allocated in the general budget, the FESA was authorized (up to predetermined limits) to plug any gaps in funding by issuing what were labeled *gaikoku kawase shikin shoken*, or foreign exchange fund financing bills, which were bought by the BOJ.

In a typical developing country where the central bank monopolizes foreign exchange holdings, the central bank will be the sole buyer of foreign exchange from exporters and their banks. As bankers say, the central bank "funds" its foreign exchange purchases by issuing currency in circulation or creating deposits in the name of authorized foreign exchange banks at the central bank. Thus foreign exchange earned by exporters directly increases the domestic money supply. But to cope with the inflationary dangers posed by the Korean War, the BOJ, rather than acting independently, became the FESA's dealer. Exporters were still required to turn over all dollars to authorized foreign exchange banks that, in turn, still sold the dollars to the BOJ and were paid with yen deposits made to their accounts. But the BOJ then turned the dollars over to the FESA. That arrangement has significant implications for the conduct of monetary policy.

We have argued that the broadly defined money supply in Japan has been steered for most of the postwar period not by the BOJ's open market operations but by its window guidance, which is administered to banks under the direction of the MOF. Dollars did serve as backing for currency in circulation, but the ultimate level of economic activity (and therefore the broader money supply), which in most countries is linked directly to currency in circulation and bank deposits with the central bank, was determined in Japan by window guidance. To some extent, that already helped keep a lid on the inflationary potential of the dollars flooding into Japan. Funding for the FESA's dollar purchases came out of the government's general budget and thus directly out of taxes; the MOF thereby acquired the power to sterilize Japan's official foreign exchange holdings, counteracting any impact on the domestic money supply. The yen created by the BOJ to pay the banks for dollars could be counteracted if necessary by removing money from the system by allocating tax revenues to fund the FESA's dollar holdings. (The FESA also had the alternative, as noted, of issuing notes if the MOF preferred not to sterilize foreign exchange earnings.) Ikeda wrote that since the domestic value of Japan's currency in circulation should mirror its external value, giving the MOF power over foreign exchange policy helped concentrate monetary and fiscal policies in the hands of the MOF.[21]

The FESA thus served a critical purpose in permitting Japan to take advantage of the Korean War boom to build up its foreign currency holdings without an inflationary impact on the money supply. Because a surge in exports can put money into peoples' pockets through increased wages without increasing the supply of domestically available goods, it can be inflationary—particularly if imports are deliberately suppressed and therefore are unavailable to mop up surplus liquidity. But the absence of a genuine labor market coupled with tight control of wages kept labor costs from rising, while holding dollars in the FESA instead of the BOJ ensured that Japan's dollar-denominated current account surpluses did not translate into more domestic money. Of course, once the Korean War was over, Japan's current account went back into the red and inflationary pressures subsided. But the architecture put in place at the time survived.

## Monetary Policy During the High-Growth Years

As noted above and in chapter 3, actual monetary policy in Japan in the postwar years was conducted not through interest rates but through *madoguchi shido*, or window guidance, the term given to the direct control of credit made available to banks. Interest rates were set much lower than they otherwise would have been by the Ministry of Finance, the BOJ, and the cartels of banks they administered. Demand for credit therefore always exceeded supply. The authorities rationed credit, allocating most of it to finance exports and capital outlays by manufacturers.

In most countries, when the authorities loosen monetary policy, money finds its way into the hands of consumers, who use the money to buy goods; the money thus ultimately ends up in the accounts of the producers of those goods. In Japan, however, the process was short-circuited, with funds going through the banking system directly to producers—producers of goods for export rather than domestic consumption. Before 1970, during the decades when Japan was a net debtor, it had needed to run its currency system and monetary policy on a gold and then, in the postwar years, a dollar exchange standard to maintain its credit standing with its trading partners. Once the threat of inflation stemming from the Korean War had receded, the FESA-centered exchange rate system functioned again much like a currency board to ensure that monetary policy dovetailed with the need to support the fixed exchange rate.

In Japan, high-powered money (according to the BOJ's definition, noted in chapter 1, as currency in circulation plus deposits with the central bank) was a function of bank credit, and banks did not increase or decrease loans due to changes in interest rates: rather, they did so in response to the lending quotas they received through window guidance. The BOJ's open market operations and interest rate changes were therefore largely irrelevant, as noted, to the availability of credit. Because monetary policy was implemented through direct controls on credit availability, the MOF had, as we saw in chapter 3, ultimate control of all significant monetary policy tools—as well as the power to determine the impact of Japan's official foreign exchange holdings on the domestic money supply through the FESA's operations. The MOF controlled tax revenues and government spending while determining the disposition of much of Japan's social security funds and postal savings. Together, social security funds and postal savings funded off-budget expenditures known as the Fiscal Investment and Loan Program, or *zaito*, to use the Japanese acronym, a pool of money under the control of the MOF's Trust Fund Bureau that would ultimately reach the equivalent of trillions of dollars. *Zaito* funds went into JGBs, government banks such as the Japan Development Bank, and the ninety-two *tokushu hojin*, or special public corporations.[22] The MOF micromanaged both the loan and securities portfolios of the institutions it licensed—banks, insurance companies, and securities firms—set deposit rates, and approved all bank and insurance products. To be sure, the BOJ distributed lending quotas to individual institutions, but aggregate lending was determined together with public sector spending inside the MOF in a manner that ensured the smooth meshing of credit allocation and monetary policy.

## The FESA and the Collapse of Bretton Woods

Since 1973, the Japanese economy has slowed despite rapid expansion of the money supply. The explanation for that contradiction lies with the buildup of both official and unofficial reserves that far exceed Japan's import needs or any requirement to back the yen. In the first postwar decades, Japan ran, as we have seen, a dollar exchange standard with the dollar reserves held by the FESA used to pay for imported capital goods and commodities. Domestic economic activities were governed by the ultimate need to retain dollar reserves as foreign exporters insisted on payment in dollars. Currency in circulation was limited, as noted, to a level some three times that of Japan's dollar holdings.

By the late 1960s, however, Japan had learned to make most capital goods for itself and its current account moved permanently into the black, with the exception of a few quarters during the 1970s oil crises. The country did not really need to hoard dollars any longer; the yen was becoming an internationally accepted currency and no longer required backing. Japan's dollar holdings continued to mount, however—as noted, if currency in circulation had risen concomitantly, it would now be at twenty times its present level. That portion of Japan's total dollar holdings in the accounts of the FESA that exceeded one-third of currency in circulation could be funded through direct appropriations or by issuing bills that were bought by the BOJ. To this day, the FESA is authorized to raise funds by selling its own bills—mostly to the BOJ—up to a predetermined limit. These bills carry such low interest rates at the insistence of the MOF that they are unattractive to profit-driven investors and—according to conventional wisdom, including the BOJ's own rationales—that is why they end up mostly in the accounts of the BOJ. The BOJ can either redeem the bills at maturity, thereby reducing the money supply, or replace them with other BOJ assets. Shifts in the value of Japan's official foreign exchange holdings as a result of exchange rate fluctuations are thus reflected not on the books of the Bank of Japan but in the accounts of the FESA and made up by the appropriations from the national budget to fund the FESA. Sterilization of Japan's dollar holdings ultimately occurs when tax revenues are diverted into the funding of the FESA's holdings.

In 1971, the entire system designed to cope with Japan's foreign exchange holdings threatened to unravel. The story has been told elsewhere of how the Bretton Woods regime collapsed, of how Japan found itself bearing the brunt of the blame for its seemingly stubborn refusal to consider a revaluation of the yen in order to help preserve the global fixed-rate system that had been of such benefit to the country.[23] Japanese commentators such as Yoshino Toshihiko, formerly a director of the Bank of Japan and once the head of its research division, have complained that the United States threw its weight around during the crisis as if it were a surplus country rather than the deficit nation it had actually become.[24] But such complaints ignore how Japan plugged its ears to appeals that it help save the Bretton Woods system by agreeing, as West Germany had done, to revalue its currency and thereby reduce its surpluses. Japan's refusal even to entertain the pleas of its counterparts in other advanced nations gave the United States essentially no choice but to endure a politically unacceptable steep recession or destroy the system. Yoshino does acknowledge that the BOJ's tight money policy of 1969 aimed at reducing inflation while preserving Japan's external surpluses had been severely criticized internationally. But neither then nor during the crisis was the Japanese elite prepared to consider any measures that would entail revising the policy of maximizing production capacity. The collapse of Bretton Woods, would, however, confront Japan's decisionmakers with a new set of circumstances. Japan's economic history since that time is to a very large extent a tale of how a country whose institutional structures and mindset presupposed a fixed-rate world responded to the policy challenge of a world of floating rates.

At the heart of that policy response lay the improvised solution to the dilemma posed by the Korean War. The institutional arrangements that date from the early 1950s, most particularly the establishment of the FESA, which allowed for a sudden surge in foreign currency holdings without monetization by the BOJ, helped permit Japan to accumulate ever-growing amounts of dollars without being forced to disgorge them on the foreign exchange markets. Holding rather than selling those dollars made the dollar stronger than it otherwise would have been while, conversely, keeping the yen weaker. With costs denominated in yen and sales in dollars, Japan's exporters enjoyed an extra edge in global competition. Meanwhile, imports were made more expensive, thus reducing import purchases. The exchange rate became ever more important as Japan found itself forced under international pressure to give up many formal trade barriers.

As a consequence, Japan's dollar holdings climbed ever higher, far outstripping even the holding capacity of the FESA. Figure 4-2 shows the buildup of the FESA's reserves, which continued to be financed by allocations from the national budget and the bills it issued. But Japan's dollars also included external assets owned by the government and by government-owned financial institutions. Even more important, they included the dollar holdings of the nominally private sector banking system, which functioned effectively as an operating arm of the MOF. The real indicator of Japan's total dollar holdings is its net creditor position—for many years now the world's largest.

The historical purpose of these holdings may have been to pay for imports, but as figure 4-3, which illustrates the growth of Japan's imports compared with its foreign exchange reserves, demonstrates, these reserves have long exceeded the amount necessary to cover three months' worth of imports. From 1973 on, the dollar accumulation became the MOF's principal tool in its de facto attempt to peg the yen far below the level that Japan's trade practices would otherwise have carried it. But that created a huge and growing sterilization problem as the total extent of Japan's dollar holdings mounted far beyond what the FESA could support through appropriations. In 1929, Ishibashi had written presciently in the article cited above, "We should lend to importing countries the net receipts of our current account

**Figure 4-2.** *Buildup of Dollar Reserves in the FESA*

Dollars, billions

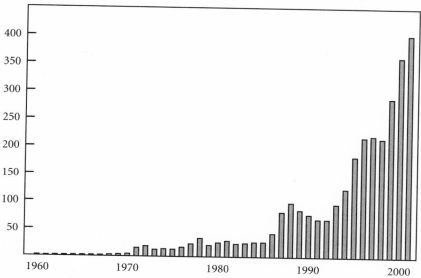

Sources: *Financial and Economic Statistics Monthly,* Bank of Japan. Calculated, arranged, and estimated by Mikuni & Co. © 2002 Mikuni & Co., Ltd.

surplus," but those "lendings"—the capital exports with which Japan would begin to flood the world, denominated in dollars that could not be monetized—would come to exert ever greater deflationary pressure on the Japanese economy. Coping with that pressure would become the dominant economic story of the last decades of the twentieth century in Japan.

## Adjusting to a Floating Rate Regime

The Japanese elite disliked it and resisted it, but since the early 1970s they have had to accept the reality of a floating rate regime. In theory, currency values in a floating rate regime are determined by the demand for and supply of the constituent currencies and will lead to a rough balance in the participating countries' external payments positions. But in Japan, most important economic players are guided not by the invisible hand of the market but by the very visible hand of the bureaucracy and the cartels it administers. As

**Figure 4-3.** *Ratio of Values of Official Foreign Exchange Reserves and Monthly Imports*

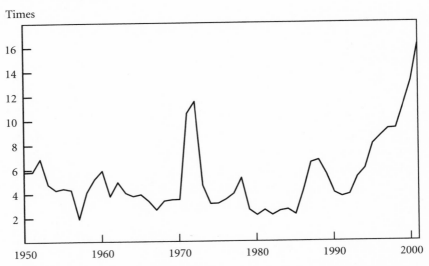

Sources: *Balance of Payments*, Ministry of Finance and Bank of Japan; *Financial and Economic Statistics Monthly*, Bank of Japan. Calculated, arranged, and estimated by Mikuni & Co. © 2002 Mikuni & Co., Ltd.

a result, Japan has succeeded in maintaining an imbalanced external trade picture by expanding credit more rapidly than the domestic economy required—a credit expansion that would provide the primary tool for support of Japan's dollar positions.

Japan's exchange policy has always been to control or peg the exchange rate not as an end in itself but as a crucial instrument in the drive to maximize production. Since the late nineteenth century, Japan has adapted itself to a gold, sterling, or dollar exchange standard in whatever manner conformed to its overall goal. When we say that Japan's goal has been to maximize production, we also imply that the profit motive has been deliberately deprived of any significant role in the Japanese economy. Banks have supported companies with strategic and political importance irrespective of their profitability and in turn have been treated essentially as public sector institutions supported by the government. The BOJ in particular has acted as the lender of last resort to banks whether they are insolvent or not. Walter

Bagehot's famous precept that a central bank should perform that function only for solvent institutions has not been observed in Japan; the BOJ has supported both solvent and insolvent institutions. In fact, criteria that would enable the BOJ to distinguish between the two have never been established. Nor can banks tell whether they themselves are solvent because they do not know whether their borrowers are solvent. Corporate borrowers cannot really answer the question either; to all intents and purposes, an independent Japanese accounting profession that could ascertain corporate financial health does not exist. In Japan, corporate viability has not been determined by the ability to turn a profit; profits, after all, acquire significance only when corporations stand or fall by their presence or absence. When every economic entity is, directly or indirectly, supported by the government, when risk is socialized, then profit seeking becomes a diversion or even a distraction. Instead, economic entities in Japan have acted like bureaucracies everywhere—doing their best to meet the expectations of those who ultimately determine their viability. And in Japan, that has meant the major ministries and the Bank of Japan.

The lender of last resort function played by BOJ therefore differed crucially from that in the major capitalist countries. That continues to be true. Under article 38 of the Bank of Japan Act, the prime minister or the minister of finance can require the BOJ to lend to a financial institution for the purpose of maintaining *shinyo chitsujo* (literally, credit order, or the stability of the financial system). The stability of Japanese finance therefore has long rested on perceptions of whether the MOF knows what it is doing; that is why the MOF has had to have ultimate say-so in foreign exchange policy as well as in all other crucial macroeconomic parameters. Currency values have thus, like income and wealth, been deliberately manipulated with both general and asset inflation, while banks have been allowed to create deposits by lending in excess of real economic requirements. Creating income independent of real economic activity and thereby creating deposits has been *the* critical tool in supporting Japan's accumulated dollar position and pegging the yen.

This ability to create income has its origins in the lending practices followed by Japanese banks during World War II. We noted in the preceding chapter that banks had been required to lend money to munitions manufacturers in whatever quantities the manufacturers specified, with the government guaranteeing the viability of the loans and making up any funding shortfall. Residual problem loans could be—and were—wiped out by inflation. Those arrangements survived the end of the war intact. Banks today can buy JGBs and other securities that technically function as secondary reserves, but the real reason for purchasing them is to create deposits. They are simply distributing money. The banks talk the way they are expected to talk about capital adequacy, but they are not actually acting as if they are at risk. To institutions that are not responsible for their own survival in a market economy, capital reserves are meaningless. A bank that tries to preserve its capital while flouting the MOF or the FSA puts, in fact, its viability at far greater risk than one with a nonexistent capital base that nonetheless diligently complies with all implied bureaucratic directives. The MOF has long informally allocated JGBs among Japan's financial institutions. In recent years, banks have helped to finance Japan's fiscal deficits by buying JGBs that fund government spending, thereby creating income for the construction companies, farmers, and rural fixers who are among the largest recipients of spending. Since these well-off people demonstrate a high propensity to save, much of their income ends up in the form of stable deposits, helping to fund Japan's dollar holdings and thereby forestalling a surge in the yen/dollar rate.

Back in the early 1970s, the Japanese authorities faced for the first time the sterilization problem created by the urgent need to fund a suddenly expanding pile of dollars in a floating rate world. They found that they could use their direct control of bank credit to provide the necessary funds through a new tactic: the deliberate creation of rapid run-ups in asset prices—that is, bubbles. In the following chapter, we will consider how they did so and the precedent it set.

# 5

## *Experimenting with Bubbles*

Japan's current account turned positive in 1966, and with two brief exceptions brought on by the "oil shocks" of the 1970s, the account has been in the black ever since. Rapid, export-led industrial growth combined with an import-suppressing policy regime gave birth to the era of surpluses. Of course, surpluses cannot exist in one country without countervailing deficits in others. The United States provided them. With the onset of the Vietnam War, the United States increased military spending without taking measures to reduce consumption. That and the inflationary methods used to finance the war led U.S. demand to outstrip U.S. production; trade and current account deficits plugged the gap. Radios, televisions, motorcycles, automobiles, and dozens of other attractive, low-priced Japanese products flooded the U.S. market, where they were snapped up by eager consumers flush with cash in a booming economy.

Much of the dollar proceeds of Japan's surpluses ended up in the accounts of the FESA, where they formed Japan's official foreign exchange reserves. In the three years from 1968 to 1970, the FESA increased its dollar hoard by

$2.4 billion, bringing the total to $4.4 billion. Meanwhile, dollar holdings by the city banks plus the Bank of Tokyo rose during the same period by $2.1 billion, tripling Japan's total dollar holdings.

In 1970, those burgeoning surpluses turned Japan into a net creditor nation. Japan had accumulated more claims on foreign countries than they had on Japan—the definition of a net creditor. As we have seen, however, it was not the first time: Chinese reparations after the Sino-Japanese War of 1895 made Japan a net creditor for a few years, and Japan again enjoyed that status during a brief period in World War I. But in 1970, unlike in the previous episodes, it appeared that the condition was likely to last quite a while. And so it has. In 1971 alone, the FESA's holdings shot up to $15.2 billion, and Japan has been a net creditor ever since. In fact, by the late 1980s, Japan would become the biggest of the world's net creditor countries, controlling the largest pile of dollars outside the United States.

Japan's willingness and ability to become the world's largest creditor with its claims largely denominated in the currency of the world's leading debtor played an indispensable role in stabilizing an international financial system based on fiat money. The final uncoupling of the world's hard currencies from gold in the early 1970s enabled central banks—including the Federal Reserve, which printed the currency in which the overwhelming preponderance of Japan's external claims was denominated—to create money without limit. Robert Triffin noted, in the words of Alvaro Cencini, that the workings of the Bretton Woods system had depended on "decisions taken by those countries that have to provide for international liquidity needs. Monetary reserves can increase only if these countries—and particularly the United States—accept a persistent deficit in their balance of trade and the accumulation of their short-term debt."[1] Cencini would go on to observe that when "fixed exchange rates are replaced by floating exchange rates, the problem does not radically change . . . parallel to the accumulation of dollars in the rest of the world the system is also characterised by a continuous expansion of the American trade deficit." And that continuous expansion was unimaginable without its mirror image: Japan's endless trade and current account surpluses. These in turn stemmed from the perpetuation without substantive modification of the policy regime put in place during the war years and cemented during the first postwar decade.

But whatever role Japan played in stabilizing a fiat dollar-based international financial order—and we argue that that role has been indispensable—Japan has, in retrospect, paid a huge price. By the late 1960s, the objectives of the postwar policy regime had largely been achieved: economic parity with the world's leading nations and liberation from structural foreign exchange scarcity. Instead of opting to continue that regime, Japanese officialdom could, theoretically, have overhauled Japan's economic institutions to permit more imports without risking any loss of the nation's newly won industrial preeminence. A number of commentators have gone beyond simply making that observation to argue that for the long-term health of the Japanese economy itself, that is precisely what should have happened. Richard Katz contends that instead, beginning in 1973, the Japanese "system . . . soured." Katz lays Japan's problems squarely at the foot of what he labels "the lunge for neomercantilism (i.e., policies that boost exports and restrict imports)"[parentheses in the original] that took place in the early 1970s rather than an "'accelerationist' response to Japan's economic shocks [that] would have . . . accelerate[d] the transfer of capital and labor from the declining sectors into the rising sectors."[2]

In the early 1970s, however, the elites lacked confidence in Japan's industrial competitiveness. Ten years later, they had acquired that confidence and even had begun to believe that Japan had cemented an unassailable lead on the rest of the world—gone "beyond capitalism" in the words of the well-known former MOF vice minister Sakakibara Eisuke in his book of that title.[3] Nonetheless, no alternative to the constant accumulation of surpluses has ever been given serious attention. If any advocates did exist back in the early 1970s for freer trade and more imports, they were silenced by the Arab oil embargo and subsequent OPEC price hikes, which brought a rapid deterioration in Japan's external position. The deterioration proved to be short-lived, although that was not obvious at the time.

As we have noted, Japan has never really accepted the logic of floating exchange rates: that foreign exchange markets should be permitted to reduce external imbalances, which in Japan's case would mean a yen/dollar rate strong enough to lower trade and current account surpluses. Instead, the policy elite worked to suppress the exchange rate of the yen so that Japan would accumulate surpluses—surpluses denominated in dollars. Exchanging the dollars for yen would have put intolerable upward pressure on the Japanese currency. It was precisely that pressure that the Japanese authorities feared most, because they worried that a strong yen would blunt Japan's export drive—the export drive that they credited with carrying their country from utter devastation to the front ranks of the world's industrial powers in just twenty-five years.

Popular understanding in Tokyo at the time held that because a current account surplus resulted in the import of dollars and dollars could back yen credit creation, a current account surplus meant easy money. That had been true as long as Japan's external position was in the red. As we have seen, Japan's monetary authorities had run a dollar-exchange standard, conducting monetary and fiscal policy with an eye to ensuring that foreign exchange reserves were always sufficient to cover about one-third of currency in circulation. Until the late 1960s, Japan had had to borrow many of the dollars needed for import payments. Japan therefore was under pressure not to increase deficits that required further borrowing, and the BOJ tightened credit whenever external deficits threatened to get out of control. Domestic spending was reduced and exports encouraged. External deficits thus spelled tight money; surpluses, easy money.

But times had changed. Elite officials understood that with Japan's emergence as a net creditor, the sterilization problem posed by ever-rising current account surpluses denominated in dollars would inevitably bring on tighter money unless counteracted by specific steps. Toyooka Tomiei, whose book *Jisho Kinyuron* we mentioned in chapter 3, had noted that in Japan it is the total volume of bank loans that determines liquidity, not the extent of foreign exchange reserves. He also went on to point out that prices in Japan were essentially set in the leading industries through cartels administered by MITI. Toyooka concluded that because MITI could control prices and a drop in foreign exchange reserves need not affect liquidity, the government should not fear measures to reduce the external surplus.[4] But the bureaucracy paid no attention.

We saw in chapter 4 how Japan had faced a similar problem back in 1918, when Japan's dollar holdings had increased following a surge of war-related foreign purchases of Japanese goods. Recall that officials had been at something of a loss because the circumstances of the war prevented them from either disposing of or easily funding those holdings. But in the intervening half-century, the bureaucracy had built up an enhanced set of instruments and controls, many of them a legacy of World War II, that made it possible to continue to expand production capacity and exports without pause, despite a deteriorating external environment. Unlike in the late 1910s, by the 1970s the banking system had come wholly under government control, and banks could literally create deposits by lending and allocating funds to des-ignated borrowers without any expectation of being paid back. Banks no longer needed to assess borrowers' capacity to service debt; MITI had plenty of practice in organizing cartels that ensured that all members could pay interest. And any problem loans that did occasionally emerge could be eroded away by rapid growth of nominal GDP.

Beginning in the early 1970s, the authorities accelerated the expansion of bank credit while boosting the already high levels of fiscal spending that had prevailed from the mid 1960s. Figure 1-10 in chapter 1 illustrates how in the early 1970s bank credit creation leaped ahead of GDP growth; that expansion appears to have been deliberately sparked in order to create deposits to fund the burgeoning dollar-denominated current account sur-plus. For it bears remembering that while an accumulating current account surplus poses no special difficulty provided that the country running the surplus receives its earnings in its own currency, the bulk of Japan's earnings were denominated not in yen but in the currency of its largest trading part-ner. Dollar deposits in the Federal Reserve system held by U.S. banks on behalf of Japan's exporters of financial capital are a form of money that can-not be used in Japan to settle claims. As long as Japan runs chronic sur-pluses and denominates those surpluses in dollars, its external assets will consist primarily of claims, directly or indirectly, on the Federal Reserve. Those assets by definition will far exceed external liabilities, which are directly or indirectly claims on the Bank of Japan. Japan is therefore not in a position to export financial capital in yen because yen, after all, constitute claims on the BOJ. Exports of capital derive from accumulated capital, and the capital Japan has been accumulating from its unbroken string of dollar-denominated current account surpluses is a huge and mounting pile of claims on the Federal Reserve. "Recycling" of current account surpluses can be done only in the currency in which the surpluses are denominated unless one wishes to change the underlying foreign exchange rate, and that is pre-cisely what Japanese authorities sought to avoid.

The deliberate expansion in bank credit in the early 1970s and the sub-sequent bubble represented the first attempt by the Japanese authorities to cope with the national balance sheet implications of Japan's accumulating dollars, which we briefly considered in chapter 3. Japan's dollar holdings were funded by domestic yen liabilities, that is, deposits owned by ultimate savers. Japan's dollar assets therefore function financially as nonperforming loans—illiquid assets as far as the Japanese banking system goes. These dollars form illiquid assets because they cannot be spent on imports without damaging domestic industries with the capacity to make intolerable political trouble, nor can they be exchanged for yen without driving the currency up. The assets must nonetheless be funded, so the deposits that support them therefore were not deployed in Japan, reducing the money supply available for a given level of economic activity. And once Japan's dollar assets outstripped the needs of the economy for currency in circulation, something that happened in the late 1960s, money to fund those assets had to be created by artificial means—that is, through means other than real economic activity—if Japan expected to offset the deflationary effects of its excess dollar holdings. Coping with this challenge has been a perennial concern of Japan's monetary authorities in the three decades since it first emerged, and their initial response was deliberately to create stable deposits.

## The Deliberate Creation of Stable Deposits

The BOJ eased money in the second quarter of 1969, encouraging banks to increase loans.[5] In December 1969, deposits began to shoot up, clear evidence of what the authorities were doing. The BOJ implicitly promised to accommodate banks that needed extra liquidity to fund the extra loans; under the regulated interest regime then prevailing, the more loans a bank made, the greater the income. Because banks in any case tended to regard credit problems as the concern of the bureaucracy, not theirs, they readily assented to the BOJ's guidance. Besides, the banks had little choice in the matter.

The loans being pushed were not the typical loans that companies take down to finance inventory creation, which are extinguished fairly quickly. The borrower puts the cash on deposit and then spends it to produce finished products, paying down the loan as it sells off the goods produced. But if instead of financing inventory the borrower uses the newly created money to buy a piece of land at an astronomical price from a farmer whose family acquired the land decades or even centuries earlier at an original acquisition cost that was effectively zero, the farmer receives a huge block of cash that he does not spend. Most of that cash almost certainly ends up as a deposit, particularly because the tax structure encourages the farmer to deposit the money. (Interest income was exempt from taxation up to a certain point, and it was long understood that the tax authorities would overlook multiple deposits opened at the post office in the names of various family members.) The farmer makes his living by farming and does not need to draw down the deposit. And unlike inventory loans, real estate loans cannot easily be paid off. Borrowers who forked out astronomical amounts of money for a piece of land typically could not generate the profits necessary to repay the loan that financed the purchase, but that was not a problem provided that they could make interest payments. And the authorities naturally kept interest rates below the level that market forces would otherwise have set them. Because the loans were never extinguished, no deposits needed to be liquidated to pay them off. As long as new asset buyers and new borrowers could be found, the system worked well. The deposits were not generated by production activities, and they were available to facilitate the funding of Japan's growing dollar-denominated claims on foreign countries.

The Japanese authorities were trying to ease credit by encouraging loans in excess of real economic activity. Whether they set out deliberately to create bubbles is a moot point; what they did resulted in the stable deposits needed to finance Japan's growing accumulation of current account surpluses denominated in dollars. But of course it also, by necessity, produced bubbles when too many loans were chasing, as it were, too few assets. Inducing extra deposits meant that bank loans had to be expanded very aggressively, beyond the needs of the real economy. By the 1970s, real GDP growth rates could be projected with a good deal of accuracy, and BOJ officials could instruct banks to increase loans in excess of whatever was needed to fund the real GDP increase—which is precisely what they did.

## Land Prices, the MOF, and Savings

As we have seen, the BOJ functions as an agent in a system ultimately controlled by the MOF. When confronted with the need to fund a burgeoning dollar-denominated current account surplus, MOF officials had to create the necessary deposits without starving the real economy of money—while continuing to ensure that manufacturers had undisturbed access to cheap, plentiful capital. "Crowding out" is a phenomenon that usually occurs when government demands for money make it more difficult or more expensive, or both, for private sector entities to raise funds for spending on real investments in factories and equipment. In Japan's case, however, the "crowding out" that threatened Japanese industry's access to cheap capital came from the need to fund Japan's dollar-denominated surpluses.

The solution lay in what we saw above: the MOF facilitated an increase in household savings through the indirect route of expanding loans in accordance with instructions given to the banks. Deposits were created from the deliberate inflation of land prices—that is, out of bubbles. Sellers of land enjoyed huge capital gains, which they put on deposit. Students of Japanese demographics have argued that the aging of the population will inevitably bring a fall in savings as retirees draw down funds to live on, but that analysis ignores the deliberate creation of huge deposits in the accounts of land sellers, deposits that constitute a critical portion of national savings and have served to offset the decline in savings rates that demographics might otherwise have produced. Meanwhile, high land prices served as a matter of course to boost housing costs. Families who bought Japan's eye-poppingly expensive houses were forced to save in order to pay back the principal they had borrowed, money that counts as "savings" in Japan's national accounts. The government encouraged homeownership not to improve living standards but as an implicit way of boosting savings. And the effects of high land prices were not limited to housing. Other household goods—food, clothing—also were among the world's most expensive, reflecting the high cost of land on which those goods were produced and sold. Japan's consumers—directly or indirectly—were squeezed as a matter of deliberate policy by the sellers and owners of land.

The typical seller of land in Japan was either a farmer on the outskirts of a city or in a resort area or the owner of a shop or small factory in a city. Lenient taxation of capital gains provided every reason for individuals to sell land, whereas tax incentives encouraged corporate borrowers to hold land.[6]

The tax system was reinforced with window guidance to increase bank loans, given first in the early 1970s and again in the 1980s with the goal of driving up land prices. Because banks are licensed by the MOF, they had little choice but to obey what amounted to orders from MOF or BOJ officials. Banks operated under the assumption that the MOF or MITI would intervene to ensure that the loans remained sound; therefore banks felt no need to assess risk through cash flow projections or credit analysis. Instead, banks most typically lent against land as collateral.

During the postwar period, economic growth gave the initial kick to land price increases. Once Japan had achieved self-sufficiency in capital goods production, imports were restricted largely to raw materials and energy while domestic production facilities expanded rapidly in order to increase exports. Production facilities required land, and with the extra credit pouring into the nation's real estate market, the notion took hold that land prices had nowhere to go but up. The banks as well as the MOF understood that their lending created land price appreciation, thus ensuring the purported soundness of loans in a self-reinforcing, virtuous circle. Land functioned as ideal collateral as long, of course, as land prices continued to rise.

The bureaucracy did everything in its power to ensure that that happened. As we noted in chapter 3, in 1969 the government introduced the *Chika Koji Kakaku Seido*, or Official Public Land Price Quotation System, based on a similar ordinance enacted in 1941 to control share prices. Hisatsune Arata, a certified real estate appraiser and president of the Toshi Keizai Kenkyujo, a think tank, wrote that the quotation system has played an essential role in boosting land prices since 1969.[7] Indeed, article 1 of the law establishing the system states that "in urban areas and their vicinities, the government selects standard spots and publicizes normal prices so that those quoted prices are to be taken as indications for all transactions." Government-certified appraisers estimated land prices independent of actual transactions, and those prices were used by the tax authorities to assess transaction taxes. Moreover, all real estate transactions connected to government spending were required to be settled at those prices.

The system provided assurance to land purchasers as well as to banks that the value of their holdings would not fall. The tax treatment of capital gains provided yet another prop for land prices; capital gains taxes were far more leniently handled than those on working income, and, as we will see below, the authorities would lower those taxes even further when they set about creating the land bubble.[8]

*Tochi shinwa*—the myth of eternally rising land prices—had already been firmly entrenched, thanks to Japan's relatively small size and the strong demand for factory sites. Plans to develop the entire Japanese archipelago— the *Zenkoku Sogo Kaihatsu Keikaku* (National Comprehensive Development Plan) of 1962 and the *Shin Zenkoku Kaihatsu Keikaku* (New National Development Plan) of 1969—reinforced the myth. But the deliberate, and successful, attempts to boost land prices in the early 1970s with what in retrospect seems to have been a practice run for the late 1980s bubble gave *tochi shinwa* the status of revealed truth.

Meanwhile, the proliferation of cross-shareholdings gave assurances that equity prices could also be supported. In 1965, during a small stock market panic that led to the near collapse of Yamaichi Securities, the government had set up two semi-public institutions to purchase shares in order to boost the market. The interventions had been successful and left the impression that they could be repeated if necessary during any future market weakness, thus further reinforcing the belief that the government could and would ensure that asset prices would always rise.

## The Ascendancy of Tanaka Kakuei

The man identified most closely with the deliberate inflation of Japan's asset prices in the early 1970s is Tanaka Kakuei, who was elected prime minister in 1972 after serving as minister of international trade and industry. He spearheaded the incorporation of the *toshi seisaku taiko* (basic policies for urban development) into the existing New National Development Plan under the rubric of "redeveloping the Japanese archipelago." This policy regime helped convert the myth of ever-rising land prices into reality by giving the government the ability to create demand for land through the construction of super-highways, bullet train lines, airports, harbors, and factory sites.

Tanaka would reign over Japanese politics for nearly two decades and play kingmaker long after he left the prime ministership in 1974 in the wake of a series of revelations in the press of his campaign financing methods. Conventional wisdom has it that Tanaka represented a kind of revolution, a successful challenge to the preeminence of bureaucratic power. The cease-less harping on what the Japanese media called the "Kaku-Fuku war" (the political struggle between Tanaka and his supposed principal rival, the ex-MOF bureaucrat Fukuda Takeo, that dominated political news in the 1970s); the obvious disdain of some of Japan's bureaucratic mandarins for Tanaka's lack of formal credentials (he never went to college and hailed from quintessentially "back country"—*ura Nihon*—Niigata Prefecture); and Tanaka's public crowing at his own skill in extracting funds from a supposedly reluctant MOF all went to feed the widespread notion that Tanaka's rise to the prime ministership marked the start of a new era.

Superficially, it is an attractive idea. Before Tanaka, Japanese industrial policy served to groom Japan's world-dominating industries. Thereafter, it served to protect industries that Japan would have done better to let die. Before Tanaka, public spending went into building the core of Japan's infrastructure; thereafter, it became a lucrative gravy train for Liberal Democratic Party politicians and construction companies. Some of Tanaka's predecessors as prime minister may have had shady connections and one of them was even an indicted war criminal, but they were also erudite men comfortable with the nuances of public policy (for example, Yoshida Shigeru, Ishibashi Tanzan, Ikeda Hayato, Kishi Nobusuke, and Sato Eisaku). And with the exception of Ishibashi, who in any case served as prime minister for only three months, they were mainstream ex-bureaucrats. Tanaka's successors have tended more to have risen through the ranks of the LDP than the bureaucracy, and—like Tanaka, from whom they learned how to do it—they climbed to power through their command of what the Japanese media labeled "money politics," the ability to direct the vast sums of money required by Japanese election campaigns to key candidates and constituencies.[9]

These observations are true, but they do not establish any kind of causal link between the conduct of policy and the occupant of the prime minister's office. Tanaka built what was undoubtedly the most formidable political machine Japan had ever seen and could on occasion browbeat the bureaucracy in a way that none of his predecessors or successors could match, but even Tanaka did not in any fundamental way determine policy. Nor was it in any sense his decision that Japan would perpetuate rather than overhaul Japan's economic system with the emergence in the early 1970s of structural current account surpluses. In fact, no one made any decision per se. Both bureaucrats and politicians simply acted as they were expected to act in protecting existing arrangements from the strains of the surpluses that helped lead to the collapse of Bretton Woods. What Tanaka did do was to serve as the public face of the only possible policy response for a country that neither could nor would dismantle mercantilist structures and yet still expected to grow. It is significant that Tanaka's protégés—most important, the late Takeshita Noboru and Hashimoto Ryutaro—have been the leading political guardians over the past twelve years of the MOF's continued control of the nation's budget and financial system.

## *Panic in Kasumigaseki*

The challenge of maintaining both economic growth and mercantilist institutions became even more acute after the collapse of Bretton Woods. Before 1971, the Japanese policy elite operated under the assumption that the yen/dollar rate of 360 was fixed forever, that the United States would never let the Bretton Woods system fail. No Japanese, of course, participated in the famous 1944 conference that gave birth to the postwar monetary order; therefore no one in the Japanese bureaucracy, as Robert Angel has pointed out, had any personal stake in or sense of authorship of the system, despite the benefits that Japan had reaped from participation in it. Bretton Woods was simply accepted as a given. As Angel writes, "Japan showed little concern over the possibility that the whole international economic system, beginning with the delicately balanced Bretton Woods international monetary arrangements, might tumble down upon its own head as well as those of the other participants."[10]

But in assuming that the United States would forever support a system that so clearly institutionalized American hegemony over the global economy, Japan's officials reckoned without considering the give and take of American electoral politics or the power that the American system gives an individual president to put his own electoral prospects above the good of the country. Coming from a world where core macroeconomic policy decisions were largely immune from electoral considerations, Japan's policy officials could not comprehend that a Richard Nixon would seek to revive the American economy in the buildup to the 1972 elections with a dose of dangerously loose money and inflationary fiscal policies. Nor could they foresee that he would be accommodated by a Federal Reserve under the leadership of an Arthur Burns who was doing his best, in the words of his critics, in "providing a prosperous climate for Richard Nixon's reelection."[11]

But that kind of inflationary jolt to the U.S. economy, following nearly a decade of inflationary financing of the Vietnam War, could come only by shaking free the restrictions of the Bretton Woods system. The Bretton Woods system forced adjustment burdens onto deficit countries, and by 1970 the United States had emerged as a deficit country.[12] To maintain the

Bretton Woods world of fixed rates, the United States would have had to halt the gold flowing out of the country not by refusing to honor its obligations to exchange dollars for gold but by tightening credit, thereby slowing down its economy in order to reverse the first appearances of trade deficits in a half-century. The political price, however, of throwing the U.S. economy into recession the year before an election was something that no American president—certainly not Richard Nixon—would easily pay.

Instead, Nixon threatened to take the United States out of the system, walking away from American obligations and pushing adjustment burdens onto surplus countries—most notably, on Japan. Indeed, Nixon took direct aim at Japan, which refused to consider resetting the yen/dollar rate and which had, in Nixon's view, reneged on a commitment to rein in textile exports. Shortly after Nixon had been nominated the Republican candidate for president in 1968, Nixon met with a group of textile industry leaders and promised them that he would do something about Japan's textile exports—a campaign promise he sought to live up to.[13] Nixon believed that he had obtained assurances that the exports would be restrained as quid pro quo for the return of Okinawa to Japanese rule from then prime minister Sato Eisaku at meetings held in Washington in November 1969. Japanese prime ministers do not, however, have the power to act on such assurances—Nixon would be neither the first nor the last American president to discover that—and he felt that he had been double-crossed. Special tariffs were imposed on Japanese goods, and the United States closed the gold window through which, under Bretton Woods, the government had been obligated to sell gold to foreign central banks for dollars.

Japanese officialdom went into a panic. The MOF kept the Tokyo foreign exchange market open for nine business days and bought dollars held by banks at the old rate of ¥360 to $1, which no one expected to survive. The incident showed clearly the role of the banks in carrying out government policies and the government's role in protecting them. The MOF bitterly opposed the appreciation of the yen and had hoped, in order to forestall foreign pressure for revaluation, to lower official foreign exchange reserves by hiding much of the reserves in Japan's nominally private banks. But when that became impossible, the MOF bought the reserves back from the banks at the old rate. The MOF was transparently attempting to shore up Japan's negotiating position in the hopes of keeping any new fixed yen/dollar rate as low as possible; at the time, no one anywhere other than a few academics actually contemplated a floating rate system. But the attempts by the major powers to fix the unbearable strains on Bretton Woods with the Smithsonian Agreement of December 1971 collapsed within six months. Japan's negotiators at the Smithsonian conference had succeeded in holding the new yen/dollar rate to ¥308/$1, but by February of 1973, Japan had been forced to let the yen float up to ¥265/$1 and the world had embarked on the uncharted territory of a floating rate system.

The introduction of floating rates made Japan's policy dilemma even more acute. A growing current account surplus would, if disposed of on foreign exchange markets, drive the yen way up. That, of course, was the whole point of the floating rate system, according to its proponents: that markets in foreign exchange would serve to reduce national external imbalances before they provoked global crises. But Japan's administrators had no intention of overhauling the economic machine that had, in their view, made their country great again, and that was what was implied in any serious reduction of Japan's surpluses. In any case, the political infrastructure that could wrest power from the bureaucracy, overhaul the economy, and lead the country in a new direction did not exist.

Policy officials continued to do their jobs as they were expected to. That meant learning how to cope with floating rates, doing everything possible to weaken the yen's value, and managing external surpluses in such a way that they did not damage Japan's economic machine.

## The Mechanics of Asset Inflation

Under the cover provided by a sense of crisis and with the prominent Tanaka as the public face for the policy, the bureaucracy began deliberately to inflate assets. Under the rubric of the New National Development Plan, bank credit, depicted in figure 1-10 of chapter 1, was aggressively pumped up by the BOJ's expansion of bank lending quotas. Most of the new lending was directed at small and medium-sized businesses rather than the large exporters that until that point typically had absorbed the lion's share. Banks also expanded loans to individuals. Although capital spending did not rise significantly, the money supply in relation to GDP (what economists call Marshallian K, or the ratio of M2 plus CDs to nominal GDP)[14] climbed rapidly (see figure 3-2 of chapter 3). The BOJ's own history admits that the "BOJ knew that most banks were allocating 30–50% of their additional lending to real-estate related borrowings."[15] Borrowers began to buy land and equities, resulting in a substantial run-up in asset prices.

The BOJ claims to have been concerned that the rise in asset prices could presage both general inflation and the appearance of bubbles: "Borrowings associated with asset purchases remain as bank deposits since they are not paid out in wages. Therefore, banks can continue to create deposits rapidly . . . liquidity is transferred from the corporate to the household sector . . . and can eventually show up as consumption and inflation."[16] But that statement need not be taken seriously. Since the sellers of land were high-net-worth individuals whose propensity to save was high, the deposits accumulating in their accounts were not contributing to consumption and rising prices. Had land sales brought on an increase in spending, it would have shown up in demand for imports—and that was what Japan's policy apparatus was geared to suppress. In fact, the authorities were trying to do precisely what they denied: to create bubbles, by inflating asset prices—specifically land prices—far beyond levels that economic fundamentals would justify. For the funds that borrowers used to purchase land remained largely as deposits within the banking system, providing the wherewithal for the banks to engage in further lending that drove land prices even higher. Borrowers could use the funds available to them to purchase land and equities, but because the sellers of such assets typically kept the proceeds on deposit, the run-up in asset prices had little effect on economic activity in the real economy while it increased available deposits.

The evidence is overwhelming that the authorities instituted a policy regime that required the deliberate creation of bubbles. Special tax incentives were put in place in 1970 to induce land sales; in particular, tax authorities announced that capital gains taxes for land, already at 40 percent, half the top marginal income tax rate of 80 percent, would be slashed for 1970 and 1971 to 14 percent, then would rise to 20 percent for 1972–73 and to 26 percent for the two years after that. Therefore, if people moved to sell fast, they would pay substantially less tax. The response was precisely what the authorities had to have wanted: between 1970 and 1973, conversion of land from farming to residential use soared from 43,000 hectares (106,210 acres) in 1969 to peak at 68,000 hectares (167,960 acres) in 1973.[17]

In a further effort to boost prices, the MOF oversaw the establishment of seven housing loan companies—the notorious *jusen*—which we mentioned briefly in chapter 1. We will discuss what happened to the *jusen* in more detail in chapter 7, but for now we will note that the MOF established the firms to create additional lending opportunities that would help pump up land prices. The *jusen* borrowed from banks and then on-lent the proceeds to finance land purchases and housing construction.

Final evidence, if any more is required, of the real intentions of Japan's authorities can be found in the measures introduced to cope with the side effects of the additional bank lending quotas. In August 1971, the BOJ was authorized to raise additional funds through the issue of bills, a form of sterilization that theoretically works to remove money from the economy. Bill issues will be familiar to observers of the current financial situation in Japan; since the mid 1990s, the BOJ has been expanding its assets aggressively at the same time that it has been selling these bills. The contemporary purpose, however, has not been to tighten credit or raise interest rates by counteracting the effects of its balance sheet expansion. Rather, the BOJ has no choice because, as Kato Izuru argues, the BOJ's monetary policy is exhausted.[18] (Kato is chief economist at Tokyo Tanshi, a leading market maker in Japan's call money market.) With the sluggishness of real economic activity, the BOJ has been unable to push sufficient currency into the economy; because it cannot issue enough currency to offset expanded assets, the BOJ has to issue the bills.

In 1971, however, when the issue of these bills was first authorized, the situation was different. The government could not control the inflow of speculative foreign short-term capital betting on a revaluation of the yen, and the BOJ believed that it needed a tool to counter the furious dollar buying it had launched to sop up the speculative capital. In fact, however, the BOJ did not take significant advantage of the powers it had been given. In other words, the BOJ had the tools to counteract the inflationary effects of the excess liquidity brought on by all the dollar buying, but it did not use them even though inflation as measured by the consumer price index would reach 25 percent in 1974. Instead, the concept of *chosei infure* (inflation for adjustment purposes) was openly acknowledged as necessary to restore the relationship between GDP and bank loans. The alternative to inflation would by necessity have involved a further rise in the yen. Of course, both inflation and a rise in the yen affect competitiveness, but inflation permits additional loans to be made that can be used to enhance production capacity, thus restoring some of the lost competitiveness.[19]

Indeed, the sum of the measures put in place to blow bubbles in 1971 and 1972 and the way the authorities deployed the tools at their disposal lead us to believe that even at the time they viewed those policies as temporary. Further, we believe that the authorities intended to counteract them once they had accomplished the purposes of stabilizing the exchange rate and funding the dollars pouring in through the current account. To be sure, no public record exists of any internal debates about how the bubble was to be deflated. Because the authorities have never admitted that they were deliberately setting about to inflate assets in the first place, they certainly were not going to reveal what they thought about the process of bubble deflation. But the policy tools that were first deployed in 1973, before the OPEC oil embargo changed everything, and deployed again after the deliberate deflation of the late 1980s bubble allow us to make an educated guess about the bureaucracy's game plan.

It appears that the authorities intended to deflate the bubble first by restoring capital gains taxes to their pre-1970 level, second by lowering lending quotas, and third by hiking interest rates. Finally, they intended to clean up any collateral damage that the bubble had created with deficit spending. Presumably the officials understood that corporate borrowers who had bought land and stock at bubble prices would suffer from losses once the bubble was punctured. Corporate borrowings would have to be serviced out of earnings generated from assets that would have fallen in value. Hiked levels of deficit spending, however, would help to compensate corporations. The government could—and did—issue bonds that banks would have no choice but to purchase. The bonds would fund generous official spending, which would find its way into the accounts of corporations that had borrowed for speculative purposes, ameliorating the losses they had sustained with the bursting of the asset bubble. Most public spending in Japan is deployed on public works that put money in bank accounts without doing much to increase wages or cause a significant uptick in demand. Spending can thus increase at a much higher rate than that of economic activity, raising government debt much faster than GDP. Indeed, government indebtedness would begin to rise in the middle of the decade from 10 percent of GDP, which it had been in the early 1970s, to some 60 percent by 1980. Such spending does not, of course, lead to sufficient additional tax revenues down the road to service the debt, but elite officials seem to have believed that the banking system could inflate its way out of the debt as banks bought government bonds to create deposits. Things did not, however, quite work out that way. Government debt as a percentage of GDP would stay at the 60 percent level until the 1990s, when it began again to climb sharply. While all the industrialized countries experienced substantial increases in government debt during the 1970s, Japan's would climb higher than that of its peers.[20]

## The Oil Shocks and the Reagan Revolution

Japan's first experiment in financing rapidly accumulating dollar-denominated current account surpluses turned out to have been fairly satisfactory. Once land and stock prices threatened to reach levels so high that the loans sustaining them could not be supported, a bout of inflation generated by the combination of highly stimulative fiscal and monetary policies reduced the real value of the loans. Large dollops of deficit spending then helped compensate corporate borrowers.

But we cannot be sure how things would finally have turned out, because the experiment had not run its course before the Arab oil embargo was imposed in October 1973. It appeared for a while as if Japan had been plunged back into the world of the 1950s, where every penny of foreign exchange was precious. The value of the yen plummeted just months after Tokyo had been paralyzed with fear that it would soar out of sight.

Because Japan is highly dependent on imported energy, the world expected Japan to be badly, even permanently damaged by the embargo and subsequent OPEC-engineered price hikes. But, in fact, Japan emerged more quickly from the oil crisis than any other industrialized economy. The bureaucracy had a century of experience in dealing with scarcity and pressure to pay for essential imports, and the shortages played right to the bureaucrats' strength in allocating goods. Rationing schemes were implemented, and by 1976 Japan astonished the world by roaring back, exporting in the face of continued global sluggishness and boasting the highest GDP growth rate and an inflation rate that was among the lowest in the developed countries.

The current account went back into the black, but the surpluses no longer seemed to pose the problems that they had in the early 1970s. The automobile and electronics industries were still growing rapidly, and GDP was still expanding at a considerable annual rate. Outlays for imported capital equipment were high enough to keep Japan's current account surpluses within reasonable bounds for the rest of the decade. Deficit spending by the Japanese government counteracted the deflationary effects, albeit at the price, as we have seen, of boosting government debt as a percentage of GDP to around 60 percent. And what came to be known as the "second oil shock" brought on by the Iranian Revolution again damped down both the yen and the current account surplus—indeed, for two quarters in 1979–80, Japan would actually run current account deficits, the last time that has happened.

Japan's emergence from the shallow recessionary trough following the Iranian Revolution and the so-called second oil shock undoubtedly would have brought the return of the current account surplus problem had it not been for unrelated events in the United States. A peculiar constellation of historical circumstances—a Paul Volcker owing nothing to anyone and free as newly appointed chairman of the Federal Reserve to pursue a zealous anti-inflation crusade; the sweeping political realignment in the wake of the 1980 elections; the dubious notion that steep cuts in tax rates would raise tax revenues, briefly popularized under the respectable-sounding rubric of "supply side economics"; and the assassination attempt against a popular president—all combined to produce a one-off event in American history: the enactment of a steep tax cut with no countervailing spending reduction at a time of historically high interest rates.

One of the authors has written about the central role that Japanese finance played in making the so-called Reagan Revolution possible.[21] For our purposes here, it is sufficient to note that the dollar proceeds of Japan's current account surplus that began burgeoning again in 1980 went initially into satisfying the sudden explosion in the American government's demand for funds. Dollars poured into the coffers of the U.S. Treasury, which was offering historically unprecedented interest rates, stemming not just from the Japanese current account surplus but from sources all over the world. The global demand for dollars led to a super-strong American currency, removing for a while the principal policy problem for Japan of current account surpluses—the threat of a strong yen. The combination of a huge cost advantage conferred on Japanese industry by the weak yen plus the recovery of the American economy that began in 1982 (a recovery that, whoever took credit it for it, vindicated Keynesian notions of the stimulative effect of deficit spending) brought on a temporary golden age for Japanese exporters.

But the good times would not last. The dollar would eventually turn down, and the problem of the accumulated surpluses would return with a vengeance. The tools first deployed in the early 1970s would be brought out again, this time to blow up the largest financial bubble in history.

# 6

# Of a Great Bubble and Its Collapse

The early 1980s saw the dollar soar as money poured into the United States to finance the burgeoning deficits brought on by the Reagan Revolution. While the beneficiaries included the U.S. Treasury and Japan's exporters, only a handful of ideologues in Washington regarded the situation either as permanent or as an unalloyed good. American industries reeled under a high dollar that not only priced their goods out of foreign markets but also subjected them to unrelenting competitive pressure at home from the Japanese. Those were the days when Chrysler's Lee Iacocca and Caterpillar's Lee Morgan stoked up the anti-Japanese rhetoric and pleaded for action on the exchange rate. A sympathetic Congress threatened protectionist legislation while anti-Japanese sentiment in the United States reached a postwar peak. Even the many economists and other observers who attributed the soaring American current account deficits entirely to macroeconomic factors feared the sheer scale of those deficits could any day trigger a catastrophic reversal in the foreign exchange markets.

Those observers surely included Japanese government officials. Both the rhetoric blowing across the Pacific and apprehension over sudden upheavals in the foreign exchange markets help explain why the Japanese authorities set about preparing for an inevitable end to the weak yen/strong dollar regime of the early 1980s. To be sure, other things being equal, Japan's ruling elite preferred a weak yen. But in an economy where profits counted for little, export volume mattered more. And the rising anger in the United States at burgeoning Japanese trade surpluses and waves of protectionist sentiment put Japan's unfettered access to the U.S. market at risk and threatened Japan's ability to maintain that volume. Cooperating with the Americans to move exchange rates into a more acceptable range probably seemed the least damaging way of heading off a protectionist storm in Washington.

Other factors also were at work in Japan's willingness to suspend for a time the weak yen policy that had prevailed since the Occupation. Japan's emergence as a net creditor nation in the early 1980s made it obvious that Japanese industry no longer needed the extra advantage of a weak exchange rate to prevail in foreign markets. After the collapse of Bretton Woods and a few years of yen strength that saw the yen reach a postwar high of ¥177 to $1, the policy mix of the early 1980s had driven the yen back down to a very weak level. But the emergence in world markets of a wide range of Japanese products that were bywords for manufacturing excellence made the weak yen seem out of date not only to many irate Americans but to some Japanese as well.

The events leading up to the Plaza Accord and its aftermath have been covered elsewhere in detail.[1] Nakasone Yasuhiro, who was then prime minister, and ex-MOF official Hosomi Takashi often are given credit for pushing the notion that an excessively weak yen could ultimately end up hurting Japan by provoking a counter spasm, and Tokyo was clearly sending such signals by early 1985. Tokyo's willingness to work with Washington to let steam out of an overheated dollar represented a major policy shift, however, and such shifts are not made by Japanese prime ministers on their own initiative. The ramifications had undoubtedly been discussed for some time by a significant cross-section of elite MOF and ex-MOF officials of whom Hosomi was only the most visible. Whoever may have been precisely responsible for the shift, considerable circumstantial evidence exists that the MOF anticipated an inevitable strengthening of the yen that would take the

Japanese currency back to the 180 rate that had been briefly breached at the depth of the 1978 dollar crisis. MOF officials seem to have believed that they could prevent further appreciation beyond that rate.[2]

Washington was not receptive, however, to the idea of something like the Plaza Accord until the beginning of Ronald Reagan's second term as president. James A. Baker III became secretary of the treasury, and he installed a pragmatist regime at Treasury in contrast to the ideologically rigid market fundamentalism that had prevailed there during Reagan's first term. The new regime's immediate predecessors had refused to consider any sort of coordination with other countries or any kind of market intervention to reverse a soaring dollar. The high dollar had been fingered by most sectors of the business and policy communities in the United States as the culprit behind yawning American trade deficits—in particular the trade deficit with Japan—and what appeared at the time to be the crippling of whole sectors of American industry at the hands of Japanese competition. When Baker took over as secretary he responded with alacrity to the growing political pressure to do something about the problem. On a visit to Tokyo in June 1985, he found the Japanese elite already prepared to work with him.

Japan's financial mandarins were ready to respond, however, only because they had been preparing for such an event for several years. Indeed, the foundations had been laid as early as 1981, when the authorities repeated what they had done in the early 1970s: prompted the city banks to lend aggressively as Japan's current surpluses mounted in the wake of the dollar's strength. The BOJ's quarterly lending quotas for each city bank rose sharply. As a consequence, outstanding loans soared from about 30 percent of GDP at the beginning of the 1980s—the norm during the postwar period—to almost 50 percent by the end of that decade. That additional lending flowed into asset markets—principally equities and real estate— where it drove up prices, providing the collateral for the waves of investment in plant and equipment that would be needed to counteract the effects of a climb in the value of the yen. Japan's traditional export manufacturing champions typically had extensive land holdings that had been purchased decades earlier and were carried on their books at practically zero valuation. The high land prices engineered by soaring asset markets conferred gigantic unrealized capital gains that helped mitigate any losses that might be suffered from a suddenly strengthening yen. And of course those landholdings provided collateral for the borrowing required to finance any needed upgrades of plant and equipment. Meanwhile, asset sellers enjoyed the huge capital gains, and the proceeds of their sales were typically put on deposit in the banking system, where they increased the capacity to finance dollar holdings, burgeoning again in the wake of the current account surpluses Japan had begun racking up since 1980.

Japan had to some extent insulated itself from the inevitable hike in the yen—and the proof could be found in the wake of the Plaza Accord. Despite the dire predictions beforehand, no large export manufacturer encountered any financial difficulty as the yen's dollar value nearly doubled between 1985 and 1987. Japanese industry embarked on what was probably the greatest wave of plant and equipment investment ever undertaken by an economy during peacetime. And as for Japan's current account surplus, not only did it fail to drop, it actually increased. That increase may have flown in the face of the wisdom economists had accumulated about the relationship between exchange rates and trade numbers since David Hume first laid out the connection in the 1740s with the price-specie flow theory, but it happened anyway.[3] In a system where profits matter little and where bank loans that do not have to be repaid can be increased by bureaucratic decree, the increased cost pressure placed on Japanese exporters after the dollar halved in value did not prevent them from churning out yet more exports and thus continuing to widen the current account surplus. In particular, American enthusiasm for high-quality, energy-efficient Japanese automobiles enabled Japan's automakers to pass on the costs incurred by the strengthening yen without ceding market share.

## Raising Dollars Abroad and the FESA's New Role

The tactics used to prepare for the rise of the yen and to support Japan's dollar holdings were not confined to the domestic market. Japanese bank activities overseas also played a crucial role, and the development of the late 1980s bubble as well as its aftermath cannot be understood without looking at what the banks were doing outside Japan. During the 1980s, banks expanded overseas with the explicit backing of the authorities in the form of a sequence of liberalizations of foreign exchange regulations, the most important of which was the 1979 revision of the Foreign Exchange and Foreign Trade Control laws.

These revisions were not made to free banks from bureaucratic oversight but rather to enhance the ability of banks to play their necessary roles in the funding of Japan's soaring external assets. The historical record reveals that since the 1880s the Japanese government has consistently attempted to expand external assets, that is, to promote capital outflow. As we have seen, acquisition of the means to expand those assets—export revenues—has been the be-all and end-all of Japanese economic policy for more than a century. In deploying export revenues, the government historically had tended to favor either direct investment in projects abroad with minimal impact on domestic employment levels—for example, real estate and leisure facilities—or securities investments by the likes of insurance companies and pension funds. Factories that would compete with domestic plant and equipment were discouraged. Naturally, Japan's administrators ensured that they and their licensees—banks, insurance companies, and securities firms—would intermediate the process of foreign investment and that the role of Japan's households would be limited to turning over their savings to licensed financial institutions. Households were deliberately frustrated by tax, reporting, and other measures from undertaking direct investments themselves; the managers of financial institutions to whom they entrusted their savings could thus be "guided" by bureaucrats whenever the need arose. The bureaucracy has always worked to ensure that wholesale capital flight cannot occur, something that foreign brokers and bankers are now learning, at their cost. Looking to make money from intermediating the restructuring of Japanese savings, which had been widely predicted, the gaijin in the 1990s set up mutual funds and opened a rash of brokerage offices and retail banking branches. But the hoped-for stampede of customers seeking higher returns never materialized.

So while the export of capital properly intermediated by institutions under the direct control of the bureaucracy—or, in other words, the acquisition of external assets—has always been a central goal of Japan's economic management, capital inflow—that is, the buildup of external liabilities—traditionally had been deliberately discouraged. The policy of discouraging capital inflow dates back as far as 1881, when incoming finance minister Matsukata Masayoshi insisted that Japan pay back loans floated in the London markets even at the cost of a severe domestic recession that nearly spelled the ruin of the Meiji government. The eschewal of foreign capital was reaffirmed in the late 1940s with the approval of Occupation authorities when, despite Japan's desperate need for money to finance rebuilding, "capital controls far stricter than those imposed by the Allied Occupation in Germany" were instituted in Japan.[4]

The inflow that did occur came mostly as "equity" investments or through banks. The word "equity" has to be put in quotes since actual ownership and control of Japanese companies has, except in very rare circumstances, never been for sale.[5] The majority of shares are locked away in the hands of friendly shareholders through interlocking shareholding arrangements or, in some cases, in the hands of the company founder and/or his heirs; the shares that do trade on the Tokyo Stock Exchange are to all intents and purposes tracking stocks. As long as foreign purchases of tracking stocks posed no threat to management control of Japanese companies and helped boost the Tokyo stock market, they were ignored or even welcomed by Japanese officialdom. But when the Japanese policy elite determined that the buildup of accumulated current surpluses required reversal of the traditional policy of discouraging capital inflow, the equity market was not a suitable vehicle. The amounts involved were too large and could have threatened the informal norms of the Japanese system—norms that give complete freedom to Japanese managers from shareholder scrutiny while profits were considered only as an afterthought.

Nor did the authorities wish to see foreign banks play a major role in importing capital because they could be difficult to control and often were deliberately deaf to the informal "guidance" administered to Japanese institutions. It was a relatively easy matter to confine the gaijin to a marginal role in Japanese banking by making it difficult and costly for them to take yen deposits. The inability to fund Japanese assets with yen liabilities automatically reduced what foreigners could do, and the gaijin had been complaining for years about the onerous restrictions on opening branches and taking deposits. Those restrictions were relaxed slightly in 1977. At the same time, the authorities broke up the single most lucrative business for the major U.S. banks in Japan: impact loans, dollar loans booked in Japan to Japanese companies. Japanese banks were allowed into the business, and the fat spreads enjoyed by the foreigners disappeared. The message was clear: further agitation for yen funding powers would lead to the stripping away of the remaining profitable lines of business.

**Figure 6-1.** *Total Assets, Breakdown of Assets, and Deposits + CDs at the Foreign Branches of the City Banks*

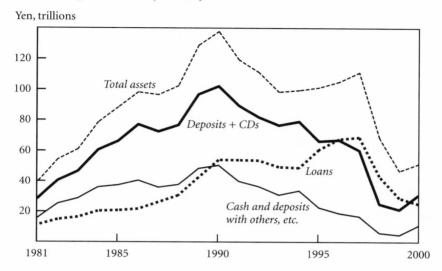

Yen, trillions

Source: *Financial and Economic Statistics Monthly,* Bank of Japan. Calculated, arranged, and estimated by Mikuni & Co. © 2002 Mikuni & Co., Ltd.

Instead, when the Japanese authorities decided that they needed to import capital in order to help suppress the rise of the yen, the authorities turned to the Japanese banking system. Japan's banks began to do more than simply recycle the dollars earned by Japan's exporters; in the 1980s, they started borrowing dollars in very substantial quantities, dollars that financed investments abroad above and beyond those that the current account surplus itself could support.

Figure 6-1 demonstrates how rapidly the assets and liabilities of the overseas branches of the city banks rose in the 1980s. Their activities were undertaken mostly in dollars, leading to oversight and "safety net" problems. Loans are not easy to liquidate at a moment's notice, and that could make for problems during a crisis; the dollar loans made by Japanese banks are no exception. (Figure 6-1 demonstrates that in the 1990s when concerns over the health of the Japanese banking system mounted, Japanese banks' overseas branches could not liquidate their loans right away in the wake of deposit withdrawals; as the chart shows, there was a considerable lag between the downturn in liabilities and the downturn in loans.) The Federal Reserve has no obligation to supervise foreign banks or play lender of last resort should they get into difficulty. But with respect to Japanese banks' dollar businesses overseas, the BOJ cannot easily play that role either; it cannot, after all, "print" dollars.

Japanese banks—undoubtedly at the expressed request of the authorities—dealt with the problem in two ways. First, the banks themselves put funds on deposit with U.S. banks (see figure 6-1) that could be drawn down when needed. Until 1990, those assets actually exceeded the dollar loans made by the Japanese even though, of course, the banks earned little or nothing on the assets.

Second, the FESA made a pool of dollars available to Japanese banks that needed them. Instead of having to worry about their ability to raise funds on international markets, Japanese banks could expand their dollar activities confident that they had the ultimate backing of the FESA. During the 1950s and 1960s, the FESA's dollar holdings had served to back Japan's currency in circulation. That was no longer necessary. Instead, in the 1980s, the FESA provided the ultimate backing for Japan's dollar raising and investments overseas, thereby providing a central institutional pillar for the strong dollar regime that would prevail after the stock market crash of 1987.

Those investments played a key role in propping up the dollar and suppressing the yen, particularly in the later part of the decade. Thus, in addition to their usual international business of financing the overseas activities of Japanese corporations, Japan's banks emerged in the 1980s as major, even dominant players in a host of dollar markets, from syndicated loans to eurodollars to Industrial Revenue Bonds to bank guarantees for U.S. municipal securities. In fact, Japanese banks grabbed so much dollar business— usually by offering to cut interest rates below any level that their Western competitors could match—that outraged American and European banks turned to their governments for help.[6]

Some of that dollar financing was actually yen finance in disguise. Pressure from both foreigners and Japanese insurance companies seeking to diversify their lending led the MOF to announce a series of ostensible deregulatory measures in the early to mid 1980s.[7] Many Japanese corporations accordingly switched sources of financing from domestic bank loans to various forms of bond issues and private placements launched abroad. Most of

**Figure 6-2.** *Short-Term External Assets and Liabilities of Banks and Other Financial Institutions*

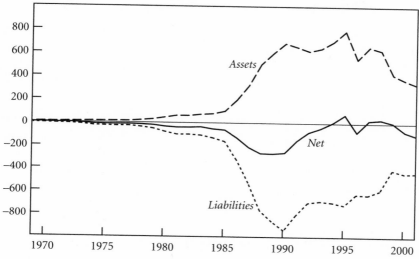

Source: *External Assets and Liabilities of Banks, Etc.,* Ministry of Finance and Bank of Japan. Calculated, arranged, and estimated by Mikuni & Co. © 2002 Mikuni & Co., Ltd.

those deals were actually intended for Japanese lenders—particularly insurance companies—but trotting the transactions through London or Hong Kong and then swapping them back into yen was deemed preferable by the MOF to a real deregulation-cum-internationalization of the Tokyo financial markets. Investment bankers at the time dubbed them "black-eye" or "sushi" bonds because they were fundamentally domestic deals—Japanese companies borrowing from Japanese financial institutions.

But the Japanese were also buying up all kinds of other dollar-based business with low interest rates and other pricing conditions (management fees and the like) that their European and American competitors could not or would not meet. They financed their lending not through additional yen creation from the BOJ or from their domestic deposit base but primarily through the expansion of dollar liabilities. As shown in figure 6-2, which illustrates the rapid growth of external assets and liabilities of the banking system in the 1980s, Japanese banks began aggressively taking dollar deposits in the major dollar markets—London, Hong Kong, and New York.

This dollar funding would accelerate yet further in the wake of the Plaza Accord.

Commentary on the Plaza Accord and its aftermath has tended to focus on the links between the rapid fall in the dollar's value and the October 1987 New York stock market crash. Once markets digested the strength of the G-5 commitments to pushing the dollar down, the dollar went into something of a free fall, ultimately dropping much farther than at least the Japanese had been prepared for. The dollar plummeted from 240 to less than 140 yen within eighteen months of the agreement, yet that had little effect on U.S. aggregate trade numbers. When market participants worldwide realized this in the wake of the announcement of the August 1987 American trade results, they dumped dollar assets, leading to a sharp rise in dollar interest rates and a flood of money out of stock markets.

The MOF is usually given credit for helping to halt the global equity meltdown and for setting a floor under the dollar through the "guidance" administered to Japan's insurance companies and other institutional investors to buy dollar instruments. While there is little doubt that the MOF did use its extraordinary powers of suasion to stop the erosion in both equity markets and the value of the dollar, the effort probably would not have succeeded had it not been for the policy regime in place. That policy regime flooded the economy with money, enabling the MOF, working through the banks and other financial institutions, to allocate that money wherever it was needed to prop up sagging prices—including prices of U.S. Treasury bonds, Japanese equities, and, indeed, the price of the dollar itself. The result would come to be known as Japan's "bubble" economy.

## Creating the Bubble Economy

Understanding how Japan's monetary authorities launched the greatest bubble in history starts with understanding the pricing of land in Japan. As we have noted repeatedly, in Japan, banks by and large lent money against the collateral of land, the value of which was not determined by the actual or potential cash flow generated by its use. Land prices were set without regard to the economic activities that took place on the land involved. Banks arbitrarily assigned collateral value to land, while buyers would bid up land prices as long as the banks were willing to lend them the purchase money, creating a self-reinforcing circle of asset inflation that reached nonsensical heights. The Official Public Land Price Quotation System in effect since 1969 served, as we saw in the previous chapter, to enlist the power of the tax authorities in setting a floor under prices.

Of course, collateral does not theoretically matter much when debt is being serviced promptly, and the ability to service debt is ultimately a function of a company's ability to generate cash flow, not of the collateral that secures the debt. But in Japan, the existence of collateral did help corporations service debt even if the collateral was seldom actually used. The reason lay in the "evergreen" nature of Japanese lending; as we have noted, banks did not typically expect their borrowers to retire debt but simply to service it with current interest payments. As land prices rose, any landowning company encountering any kind of temporary cash flow constraint could solve the problem by simply borrowing more money—something rising land prices enabled it to do. Corporations would not sell land to raise cash, they would use it to borrow more money. Well-established corporations—particularly manufacturers—have long been the privileged darlings of the Japanese economic system. Even so, they have been required to treat all capital gains, including long-term gains, as taxable income, and thereby discouraged from selling corporate land. Rather than sell land—and thereby increasing the supply and putting downward pressure on prices—they were encouraged instead to use it as collateral to borrow money. As long as all players had confidence in the ability of the bureaucracy to use its extensive tools to prop up land prices, there was no one to call a halt. The collateral system of Japanese finance—ultimately based on the twin convictions of eternally rising land prices and the infallibility of the bureaucracy—served as the foundation for a seemingly inexhaustible money pump.

Absent the restraints of market forces, land prices could thus climb to stratospheric levels, giving banks the confidence to lend limitless amounts to borrowers provided that the loans were secured by land whose price could be hiked at will. As they had done in the early 1970s, the authorities began to use the tools at their command to push land prices up. In particular, the capital gains tax burden, which had been increased back in 1975 as part of the deflation of the early 1970s bubble, was again brought down. In 1982, the percentage of income from capital gains to be added to working income in order to determine total taxable income was reduced from 75 percent to 50 percent just at the time that bank lending quotas were again being raised.[8] As we have stressed repeatedly, banks did not look at the borrowers' cash flow in assessing their capacity to service debt and they lent money irrespective of the economic activity of the borrowers.

This land-based system of lending gave the BOJ the ability to engender additional lending independent of any rise in demand from the real economy of production and trade. We noted in the previous chapter how the MOF and the BOJ experimented in the early 1970s with deliberate asset inflation through excess lending steered into asset markets. When banks lent more than required by production activity, the excess credit inevitably went to bid up land and equity prices. The capital gains and increases in bank deposits generated from transactions consummated at these "irrational" levels were completely independent of real economic activity. The utility of the deposits thereby created should now be obvious: they went to fund Japan's burgeoning external assets. For a while, the BOJ could have its cake and eat it too; because there seemed to be no limit on the ability of banks to extend credit, the BOJ could ensure that banks financed production and trade in the real economy while simultaneously funding the growing dollar asset hoard.

There were, however, side effects. Loans outstanding were increasing at 15 percent a year, while the nominal GDP growth rate was only 5 percent. To induce borrowers to continue to accept money at that pace, banks had to offer cut-rate loans priced below their cost of funds. Figure 6-3 shows how bank cash flows turned negative in 1986–87. Many of the deals were linked to the equity market, and, to be sure, banks expected that they would eventually be made whole through equity prices, which they let themselves believe would rise forever. The experience of the 1970s persuaded bankers that the government could and would precipitate a round of generalized inflation to reduce the value of all loans once the purposes of the bubble had been accomplished: stabilizing the exchange rate and providing adequate deposits to fund the accumulated current account surplus. And because banks were running negative cash flows on their rapidly expanding assets, they were in no position to add to loan loss reserves, even if they had felt it necessary, which they did not.

Meanwhile, however, borrowers were using the proceeds of bank loans to speculate in asset markets—there being no other practical use for the money—creating price spirals that had to be financed with additional loans lest the whole cycle crash. By the late 1980s, prices were rising to eye-popping levels that seemed to demand a cooling off. But instead of taking

**Figure 6-3.** *City Bank Spreads*[a]

Yen, trillions

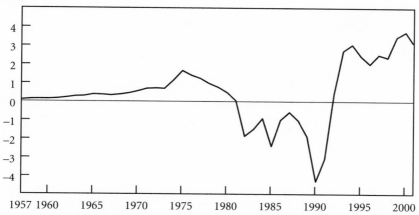

Sources: *Analysis of Financial Statements of All Banks,* Japanese Bankers Association. Calculated, arranged, and estimated by Mikuni & Co. © 2002 Mikuni & Co., Ltd.

a. Interest income on loans and discounts – interest expenses on (Deposits + CDs), for years ending in March.

steam out of overheated markets, Japan's authorities did just the reverse. We believe that the negative cash flow at Japanese financial institutions scared the BOJ and the banks into continuing to expand credit to forestall a crash in asset prices that would plunge bank loans way under water. And of course the conspicuous spending and "good times" spread to almost all sectors of the economy, creating constituencies with vested interests in doing anything to keep the party going.

While by that time asset values in Japan appeared to be riding on a runaway train, there can be no arguing with the success of the asset inflation strategy in financing the current account surplus. During the 1980s, long-term capital outflows far exceeded the surplus, as illustrated in table 6-1. Direct investment and portfolio investment, the two major components of long-term capital outflow, rose from ¥536 billion and ¥844 billion respectively in 1980 to ¥6.14 trillion and ¥15.7 trillion respectively in 1989. Meanwhile, the current account surplus, which had started the decade in the red, would rise to ¥7.9 trillion by 1989.

# Table 6-1. Japan's Balance of Payments[a]

| | 1970/12 | 1971/12 | 1972/12 | 1973/12 | 1974/12 | 1975/12 | 1976/12 | 1977/12 | 1978/12 | 1979/12 |
|---|---|---|---|---|---|---|---|---|---|---|
| Current balance | 709.2 | 2,001.2 | 2,000.1 | -33.0 | -1,329.3 | -200.4 | 1,077.7 | 2,843.1 | 3,484.5 | -1,969.5 |
| Long-term capital | -572.8 | -373.6 | -1,354.9 | -2,365.8 | -1,099.3 | -79.9 | -283.7 | -841.0 | -2,466.0 | -2,831.3 |
| Assets | -731.2 | -770.2 | -1,515.8 | -2,054.7 | -1,150.9 | -996.7 | -1,347.4 | -1,387.0 | -3,084.7 | -3,549.4 |
| Liabilities | 158.4 | 396.6 | 160.9 | -311.1 | 51.6 | 916.8 | 1,063.7 | 546.0 | 618.7 | 718.1 |
| Basic balance | 136.4 | 1,627.7 | 645.3 | -2,398.8 | -2,428.6 | -280.3 | 794.0 | 2,002.1 | 1,018.5 | -4,800.8 |
| Short-term capital | 260.6 | 840.6 | 593.6 | 584.1 | 503.6 | -334.4 | 31.3 | -183.0 | 304.2 | 606.9 |
| Errors and omissions | 97.6 | 181.9 | 192.6 | -629.7 | -12.2 | -171.6 | 35.0 | 167.5 | 62.0 | 520.4 |
| Overall balance | 494.6 | 2,650.2 | 1,431.5 | -2,444.4 | -1,937.2 | -786.3 | 860.3 | 1,986.6 | 1,384.7 | -3,673.5 |
| Monetary movements | | | | | | | | | | |
| Official sector | 406.8 | 3,568.1 | 882.3 | -1,480.4 | 385.5 | -233.9 | 1,043.0 | 1,554.5 | 1,906.7 | -2,787.2 |
| Gold and foreign exchange reserves | 325.1 | 3,740.7 | 945.1 | -1,484.7 | 360.3 | -206.6 | 1,114.8 | 1,602.0 | 2,367.0 | -2,798.2 |
| Others | 81.7 | -172.6 | -62.8 | 4.4 | 25.2 | -27.3 | -71.8 | -47.5 | -460.3 | 11.0 |
| Authorized foreign exchange banks | 131.7 | -873.7 | 597.5 | -964.0 | -2,322.7 | -552.4 | -182.7 | 432.1 | -522.0 | -886.3 |
| Others | -43.9 | -44.2 | -48.3 | | | | | | | |
| Balance of monetary movements | 494.6 | 2,650.2 | 1,431.5 | -2,444.4 | -1,937.2 | -786.3 | 860.3 | 1,986.6 | 1,384.7 | -3,673.5 |

| | 1980/12 | 1981/12 | 1982/12 | 1983/12 | 1984/12 | 1985/12 | 1986/12 | 1987/12 | 1988/12 | 1989/12 |
|---|---|---|---|---|---|---|---|---|---|---|
| Current balance | -2,577.2 | 1,147.0 | 1,774.6 | 4,960.3 | 8,350.3 | 11,517.6 | 14,178.7 | 12,541.3 | 10,192.3 | 7,853.2 |
| Long-term capital | 480.7 | -2,186.2 | -3,664.0 | -4,218.4 | -11,869.6 | -15,232.7 | -21,741.1 | -19,818.4 | -16,810.9 | -12,406.4 |
| Assets | -2,432.0 | -5,057.8 | -6,790.1 | -7,708.4 | -13,567.0 | -19,273.6 | -22,045.2 | -19,401.9 | -19,232.7 | -26,732.3 |
| Liabilities | 2,912.7 | 2,871.6 | 3,126.1 | 3,490.0 | 1,697.4 | 4,040.9 | 304.1 | -416.5 | 2,421.8 | 14,325.9 |
| Basic balance | -2,096.5 | -1,039.2 | -1,889.4 | 741.9 | -3,519.3 | -3,715.1 | -7,562.4 | -7,277.1 | -6,618.4 | -4,553.2 |
| Short-term capital | 659.4 | 454.7 | -380.9 | 2.9 | -1,009.7 | -190.2 | -313.5 | 3,433.1 | 2,530.4 | 2,965.1 |
| Errors and omissions | -719.5 | 92.6 | 1,133.3 | 490.9 | 938.3 | 983.6 | 489.7 | -485.7 | 321.4 | -3,095.0 |
| Overall balance | -2,156.6 | -491.9 | -1,137.0 | 1,235.7 | -3,590.7 | -2,921.7 | -7,386.2 | -4,329.7 | -3,766.8 | -4,683.1 |

Monetary movements

|  | 1990/12 | 1991/12 | 1992/12 | 1993/12 | 1994/12 | 1995/12 |
|---|---|---|---|---|---|---|
| Official Sector | 1,219.6 | 973.2 | −1,129.0 | 383.6 | 557.5 | −348.7 |
| Gold and foreign exchange reserves | 1,259.9 | 727.5 | −1,175.9 | 294.5 | 429.2 | 46.7 |
| Others | −40.3 | 245.7 | 46.9 | 89.0 | 128.3 | −395.4 |
| Authorized foreign exchange banks | −3,376.2 | −1,465.1 | −8.0 | 852.1 | −4,148.2 | −2,573.0 |
| Others |  |  |  |  |  |  |
| Balance of monetary movements | −2,156.6 | −491.9 | −1,137.0 | 1,235.7 | −3,590.7 | −2,921.7 |

|  | 1990/12 | 1991/12 | 1992/12 | 1993/12 | 1994/12 | 1995/12 |
|---|---|---|---|---|---|---|
| Current balance | 5,202.6 | 9,766.8 | 14,902.3 | 14,612.7 | 13,199.5 | 10,289.8 |
| Long-term capital | −6,639.6 | 4,979.4 | −3,485.7 | −8,591.4 | −7,918.8 | −7,699.7 |
| Assets | −17,661.1 | −16,354.9 | −7,280.6 | −8,063.6 | −11,116.4 | −11,651.8 |
| Liabilities | 11,021.5 | 21,334.3 | 3,794.9 | −527.8 | 3,197.6 | 3,952.1 |
| Basic balance | −1,436.9 | 14,746.0 | 11,416.4 | 6,021.0 | 5,280.7 | 2,590.2 |
| Short-term capital | 3,017.6 | −3,513.8 | −910.3 | −1,613.2 | −904.5 | 7,208.3 |
| Errors and omissions | −2,976.1 | −1,048.7 | −1,243.2 | 31.8 | −1,764.8 | 1,333.2 |
| Overall balance | −1,395.2 | 10,183.8 | 9,263.2 | 4,439.5 | 2,611.6 | 11,131.8 |
| Monetary movements |  |  |  |  |  |  |
| Official sector | −4,024.6 | −2,278.3 | −180.6 | 2,709.5 | −290.1 | 3,439.2 |
| Gold and foreign exchange reserves | −1,512.5 | −1,076.5 | −38.2 | 3,108.3 | 3,484.5 | 5,810.1 |
| Others | −2,512.1 | −1,201.7 | −142.4 | −398.8 | −3,774.6 | −2,370.9 |
| Authorized foreign exchange banks | 2,629.4 | 12,462.1 | 9,443.8 | 1,730.0 | 2,901.7 | 7,692.6 |
| Others |  |  |  |  |  |  |
| Balance of monetary movements | −1,395.2 | 10,183.8 | 9,263.2 | 4,439.5 | 2,611.6 | 11,131.8 |

Source: *Balance of Payments*, Ministry of Finance and Bank of Japan. Calculated, arranged, and estimated by Mikuni & Co. © 2002 Mikuni & Co., Ltd.
a. In yen, billions.

Long-term capital outflow was thus running from two to three times the amount of the current account surplus. Bubbles being created in Japan's domestic asset markets, particularly land, accounted for the gap between long-term capital outflow and the current account surplus. As land prices shot up, companies that owned property saw their unrealized capital gains skyrocket. The companies borrowed limitless amounts of money based on the inflated value of their landholdings from banks that essentially were being ordered by the BOJ to expand loans. With the borrowed funds, companies bought assets overseas very aggressively. That was both a direct and an indirect stimulus to Japanese exports; direct because so many of the assets acquired were factories and companies that promptly began placing orders for Japanese goods, indirect because the asset purchases supported the dollar and thus helped fund their customers' purchases of Japanese goods.

Economists typically focus on a country's net external capital flows— capital exports minus capital imports—but in the late 1980s, Japan's gross external capital flows were the more revealing. That number demonstrated the commitment to support the exchange rate of the dollar by a Japanese policy elite that had been badly frightened by the New York stock market crash of October 1987 and the concomitant dollar weakness. Japanese financial institutions, their arms openly twisted by MOF officials, were buying dollar instruments not because they thought they were profitable investments but because they were told to. As Fujii Yoshihiro, a financial reporter and editor at the *Nihon Keizai Shimbun* points out, for years banks have engaged in *shiji machi*, or "waiting for instructions," from the MOF (and later the FSA),[9] and in the late 1980s those instructions were simple: raise dollar liabilities and buy dollar instruments. The inflow of capital that funded the difference between the net and gross outflows consisted primarily of bank liabilities. The behavior of Japanese banks in raising funds overseas at higher interest rates than those predominating in Japan cannot be squared with the notion of maximizing profits, particularly when the assets being funded with those liabilities often carried lower interest rates. (Japanese banks would, of course, pay more for dollar funds than the yields on U.S. Treasury securities, so purchases of Treasury securities were automatically a money-losing proposition for banks.)

When Japanese companies bought assets overseas, they had to pay for the assets in dollars. And the banks again stepped in to fund those dollars, which they did with their short-term dollar-raising activities. The evidence can be seen in table 6-1, which sets out Japan's balance of payments statistics from 1970 to 1995. As the table demonstrates, short-term capital inflows reflecting borrowing by authorized foreign exchange banks largely plugged the widening gap between the current account and long-term capital outflows.

## The Importance of Japan's Dollar Liabilities

The short-term capital inflow—most of it in the form of short-term dollar liabilities taken out by Japanese banks—was highly important, particularly after October 1987, for it halted the dollar free-fall that in the opinion of most observers was the fundamental cause of the New York stock market crash. The frenzy of short-term dollar borrowing by Japan's banks during the months after the crash may well have helped preserve the dollar's role at the center of global finance and trade; certainly the behavior of MOF officials during the immediate post-crash months shows their concern over the preservation of the dollar's role.[10]

Overall, the expansion of Japanese liabilities overseas during the 1980s, yielding, as it did, a substantial inflow of money through the banking system, helped bring on the rapid and dramatic expansion of the banks' domestic assets. Japanese banks during that decade raised more money overseas than they lent, and the difference by definition went to fund domestic assets. Figure 6-4 shows that domestic asset increases in the banking system averaged ¥26 trillion per year between 1981 and 1985, rising to ¥46 trillion per year in the key years between 1986 and 1990. The assets of the foreign branches of the city banks alone rose from ¥40 trillion in 1981 to peak at ¥138 trillion in 1990, increasing the availability of money in the economy after the Plaza Accord.

Most of the dollars raised abroad by Japanese banks came in the form of deposits made with them by American and European banks. That wave of deposits had, however, the ominous effect of raising to troubling levels the exposure of American and European banks to Japanese bank credit risk. Efforts by Western banks to understand the nature of that risk and control it led to the rapid expansion, among other things, of the work they commissioned from Mikuni Credit Ratings in order to help them cope with that risk. At one point during the 1980s, for example, the Chase Manhattan Bank had extended more credit to the Bank of Tokyo than to any other single

**Figure 6-4.** *Average Annual Increases in Domestic Credit Extended by Banks, Including the Bank of Japan*

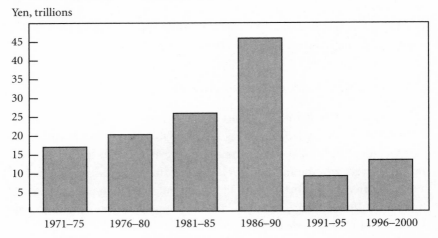

Yen, trillions

Source: *Financial and Economic Statistics Monthly,* Bank of Japan. Calculated, arranged, and estimated by Mikuni & Co. © 2002 Mikuni & Co., Ltd.

entity in the entire world.[11] When worries over the health of the Japanese banking system burst forth into full-fledged panic in the 1990s, Japan's banks were forced to curtail their dollar borrowing overseas, leading to a rapid shrinking of the dollar assets those borrowings had financed and a drastic increase in the deflationary pressures stemming from the current account surplus.

But we are getting ahead of our story. For in the 1980s, the heavy dollar borrowing of Japan's banks, funding the waves of dollar investments by Japan's corporations, counteracted the effects of the near halving of the yen/dollar rate in the wake of the Plaza Accord. As a result of the high yen, export proceeds to Japan's corporations in yen terms were cut in half. But in order to keep production going, Japan needed export volume. Aggressive measures therefore were required to halt further erosion in the dollar's value and to expand the credit available to Japan's export customers—most important, the United States. One more time, as Ishibashi Tanzan had proposed back in 1929, Japan was lending the proceeds of its current account surplus to its customers so they could continue to afford to buy Japanese products. Except in the late 1980s Japan was going one step further—using the land-based credit-pumping mechanism to pour out additional credit so its customers could enjoy endless "deficits without tears" while Japan's manufacturers churned out exports. Who cared so long as money seemed to fall out of the sky—or, to be specific, out of Japan's financial institutions—like rain? Who needs profits when banks and securities firms were throwing around vast quantities of what amounted to free money in order to meet their BOJ quotas?

Japan's corporate borrowers borrowed money simply because banks lent them money. They stayed in business only because banks continued to lend them money. In the West, companies would worry about bumping into credit ceilings that prevented them from borrowing what they needed. In Japan, conversely, borrowers worried about finding uses for loans they could not refuse. For if they turned down the funds, the banks would cut the safety net that underwrote corporate viability. The admonition "Borrow or die" came to characterize the relationship between customers and banks. Banks and borrowers were left with the choice between lending and investing recklessly or dying without help from, respectively, the BOJ or banks. As an old Japanese folk song put it: "Those who dance are fools; those who don't are fools. Since both are fools, it's better to dance." Things reached the height of the absurd when a major real estate company astounded American sellers by insisting on paying more than the asking price for a trophy building in Manhattan just to get the company name in the Guinness Book of World Records.

Japan seemed to be defying the law of gravity. The soaring of the yen had brought in its wake not a reduction in the current account surplus, but an increase; the entire underpinning of the floating rate system seemed to have gone completely awry. Floating rates were supposed to provide an adjustment mechanism for payment imbalances; instead, the imbalances just kept increasing. For a while, the result was a virtuous circle. The rapid expansion of domestic credit resulted in an astronomical run-up in asset prices. Asset sales created deposits that funded the current account surplus, allowing the surplus to expand and bring with it yet more credit creation. The cost of capital to Japanese industry fell to what was perceived as negative levels; thanks to financial game playing such as equity warrant deals, Japanese corporate treasurers believed that they were being offered free money that they would never have to pay back.[12] Corporations did not seek profits but instead indulged in an orgy of investment spending in a booming domestic economy. High utilization rates for plant and equipment helped exporters minimize profit declines due to the shrinking yen proceeds from dollar sales. Japan found that it could cope with the Plaza Accord without reducing either the current account surplus or its production levels.

## Paying the Price

While prices of land and stocks soared to stupifying levels, there was virtually no inflation in the cost of other goods and services. But there was still a toll to be paid. The absurdly high prices for land and equity occurred without anything resembling a corresponding rise in economic activity or profits. At the beginning of the 1990s, it became harder and harder to expand bank loans because the bubbles had become so transparent. The BOJ was forced to concede publicly the existence of the bubbles, which it did with the well-remembered interest rate hike of Christmas Day 1989. But because interest rates have little direct bearing on the level of lending in Japan, the hike was more of an open acknowledgement of an underlying reality: that it was becoming more difficult to flood the economy with bank lending and continue the upward credit spiral.

Much of the problem could be traced directly to Japan's ever-growing hoard of dollars. By denominating exports of goods in dollars and exporting capital in dollars, Japan received dollar deposits in the U.S. banking system. Because Japanese banks typically will not lend against the collateral of dollar assets, borrowers had been using domestic landholdings as collateral instead to raise money and buy dollar assets. But the interest, earnings, and dividend income from dollar assets had to be reinvested in dollars rather than exchanged for yen. Otherwise the yen would soar in value; preventing that from happening had been the underlying reason for the accumulation of dollar assets in the first place. Dollar assets were therefore useless in servicing yen debts; to continue to hold the dollars, the level of yen borrowings had to be increased. Banking practices that did not require cash flow to pay back loans enabled Japan to hold more dollar assets without causing a monetary squeeze. But once, for whatever reason, additional lending faltered, the holders of dollar assets—dollar assets that yielded no yen cash flows—would need to dispose of their landholdings in order to raise the cash to service or retire yen borrowings.

A key factor in reducing the ability of the banks to continue to pump out credit was the capital adequacy requirements recommended for any private sector bank engaged in cross-border business by March 1993 by the Basel, Switzerland–based Bank for International Settlements (BIS)—the "central banks' central bank," where the world's major central banks settle claims against each other. Much of the impetus behind the "BIS ratios," as they came to be known, had come, as noted, from the practices of Japanese banks buying up business at rates that seemed irrational or even dangerous to Western banks and regulators. Japanese banks were expanding their cross-border business during the 1980s at an annual clip of 30 to 50 percent; the share of all external lending to total assets rose from 10 to 40 percent. Cross-border business on both the asset and liability sides had become so important to Japanese banks that authorities believed that they could not flout the recommendations, and therefore they took steps to ensure that the banks at least gave the appearance of compliance.

Paradoxically, the initial effect of the BIS ratios was to accelerate, not retard, the expansion of Japanese bank assets. Japanese negotiators, arguing that reported capital ratios did not reflect the true equity cushions of their banks, had secured an exception: Japanese banks would be allowed to count 45 percent of the unrealized value of the gap between the book and market value of their equity holdings as Tier II capital (defined as subordinated debt and other forms of nonequity capital). Because bank lending fueled the Tokyo bull market of the late 1980s, the more lending the banks did, the higher equity prices rose and the higher the banks' Tier II capital rose. And the banks could issue new equity at those inflated prices that would boost their Tier I capital as well. The banks historically had been loathe to raise new equity—and presumably had been discouraged by the authorities from doing so—because they did not want their industrial customers following suit and raising funds themselves through the equity market rather than through bank loans. Corporations and their "main banks" held large chunks of each other's shares in fixed ratios. If any one entity in a bank/business group (the *keiretsu* or *guruppu gaisha*— literally, group companies, with "group" referring to bank group) raised new equity, all others had to follow suit in order to maintain the specified equity ratios. But the pressure of the BIS ratios proved irresistible. The MOF organized the banks into queues, and one after another they went to the market with huge new issues. Eventually, market players realized the flood of bank new issues posed a deadly threat to the entire market, but by then it was too late.

For once the market turned sour, the BIS ratios forced the banks to cut back on lending in order to bring their ratios into line. The BIS ratios were not the only reason they had to do so. In the past, banks had relied on inflation to reduce the value of loans on the books, but despite the soaring of the asset markets, inflation in the prices of goods and services was, as noted, nowhere to be seen. The revving up of the BOJ's credit-pumping machine was not solving the negative cash flow problem, it was only making it worse. Banks began to scramble for additional funds, aggravating the situation further at a time when the expansion of the real economy was demanding more and more bank credit.

Meanwhile, the banks also were being called on to pump up the stock market. In the wake of the October 1987 market crash, the banks had begun to buy shares aggressively. They were doing so, of course, at the tacit direction of the authorities who were providing the necessary credit. In a manner of speaking, the BOJ was monetizing equity. The Tokyo market sharply rebounded from the crash, helping to stop the global meltdown, but from then on the health of the banking system and that of the market became closely intertwined through Japan's peculiar institutionalization of cross-shareholding.

As noted above, major corporations and banks tended to hold each other's shares in fixed ratios. The system dates back to the early 1950s, when the prewar *zaibatsu* were reconstituted as *keiretsu* or *guruppu gaisha*. Under cross-shareholding arrangements, blank proxies are exchanged among *keiretsu* members so that the management of each company can be assured of a majority vote in any shareholder meeting and can act as if there were no external shareholders. The cross-shareholdings permitted Japan to boast that it had stock markets without risking interference by profit-seeking outside investors in the bureaucratic administration of the economy. For while shares were, to be sure, traded on the markets, corporate control was never for sale. Cross-shareholdings formed a key element in the thorough bureaucratization of the uppermost levels of the Japanese economy, removing the pressure for profitability on Japanese corporations and attuning Japanese managers to bureaucratic rather than market norms.

But cross-shareholding turned out to have set a kind of booby trap for the Japanese banking system once it became impossible to prop up share prices. For group company holdings of bank shares amounted ultimately in financial terms to treasury stocks—shares of a company that are held by the

company itself. When each share of bank equity held by a company is balanced by a share of the company's stock held by the bank, when one of the
shares cannot be sold without triggering the sale of the other, then neither
share represents genuine equity. That is to say, neither share represents any
outside infusion of ownership capital.

Banks were ensnared by the system. Any selling of the corporate shares
they owned would be met with retaliatory sales of their own shares. The
only allowable exception involved selling a share that had been bought
decades earlier at a tiny fraction of its current market value, recording the
sale proceeds as a capital gain to cover up losses elsewhere, then buying the
share back at current prices. Not a great deal of that could take place, however, without damaging the bank's real equity cushion, much of which
rested in the gap between the book value of the corporate shares it owned
and the market value. But if the shares were sold and not bought back, the
banks risked driving down the market, seeing their own shares dumped,
and unraveling the network of cross-shareholdings that provided the illusion that there was positive equity in the banking system. And as the 1990s
proceeded, an illusion is indeed what it turned out to be. While corporations and banks have never been required to disclose details of cross-shareholding, by June 2000, city banks' corporate equity holdings—a reasonable
proxy because most banks hold most shares in other group companies—
amounted to ¥27.8 trillion (valued at their cost of acquisition). That exceeded total shareholders' equity in the banks themselves, which amounted
to only ¥18.1 trillion at the end of March 2000. If finance theory is correct
that the ability of a bank to create liquidity is a function of its equity, then
the Japanese banking system had by that year lost the ability to create liquidity; the entire burden had fallen on the shoulders of the BOJ.

Meanwhile, the equity and real estate markets in Japan became more and
more tightly linked. In the 1980s, equity prices had been driven up on the
basis of landholdings; corporations would float new equity issues into the
soaring market. Banks would buy the new issues or provide credit collateralized by landholdings to finance purchases by others. Proceeds of the
equity issues would be used to purchase land, starting the cycle over again.
But just as the two markets drove each other up, so they drove each other
down. When bank lending faltered in 1990 and the stock market began to
plunge, it took the real estate market down with it, which in turn exacerbated the fall of the stock market. The entire superstructure of Japanese real

estate values had been based on a relatively modest number of transactions; just as a few purchases had raised land prices to stratospheric levels, so would a few sales send prices plummeting.

Deals stopped, and suddenly everyone wanted to be a seller. Companies that had borrowed heavily to acquire real estate started to lose money. Real estate in Japan—like external dollar holdings—had rarely generated sufficient yen cash flows to cover the cost of financing. With companies unable to service their debt, the banks found themselves facing rising levels of nonperforming loans. Under pressure, banks began to demand full repayment. With the value of their landholdings plummeting, borrowers could not convince banks to wait for a future recovery, and their scant profits, which they had never attempted to maximize, were woefully inadequate to support repayments. In order to survive, in order to pay wages, they had to sell anything they could, driving prices down yet further as banks refused to lend.

In the bubble of twenty years earlier, once asset prices had peaked, once companies began to falter in their ability to service debt, Japan's authorities had succeeded in spreading inflation from asset markets into the general economy. As prices of goods and services soared, companies could raise their own prices and thus service their debt more easily. The percentage of total loans held by Japan's banks that had nonetheless become nonperforming could be reduced as the nominal size of bank assets grew with the advent of general inflation. But in the early 1990s, the authorities found they could no longer create inflation.[13]

To begin with, the near doubling of the yen's value in the mid 1980s had finally started to erode the dikes that kept imports of manufactured goods out of Japan. Before the late 1980s, imports had consisted primarily of oil and other raw commodities. Intense foreign pressure had forced Japan to dismantle most formal protectionist barriers, such as tariffs and quotas. A vast network of distribution cartels, industrial associations, and extra-legal bureaucratic and political pressure had, however, continued to suppress unwelcome imports despite the removal of the formal barriers. But beginning in the late 1980s, the price gaps that opened up between foreign products and their domestic equivalents became so high in various sectors that imports began to wash away even those carefully constructed dikes. Such imports had little impact on Japan's overall external payments position, but waves of imports for a particular product, flooding in as a barrier finally crumbled, typically brought in their wake abrupt and startling price reductions labeled "price destruction" by distraught Japanese businessmen. Prices on goods as disparate as men's suits, personal computers, alcoholic beverages, and gasoline tumbled, with adverse effects on production. And not just production. For, in a manner of speaking, as Japan imported goods it was simultaneously "importing" foreign land—the land abroad on which the cheaper goods were being made. The phenomenon helped spell the end of *tochi shinwa*—the myth of eternally rising land prices.

The efforts by producers to reduce production costs also backfired. With land and other production costs soaring in Japan, manufacturers moved into neighboring Asian countries to produce components and labor-intensive products, helping to bring on economic booms in those nations. But companies were prevented by custom and pressure from retiring production capacity in Japan, thus further eroding their profitability. Companies in assembly industries such as automobiles and consumer electronics expanded capacity and then increased production volume to achieve efficiency, causing more price pressure.

## The Failure to Create Inflation

Plenty of evidence exists that the authorities deliberately tried to inflate the general economy in the early 1990s. They hiked virtually every price they controlled directly—transit fares, utility charges, expressway tolls, access fees. To be sure, interest rates went up as well—usually a deflationary development—but then the BOJ reversed course, slashing rates below the levels they had been at the height of the bubble. So much money was sloshing about that the BOJ abandoned the practice of passing out quarterly lending quotas to the banks; it had become an empty exercise.

Yet inflation could not be created. Part of the problem lay with the outside world. In 1974 in the wake of the collapse of Bretton Woods, general global inflation had made the job of Japan's authorities much easier. Two decades later, a tight-money Federal Reserve had succeeded in largely purging the United States of inflation, while European countries had already begun implementing the series of anti-inflationary steps that had been decreed as a prerequisite for membership in the Euro bloc. Commodity prices, led by oil, were soaring in 1974; by the early 1990s, they were falling.

Meanwhile, Japan was stumbling under a kind of double weight of excess capacity. Companies in the United States tend to build and produce for the domestic market and export what is left over. But from the beginning Japanese manufacturers have viewed domestic and export markets as distinct, revving up separate production lines to supply the demands of both. By the late 1980s, however, capacity far exceeded both domestic and export demand; there was no option to dump the excess of one market into the other. Excess capacity will, other things being equal, lower prices as businesses seek to sell whatever they can. And the current account surplus produced by that excess capacity exercises downward pressure on prices, no matter what is done with it. If it is spent on imports, the imports will, as we have seen, drive down prices. If it is exchanged for yen, the yen will get stronger, driving down prices. If it is allowed to accumulate, as we have discussed repeatedly, the accumulated dollars drain yen from the domestic system; dollars not spent and not exchanged must be backed by yen. And draining off money drives down prices.

In fact, Japan has suffered from all three deflationary pressures. Imports in volume terms have risen. Despite their best efforts, Japan's authorities have been unable to prevent periodic surges in the yen's value. Yet surpluses have continued to accumulate, requiring deflationary draining of money out of the domestic economy. The real core of the inability to create inflation, however, lay with the growing doubts in Japan about the ability of the authorities to sustain the Japanese system. Remember that money in Japan is pushed into the Japanese economy through the banking system—through the creation of deposits that the banks then on-lend, leading to further deposit creation. Before the 1990s, the banks had simply lent money as directed by the authorities and their major borrowers or on the basis of the value of land put up as collateral. But with land prices tumbling and bankruptcies accelerating, banks became fearful that the authorities might not, after all, bail out their borrowers. The borrowers themselves, afflicted with excess capacity, had no use for funds, and with asset prices beginning to plummet, they were no longer willing or able to buy land and equities. And thus the banks themselves feared—correctly, in retrospect—that they themselves could be at risk. Lacking any experience in cash flow–based lending, never having had to do what a Western banker would recognize as genuine credit analysis, Japan's banks froze like deer caught in the headlights. Lending stopped, and with it any hope that inflation could be accelerated. And the jaws of the policy trap that had been kept open with waves of credit since the collapse of Bretton Woods began, inexorably, to close.

# 7

# *The Downward Spiral*

Duuring the late 1980s, the Japanese economy had ridden high in a virtuous circle that saw floods of credit lead to higher asset prices that in turn led to a buildup of deposits and yet more credit. But in the early 1990s, the dynamic reversed itself. With bank lending beginning to falter, a vicious circle set in. Many could not obtain credit, and asset prices fell, leading to yet further shrinking of credit. Bankruptcies began to climb.

Economic history is studded with examples of booms that become slumps overnight, of "manias, panics, and crashes," to use the title of perhaps the most famous book ever written on the subject.[1] In retrospect, the end of the Japanese bubble seems inevitable. No matter how many levers Japan's administrators controlled or how skillfully they deployed them, they could not sustain forever conditions that saw the theoretical land value of Tokyo's Imperial Palace grounds exceed that of the whole of Canada. Once even the smallest indications surfaced that the administrators could not or would not keep the virtuous circle in motion—indications such as the BOJ's Christmas 1989 interest rate hike, the growing publicity given to the banks' negative cash flow, the slowdown in lending—the vicious circle set in. And to this day, Japan is still in its grip.

The clearest sign of the circle's inexorability lies in the growth of total liabilities of newly bankrupt companies, which had run between approximately 0.5 percent and 2 percent of GDP from the early days of postwar recovery until 1990. During the 1990s, the number began to climb, and by the end of the decade it would be well over 2 percent. In the year 2000, ominously, it rose to 4.7 percent.[2] The first wave of bankruptcies appeared among firms that had speculated in land and stock, beginning with the sensational collapse in September 1990 of Itoman, a trading company-turned-property-developer and a major client of the Sumitomo Bank. The Itoman saga unrolled like a third-rate potboiler, with revelations of massive fraud, gangster connections, prison sentences, and a suicide, making it easy to dismiss initially as a one-off event.[3] But such complacency did not last long. Within a few months, a string of other developers and speculators—the steel trading company Hanwa Steel; Asahi Juken, Japan's second-biggest condominium developer; Azabu Building, a large property developer; Ikeda Bussan, a Nissan affiliate that manufactured car seats and had speculated heavily—were either bankrupt or the subject of massive rescue operations.

The rot inevitably spread into the financial sector as speculators began to take their bankers down with them. During the postwar period, the MOF had always given tacit reassurances that no bank would be allowed to fail.[4] And indeed, the initial bankruptcies to appear in this sector started among the weakest and most peripheral entities in Japanese finance: nonbanks such as Esco Lease, the biggest leasing company on the northern island of Hokkaido, and several other middle-sized leasing companies; *shinyo kumiai* (credit associations); and second-tier regional banks. Once those institutions started to crumble, however, the central pillars of Japanese finance could not remain untouched, despite the widespread assumption that their position as direct licensees of the MOF gave them a greater degree of protection. For the failing credit associations, leasing companies, and local banks were linked with the major city banks in countless ways: Many of the deposits created by city bank lending ended up with the smaller institutions. Farmers and other holders and sellers of land were among those who usually banked with smaller institutions, and the proceeds of property sales often end up as deposits there. The city banks introduced lending opportunities and raised funds from these firms; in turn, the nonbanks and local banks invested heavily in long-term bank debentures, trust bank securities, and insurance policy contracts as well as dollar-denominated foreign securities. And they were lenders to real estate developers, usually at the invitation of the city banks. When the smaller institutions began to collapse, the MOF itself attempted to staunch the hemorrhage of bad debt by pushing the city banks to lead the rescue efforts. Four city banks were dragooned into bailing out the collapsing Taiheiyo Bank, while the MOF engineered the Tokai Bank's takeover of Sanwa Shinyo Kinko.

But the metastasizing credit problems could not be contained, and eventually the core institutions of Japanese finance would themselves begin to fail. The first of the city banks actually to collapse was Hokkaido Takushoku—Takugin, to use its Japanese acronym—which went under in November 1997. Takugin was, to be sure, an unusual entity. Although it was nominally a city bank, unlike the others it had no roots in any of Japan's three main metropolises, Tokyo/Yokohama, Osaka/Kobe, and Nagoya. Instead, it had been set up by the Meiji government to finance the development of Japan's northernmost "frontier" island of Hokkaido, where Takugin's franchise was still largely based. No major Japanese manufacturer is located in Hokkaido (even the island's most famous company—Sapporo Beer—is run from Tokyo), and Takugin's business lay mostly in resort developments, golf courses, and land investments—precisely those sectors of the economy hurt the worst by the collapsing bubble. Yet despite its unusual features, no one had ever questioned Takugin's status as one of the country's core twenty banks. And it played an essential role, as we have noted, in Hokkaido's economy. That the MOF would stand aside while Takugin collapsed—or felt that it had no choice but to allow Takugin to collapse—came as a shock that reverberated throughout the world of Japanese finance. Clearly the old order was crumbling.

After the failure in the early 1990s of the smaller deposit takers, the MOF had changed its tune from "No bank will ever fail" to "None of the top twenty banks will fail." But with Takugin's collapse, it was obvious that the MOF's commitment to keep even the core banks afloat could not be honored. And indeed, the Long-Term Credit Bank of Japan and the Nippon Credit Bank would follow Takugin into bankruptcy within a year. Meanwhile, the MOF closed Yamaichi Securities, one of Japan's Big Four brokers, the same week that Takugin failed. The MOF had, back in 1965, once rescued Yamaichi from bankruptcy, but it could not—or would not—do so again in 1997.

The MOF's "commitment" to keep its core licensees from failing turned out to be backed by little more than the prestige the ministry historically enjoyed. The MOF had never, of course, had to describe precisely how it would meet that commitment nor was there any institutional mechanism to force it to do so. The MOF bore much of the responsibility for what had happened, having done everything short of ordering the banks to make the loans that had turned sour. But with the escalating series of bank failures, the financial community gradually began to understand that the MOF had no way of alleviating the burden of problem loans other than to create economy-wide inflation. And it had become clear, as noted in the previous chapter, that it could no longer do that, the hectoring of foreign economists notwithstanding.

The failure of the core banks was particularly ominous. A major Japanese company typically had a core bank as what is called its "main bank"—a Japanese-English term to describe a unique Japanese institution. A main bank was expected to stand by its customer come what may; in particular, it was expected to step in and provide funding in the event that the customer encountered any kind of cash flow difficulty. Companies raised funds from creditors other than their main bank simply on the strength of the name of that bank, which provided what amounted to an informal guarantee of all the liabilities of all customers with whom it had a main bank relationship. Once a bank failed, however, those customers would find other sources of credit drying up. And if to forestall failure a bank did not honor the implicit guarantees it might have made to collapsing companies, then other banks would not feel bound to honor any guarantees that they might have made to that bank about their own customers.

Nor did the banks have any way to recover substantial portions of loans made to failing customers. Banks have rarely resorted to foreclosures and seldom initiated legal proceedings against defaulting debtors until the final collapse. As we have noted several times, they never really expected their main borrowers to pay them back anyway, just to service current debt and roll loans over. No serious efforts were therefore ever undertaken to develop meaningful procedures to recover bad debt.

In a country where asset "prices" have been rigged without any reference to the earnings they generate, where the number of courts and lawyers is, through deliberate arrangement, woefully inadequate to handle any serious volume of economic disputes, no means exist by which the assets of bankrupt companies can be seized, assessed, and assigned. By the late 1990s, collateral lending, the base of the entire superstructure of Japanese finance, stood revealed as a fiction. Collateral turned out to have meaning only as long as companies did not go bankrupt and banks did not need to foreclose on the collateral.

## The Bond "Market"

Meanwhile, just as supposedly rock-solid banks were teetering on the edge of collapse, the peculiar Japanese bond market—also long regarded as immune to default—was caught up in the general deterioration of credit. With the harrowing bond market collapse of 1927 seared into its institutional memory, the MOF had insisted in the postwar era that corporate bonds be almost as safe as currency or JGBs. Eligibility standards for bond issues were extremely tight, and only selected companies were allowed to issue them, with the understanding that no Japanese bond issue would ever default. On the rare occasions when the bond issuers themselves did in fact fail—the bankruptcy of Sanko Steamship in 1985 being a good example— main banks bought back the defaulted bonds from investors. In Sanko's case the banks bought the bonds at face value together with accrued interest. Until the 1990s, no investor in the postwar period had ever suffered a principal loss from holding a Japanese corporate straight bond.[5]

But in December 1998, Nippon Kokudo Kaihatsu, a middle-sized general construction contractor, filed for reorganization with straight bonds outstanding. The company's banks did not redeem the bonds, and investors were left holding defaulted paper. A legal settlement of the company's affairs had to wait until October 2000. As a result of the settlement, bondholders are receiving some 6 percent of the face value of the bonds. (Indeed, it is rare for unsecured creditors to bankrupt Japanese companies to recover more than 10 percent of the value of defaulted debt.)

The unique features of the Japanese bond market make it a tricky matter for Japanese authorities to follow the oft-heard advice of Western economists to create inflation by issuing floods of bonds to be purchased by the BOJ. As we have noted several times, banks in Japan lend to the government through their purchases of JGBs. Individuals do not buy significant numbers of either JGBs or corporate bonds. Household savings in Japan are intermediated by deposit-taking institutions, while JGBs and corporate bonds end up almost entirely in the accounts of MOF-licensed financial institutions and the postal savings system—and not because the bonds have attractive yields. The majority of corporate bonds are bought by banks, insurance companies, and other MOF-licensed financial institutions and are not often traded,[6] while JGBs are usually force-fed by the MOF to the post office and syndicates of MOF licensees. There is no secondary bond market comparable to those in New York or London; the few instruments that do trade continually—the ten-year JGB being the prime example—function as benchmark securities. As in so many other "markets" in Japan, bond "prices" are determined by licensed financial institutions acting under guidelines from the MOF and the FSA. The prices therefore have little meaning from the standpoint of market forces; nonetheless, they are used as benchmarks in determining other interest rates.

Creating inflation through this hobbled and distorted market leads back to the same problem that authorities have encountered in creating inflation by pushing money directly at banks. If the intention is to create money by having the BOJ buy vast quantities of new bonds, the BOJ must still figure out how to get that money out into the wider economy if inflation is to result. That can be done in today's Japan only through the banking system.

Banks, the primary buyers of JGBs, purchase them in order to create deposits in the accounts of the government; the government must then disperse the funds into the market. Fiscal spending is the only means of doing that. If the government is serious about creating inflation, it will have to spend without limit, as it did during the war years, while the BOJ and the banks buy bonds that finance the spending, flooding the economy with liquidity. But of course the Japanese government, already facing the highest relative national debt figures among the OECD countries, would run the risk of destroying Japan's credit worldwide; for that reason, the MOF has tried to reduce fiscal spending. Meanwhile, the banks have become chary of lending now that the bureaucracy has demonstrated that it no longer can support all corporate borrowers or all banks.

Theoretically, the government could try to find new buyers for the bonds, bypassing MOF-licensed institutions, but that would require pricing the bonds at levels that would be attractive to outside investors. Doing so would be no easy matter if at the same time the authorities effectively announced their intention to destroy the value of existing bonds, which is what they would do if they issued a huge flood of new ones. And permitting outside, profit-driven investors to determine bond prices and thus the structure of interest rates would involve the surrender by Japan's policy elite of perhaps its most important tool in preserving its power: its control of credit and its ability to allocate credit at will. Real bond markets—complete with deep, liquid secondary markets and both foreign and domestic bondholders—sensitize investors to all kinds of risk: credit, maturity, and market. Accordingly, investors learn how to manage risk and watch out for themselves. The entire historical record argues that Japan's bureaucrats have deliberately sought to socialize and control risk, and the "privatization" of risk inherent in a deep and broad bond market would make it impossible for them to continue to do so.

## *The* Jusen *Scandals*

The woes of the Japanese system culminated with the collapse of the seven large housing loan companies—*jusen*, to use their Japanese acronym. Because it illuminates almost everything that went wrong with Japanese finance in the 1990s, the tale of the *jusen* scandals is worth going into in some detail. The scandals spelled a highly significant systemic failure, for the announcement that the banks could not support their *jusen* affiliates demonstrated that no one could rely any longer on the ability of larger players in the Japanese system to protect their protégés. It had never been easy to ascertain creditworthiness by Western standards of analysis because the necessary information was not available and pro-forma disclosure requirements were rarely enforced. Instead, credit flows were a function of land value, which was thought to appreciate forever; credit analysis of individual borrowers was therefore irrelevant, and credit was allocated on the basis of affiliation. But when land price declines destroyed the basis of credit extension, new credit could not be raised. Because the cash flow to retire debt did not exist, borrowers had to rely on the soft guarantees of affiliation and protection from more powerful entities to obtain fresh credit. The *jusen* bankruptcies made it clear to everyone that informal guarantees based on affiliation and protection of protégés were hollow. Credit dried up regardless of what the BOJ might be doing.

The first of the *jusen*, Nippon Jyutaku Kinyu, or Nichijyukin, to use its Japanese acronym, had been established in June 1971 by a group of city and top regional banks; other city banks that had not been involved with Nichijyukin set up Jyutaku Loan Service three months later. The banks themselves had been discouraged from direct mortgage finance, but as we noted in chapter 5, the MOF was seeking a means to expand Japanese bank lending. The *jusen* were therefore set up, with the notion that they would fund themselves from their sponsoring banks and smaller deposit takers, then on-lend the proceeds to house purchasers. In 1978, regulatory responsibility for the *jusen* was shifted from the prefectural governors to the MOF.

The shift was significant. The role of the prefectural governments in regulating nonbank loan companies is somewhat comparable to that played by regulators in Western countries—they supervise the activities of finance companies to prevent wrongdoing. But once a financial institution comes under direct MOF oversight, it is understood that the institution is covered to some degree by the protective umbrella of the MOF. While the *jusen* stood near the back of the group of MOF protégés, the fact that they had become MOF regulatees enhanced their credibility and fund-raising powers; liabilities of the *jusen* thus came to be regarded as being to all intents and purposes as sound as bank deposits. Limits on the ability of the *jusen* to borrow money essentially disappeared.

In 1982, with the blessing of the MOF, the city banks muscled into the housing loan business, competing directly with their *jusen* affiliates. By the early 1980s, with the flood of new money being pushed by the BOJ into the banking system, banks needed new borrowers. Almost since the inception of the *jusen*, the banks had in fact been chafing to get into the lucrative housing loan business too, leading to howls of outrage from Niwayama Keiichiro, president and founder of Nichijyukin.[7] Niwayama's outbursts, however, need to be taken with a grain of salt. Niwayama himself was an ex-MOF official and presumably understood why the MOF felt it had to let the banks into the housing market in order to boost loans; furthermore, he surely understood that he and his company had no choice in the matter. But he went through the ritual of protest in order to appear "sincere" in front of his employees, who could not understand why their sponsoring banks had suddenly started taking business away from them. Niwayama's pro-forma complaints notwithstanding, the MOF gave the banks the go-ahead in the early 1980s. We believe MOF officials may have feared a sudden surge in the value of the yen and concluded that bank lending must rise yet further to offset the growing dollar hoard. And the MOF decided to open up the housing loan market to aggressive lending by banks as one means of increasing lending opportunities. Meanwhile, the *jusen* were, by implication, to be shown other ways of shoveling credit into the economy. That decision created the conditions that led to the *jusen* crisis fifteen years later.

The *jusen* had been established, among other things, to strengthen the solidarity within the various "convoys" of Japanese finance. The city banks had Nichijyukin and Jyutaku Loan Service; the trust banks, Jyu Sou; the first-tier regional banks, together with the life companies, had Chigin Seiho Jutaku Loan, and so forth. Put together, those convoys encompassed nearly the entire financial system. The *jusen* had existed specifically as vehicles to expand bank lending; that meant that once the banks entered the housing loan field themselves, they had an unwritten obligation to help the *jusen* make up for their lost housing loan business. The *jusen* were openly encouraged to direct their lending to entities seeking to finance speculative real estate purchases. They could not refuse the request of their *botaiko*—literally "mother banks"—to do so. They were highly leveraged and their viability depended on access to bank credit.

And the banks did provide that credit. The *jusen*'s ability to raise funds from their sponsoring banks served as a signal in the Japanese system that both the banks and, ultimately, the MOF would stand behind them, permitting the *jusen* to tap other financing sources. In essence, of course, the sponsoring banks were indirectly lending through the *jusen* to final borrowers. That was the whole point of the exercise—to provide the banks with additional outlets for monetary creation. It suggests, in fact, that the entire financial system was involved in a giant "project" to inflate land prices. And not just land prices: insiders probably understood at some level that earnings could not justify existing asset prices and that more rapid nominal GDP growth was absolutely necessary, even if it required economy-wide inflation.

Thus the late 1980s saw the values of "old Japan" stood on their head. Conspicuous spending was positively encouraged, and for the first time in the postwar period, the authorities gave the impression that they were encouraging imports of such luxury items as Mercedes automobiles for display, items that would once have attracted tax audits. Gorgeous resorts were built. Egalitarian and frugal values were thrown out the window—anything to enable the banks and the *jusen* to continue to shovel out the loans in a frantic effort to keep the party going and spark price increases.

For as long as land prices continued to rise, the credit quality of the *jusen* borrowers did not matter—borrowers would be solvent. But once prices stopped rising, once waves of bankruptcies swept Japan's real estate–related firms, the *jusen* found themselves holding what amounted to worthless assets that generated no cash. The troubles of the *jusen* had been clear to everyone since July 17, 1992, when the *Asahi Shimbun*, Japan's preeminent general circulation newspaper, had run a front-page article noting that the *jusen* had accumulated some ¥4.5 trillion in nonperforming loans. The *Asahi* accompanied the article with a detailed chart showing ¥14 trillion in loans made by a wide range of banks to the *jusen*. Emergency transfusions kept the *jusen* alive until the summer of 1995, when they finally ran out of cash to pay wages. MOF examiners descended on the *jusen* and "discovered" loan losses totaling ¥6.4 trillion, nearly half the total assets of the *jusen*. There was no alternative but to close them.

Because the *jusen* had ultimately been instruments of MOF policy, the MOF was forced to take action to mitigate the losses suffered by related parties, some of the biggest of whom were agricultural cooperative associations. The associations are the financial affiliates of what is known as JA (from "Japanese agriculture") or *nokyo*, cooperatives that control virtually every aspect of the farm economy from distribution of seed and fertilizer to the marketing of produce to the financing of agricultural machines. The *nokyo* in turn form one side of one of Japan's most formidable iron triangles, the other two sides being the Ministry of Agriculture, Forestry, and Fisheries (MAFF) and the Liberal Democratic Party, which is heavily reliant on a declining rural vote that plays a central role in the gerrymandered Japanese political system. This triangle helps to siphon wealth away from urban centers and lavish it on the countryside, where it takes financial form in the large, stable deposits held by land-owning farm families on the edges of Japan's major cities and by rural construction executives.

The agricultural cooperative associations had been invited by the banks to help fund the *jusen*; when the *jusen* collapsed, the associations expected that, in time-honored Japanese fashion, they would be made whole. After all, they had lent money to the *jusen* only at the request of banks—banks that might even have ex-MOF officials on their board of directors—and they correctly understood that the original requests for funds had been blessed by the MOF. For a while the MOF and MAFF officials assumed Kabuki-like poses of confrontation as the MOF made pro-forma demands that the cooperatives assume a share of the *jusen* losses. But each ministry is in effect a sovereign power, and it is responsible for what its own protégés do. The *jusen* were MOF-blessed entities and the MOF, not the MAFF, had to cope with their collapse. The real objective of all the drama was to ensure that the LDP was on board in a plan to use public funds to bail out the banks from the consequences of the *jusen* debacle and that the ruling party would acquiesce in an unpopular hike in the consumption tax to provide the necessary money. Once that had been achieved, the associations were bailed out with ¥ 685 billion in tax money.

The *jusen* had been *yoshingendo shoryaku saki*, the term we encountered in chapter 2 for borrowers considered so safe that they were "entities outside credit limits." Their failure heralded the future collapse of core banks. No one was safe anymore. The MOF was acting like a losing general defending a walled city. First the outer ramparts—the *shinyo kumiai* and leasing companies or, in the case of bonds, Swiss Franc and euroyen convertible instruments—had been surrendered. Then the inner walls of second-tier regional banks and domestic yen convertible bonds had been lost. With the collapse of the *jusen* and defaults on domestic straight bonds, the invaders had breached the city's defenses. Only the keep that defended the core institutions of Japanese finance—the city banks—remained standing.

## Foreigners Flee; Bank Assets Shrink

With MOF protégés now tottering on all sides, both borrowers and lenders froze, waiting for inflation that never came. As a tidal wave of negative cash flow loomed, banks simply stopped lending and borrowers collapsed. Meanwhile, the BOJ and the Japanese government could not forever pour good money after bad into the black hole of the nation's banking system. In a society in which contracts and the rule of law are not accorded the ultimate authority to resolve disputes, those who could manage to simply walked away from their tacit obligations while their dependents were left to twist in the wind of bankruptcy with little recourse to courts. They were certainly unable to bring suit against the bureaucracy itself. Outside observers find it difficult to understand that the MOF has never publicly explained why and how it could not keep its word to maintain the integrity of Japanese finance. But the MOF does not regard itself as accountable to its inferiors, and it does not recognize the existence of any superior entity to which it is bound to give an accounting. The ministry certainly does not believe it owes anything to politicians, courts, "public" opinion, or journalists.

But while no one in Japan could call the ministry to account, the confidence in the soundness of the Japanese banking system of the international community on which the MOF had relied to fund its external buildup of dollar assets had been destroyed. As Japanese share and land prices declined, as well-established Japanese financial institutions began to totter and collapse, Japanese banks found themselves paying premiums for funds overseas or frozen out altogether from foreign markets. We noted in the previous chapter how Japanese banks had, in the 1980s, begun to raise vast quantities of dollars overseas as a means of financing a surge in Japan's gross capital outflows that outpaced the current account surplus and helped suppress the exchange rate of the yen. We saw that as the banks expanded overseas, they understood that the BOJ could not and the Federal Reserve would not serve as a lender of last resort if they had difficulty raising dollars, so they had kept large pools of liquid assets to cope with any potential withdrawals. But those assets were not adequate once international confidence in Japanese finance collapsed. With the souring of money and bond market sentiment on Japanese banks, the international ratings agencies cut the ratings assigned to the banks, while their foreign branches began to hemorrhage deposits. These deposits had indirectly played a key role in funding both overseas portfolio investments and the soaring of domestic asset prices. The steep drop in deposits, particularly after 1995, can be seen in figure 6-1 of chapter 6.

The destruction of Japanese bank activities overseas proved very costly. Japanese banks were forced both to reduce credit to domestic borrowers in order to pay off their foreign depositors and to liquidate their dollar assets. The yen shot up several times as a consequence—in early 1993, in the spring of 1995, in the fall of 1998. Banks could no longer do what they had done in the 1980s—raise extensive dollar funds to support dollar assets. While the ability of the banks to call on dollar reserves held by the FESA prevented any outright defaults, the MOF appeared to be losing control of exchange rates.

The retreat of the Japanese banking system abroad seemed the financial equivalent of the defeat at Midway during World War II.

Meanwhile, domestic banking assets started to shrink. We have noted the effect of the BIS bank capital ratios in forcing banks to shrink assets. Because bank liquidity had been a major factor in driving up asset prices, the drying up of liquidity helped push asset prices down in a vicious circle that exacerbated the banks' capital problems. And the outflow of money deposited overseas removed what had become a major source of bank funding.

The threat to Japan's gross capital outflow and its ability to suppress the yen helped prod the government into the so-called Big Bang of 1998, an easing of regulations designed ostensibly to make Tokyo a fully internationalized financial marketplace comparable to Wall Street or the City of London. The revisions of the Foreign Exchange Control Act that were part of the Big Bang enabled nonbanks and other Japanese players to hold dollar instruments directly without having to go through banks. And the lifting of restrictions on the issue of euroyen and on yen loans to nonresidents gave Japanese banks and securities houses alternatives to dollar financing as a means of acquiring overseas assets and propping up the dollar.

Those alternatives lay primarily in a surge of yen-denominated bond issues by nonresidents, yen-funded dollar loans to banks in other Asian countries, and unhedged yen loans to hedge funds. In the first half of the 1980s, when yen interest rates ran five to six full percentage points below comparable dollar rates, the interest rate differential had been sufficiently attractive to foreign borrowers that a considerable volume of uncovered yen financings were done—that is, the borrowers did not hedge their yen obligations with swap contracts and the like. The vehicles were mostly yen loans from syndicates of Japanese banks and what the financial press labelled the *kagonuke* lease—large private placements with Japanese nonbanks funded by Japanese insurance companies.[8] Borrowers believed that the interest rate differential was sufficient to compensate for the risk that the yen would appreciate during the life of the financing. But with the ascent of the yen in the wake of the September 1985 Plaza Accord, discussed in the previous chapter, to levels far beyond those imagined possible by anyone at the time, the deals turned into disasters for the borrowers, few of whom had any natural means of earning yen. Japan, as noted in chapter 1, typically has paid for its imports in dollars—and with the near doubling of the yen's value in the eighteen months after the Plaza Accord, borrowers had to earn nearly twice as many dollars to service the financings as they had anticipated. The result was to shut down unhedged yen financing for nearly a decade—no borrower would risk further yen appreciation.

But after August 1995, it appeared to certain borrowers—primarily the hedge funds such as Long-Term Capital Management—that the risk had been mitigated to the point that uncovered yen financing had again become worthwhile. In the wake of the Mexican peso crisis of early 1995, the yen had climbed again to previously unimaginable highs, at one point reaching 79 to the dollar. A series of brilliantly timed joint market interventions by the U.S. and Japanese authorities masterminded by then secretary of the treasury Robert Rubin, however, helped drive the yen back into the 120 range. The interventions had been agreed to and indeed urged on the Treasury in meetings held in Washington that June with Sakakibara Eisuke, just recently appointed director general of the MOF's International Finance Division.[9]

Seeing yen interest rates close to zero and convinced that the United States and Japan had both the determination and the ability to keep the yen from rising again, offshore hedge funds shorted yen in large quantities, went long dollars without cover, and enjoyed the "carry," or difference between yen and dollar interest rates. The hedge funds placed many of their bets from the dollar/yen mismatch in emerging markets such as Thailand, Korea, and Eastern Europe, helping to fuel unsustainable asset bubbles that burst with the Asian financial crisis of 1997–98 and culminated in the spectacular near-collapse and bailout of Long-Term Capital Management in September–October 1998.[10]

And Japan's banks themselves had provided even more of the fuel for at least the Southeast Asian asset bubbles. The lure of "yen carry" and hungry borrowers proved irresistible. Carmen Reinhart, an economist formerly with the International Monetary Fund, notes that Japanese banks had "played a major role in fomenting contagion" in Southeast Asia.[11]

## No Way Out?

While the measures to cope with the collapse of the Japanese banks' dollar raising smacked of desperation and proved ultimately self-defeating, during the late 1990s the current account surplus nonetheless continued to rise. As the economy slowed following the bursting of the bubble, exports and a current account surplus had been more necessary than ever to keep plant utilization high. Fortunately, the recovery of the U.S. economy under way by late 1992 and continuing right through the decade helped to sustain the surplus.

But the problems of the banking system and the inability of the government to support all players rendered the banks unwilling and unable to renew loans to those who had borrowed heavily during the bubble years. As asset prices plummeted, those borrowers had gone practically broke, and they could not service their debt. Japan had landed in a policy trap from which no escape seemed possible. A reduction in the current account surplus in the absence of a recovery of domestic demand would bankrupt many of Japan's manufacturing companies. Yet the very existence of that surplus, with the loss of the ability to deliver increases in nominal GDP, precluded a restoration of demand.

What had happened? How had Japan fallen into such a trap? Japanese workers are, like all workers who are not slaves, paid wages for producing goods and services. Those wages constitute income out of which consumption and saving take place: workers use a portion of their wages to consume some of the goods and services they produce, and the rest goes into savings. During the high-growth period, which ended in the early 1970s, those savings funded capital investments. By the mid 1960s, the savings of Japan's workers were sufficient to finance the investment needed by Japanese industry without any requirement for foreign capital. Thus the current account moved into balance. As noted, it is a commonplace of economics that the current account measures not only a country's trade and current financial flows to and from the rest of the world but also the gap between the savings its economy generates and the real investments it undertakes. An economy saving less than it invests will by definition run a current account deficit, as the United States has done for the past two decades. But when a country saves "enough"—as Japan was doing by the mid 1960s—it no longer runs a deficit. And until Japan began saving "too much" and the current account moved into surplus, financial assets and liabilities reflected transactions for goods and services. Bank loans were supporting the real economic activities of production and trade.

But as we have stated repeatedly, when Japan started to run chronic current account surpluses in the late 1960s—surpluses denominated not in its own currency but in the currency of its largest trading partner—the country needed to create money apart from those real economic activities in order to export capital and to fund that surplus. Otherwise, the money to fund the surplus had to be siphoned from the domestic banking system, resulting in deflation. Japan faced the national balance sheet problem we have noted in earlier chapters: with ever-increasing assets denominated in dollars that could neither be spent nor exchanged for yen, matching liabilities had by definition to come from somewhere. Balance sheets must, after all, balance. And the balancing liabilities could come from one of three sources: from matching dollar liabilities, a source closed once Japanese banks could no longer raise funds overseas; from domestic monetary creation through "artificial" asset inflation—that is, bubbles; or by deflation, the markdown of yen assets so that existing yen liabilities could support both dollar holdings and the yen-denominated assets of the Japanese economy.

Of course, Japan is not the only country to have run large current account surpluses. But in most countries, those surpluses either do not last very long or do not become hugely lopsided because the exchange rate of the country's currency rises. That normally works to reduce the surplus as the country's goods become more expensive in foreign markets while imports become cheaper at home. In Japan, however, as we have seen, a panoply of policy tools suppressed the yen. Even when nevertheless the yen climbed, the widespread cartelization of the Japanese economy neutralized much of the effect a stronger yen would otherwise have had on the country's trade and current accounts. So dollars have continued to pour into Japan's national balance sheet, creating an ever-larger financing problem.

Therefore, as the current account surplus accelerated in the early 1970s and then, after disappearing briefly in the wake of the OPEC oil embargo, surged again, Japan's monetary authorities had no choice but to create extra money to support the surplus. With the creation of extra money, banks found themselves lending more than economic activity required—they essentially had no choice in the Japanese system. Borrowers with access to seemingly limitless amounts of cash bid up asset prices. Japan's wealth holders reaped substantial capital gains income, which they converted into deposits.

Because their holders did not need the funds to live on, those deposits tended to stay in place, and banks mobilized them to fund the recycling of Japan's current account surplus. Since ultimately the deposits funding the recycling were created apart from the real economic activities of production and trade, the recycling—or to put it in other words, Japan's capital exports arising from capital gains—did not immediately affect activities in the real economy. That is why in the GDP tables drawn up by statisticians, capital gains are not recognized as part of national income—they do not stem from real economic activities. But in the real world, capital gains income ends up competing with working income.

Buyers of land anywhere typically borrow money to finance their land purchases. The debt has to be serviced, which means borrowers are forced to save. In Japan, however, there were two classes of buyers that borrowed money to purchase land: households that had to save in order to pay back loans they had taken down, thus boosting national savings, and corporations that until the late 1990s never needed to pay back the principal on their debt. Borrowers and other purchasers of high-priced land do, however, pass on the high cost of doing business brought on by expensive land. That helps explain why Japanese consumers are forced to bear the burden of the world's highest living costs. And the purchasing power of the deposits generated by a land sale will eventually compete with the purchasing power of working income. Assuming a fixed level of economic activity, with the growth of deposits generated by capital gains, the purchasing power of working income is diluted—and that eventually lowers aggregate demand in the economy.

Japan sidestepped that dilemma during the bubble years as demand increased. Flush with cash, those who had profited from land sales increased their spending somewhat. Meanwhile, those who borrowed money to purchase land tended not to worry about servicing their debt, assuming that they could repay their loans by selling the land they had bought at a higher price. But as the bubble collapsed, borrowers suffered losses on land they had bought at inflated prices. As land values sank, it became clear that those who had sold assets at the peak of the bubble had reaped huge, undeserved windfalls. Those sellers had their windfalls deposited safely—so they thought, and so they continue to think—in banks. After all, the government guaranteed the banks, and even when that guarantee turned out to be hollow, no depositor at a core bank lost his money.

The air leaked out of the bubble. Borrowers went bankrupt, and some of their lenders went bankrupt, yet the deposits that resulted from the chimerical capital gains of the bubble years still sit there at face value. They finance assets whose intrinsic economic value (measured in terms of their ability to generate the cash flow of rents or dividends) was very low to begin with and whose nominal values have now collapsed as well. But the deposits have yet to be written down. The American with a mutual fund sees its value drop instantly as the values of the equities that it comprises drop. He adjusts his economic expectations accordingly. The Japanese housewife with ¥1,000,000 (some $8,000) in the bank does not, however, yet understand that that deposit supports assets that are probably not worth even ¥500,000. Because she can go to the bank or the post office and withdraw money whenever she needs to, she does not realize that the money she saved has actually disappeared. She or her husband may have earned it doing something real and valuable, or perhaps she received it as the proceeds of the land she sold when her parents died. Whatever the source, she put it on deposit with a bank that then lent the money to a developer. That developer is now bankrupt because it bought land at prices that were three to four times today's levels. The money is gone, but if the authorities were to tell her and millions of other Japanese depositors like her that their savings have been wasted, the Japanese financial system would melt down.

For the deposits she and millions like her made ultimately went to finance not just land and "equities" at absurd prices but Japan's ¥200 trillion in accumulated current account surpluses. Unfortunately, that is worthless too. Or, to be more precise, it can be converted into things of worth—foreign goods, foreign land, and foreign services—only by destroying the Japanese economic system, by forcing Japanese land values down to the point that it would be profitable in an open economy to make or grow things on that land and by wiping out those very large parts of the Japanese economy that could not withstand competition from foreign counterparts.

In the interests of its own survival, therefore, the government has no choice but to guarantee all deposits and to continue piling up excess loans, amassing additional external surpluses, and doing what it takes to stabilize the exchange rate. After the collapse of the bubble, it found other ways to keep the game going for a few more years.

# 8

# The Policy Trap
# Revisited

I n the first chapter of this book, we laid out the dimensions of the trap that has gripped the Japanese economy
since the early 1990s. A century-long policy of accumulating
production capacity and claims on other countries without
regard for profitability or return has saddled Japan with a
huge pile of dollar assets. Those assets can be neither exercised nor exchanged without destroying the political and
economic base of the Japanese system, yet their sheer weight
has defeated every attempt to restart the economy. Japan can
live neither with its dollars nor without them. Meanwhile,
the economy has staggered under the weight of excessive
capacity supported by vast pools of yen deposits that cannot
be written down, while working income has shrunk. By the
summer of 1992, as it became impossible to hide the volume
of bad debts on the books of the country's financial institutions, the iron grip of the trap had become clear. The capital
in the banking system had been dangerously depleted, and
many—even most—banks would have been wiped out if
their assets had been realistically valued. If, as many urged,
profits were to govern investment decisions, if corporations

were required to retire debt out of current cash flow, Japan's current account surplus would vanish—and take much of Japan's industrial capacity and employment with it. That would plunge the economy into deep recession, destroy any remaining illusions about the viability of the financial system, and destabilize the foundations of the political order. Yet perpetuating excessive, unprofitable capacity meant an accumulating current account surplus and an increase in the net creditor position—a position that would have to be funded by domestic liabilities. But revving up those liabilities was no easy matter as the economy sank into the grip of deflation.

Banks could not increase loans to companies that had borrowed heavily during the bubble years; as asset prices plummeted, those borrowers had gone practically broke anyway and could not service their debt. Banks in the early 1990s were initially willing and, presumably, encouraged by the MOF to shovel credit at anyone else who would take it. Loans were increased to small and medium-sized firms in nonmanufacturing industries and in the housing loan market. But those borrowers were in no better position to pay back the money they had borrowed than their larger brethren; with land prices continuing their relentless decline, neither big nor small real estate–related firms could service their debts. Far from taking up the slack, the lending to small and medium-sized firms would end up compounding the bad loan problem.

As we saw in the previous chapter, in the 1980s Japanese banks not only had sharply increased their domestic deposit taking but also had raised liabilities abroad in vast quantities. Those liabilities—mostly denominated in dollars—financed a wave of global investment under Japanese control that exceeded even the country's net creditor position. But as we have noted, the growing worldwide concern over the creditworthiness of Japanese banks began to cut deeply into that source of funding. The banks found themselves paying a substantial premium for dollars in international markets as foreigners pared back their exposure to Japanese institutions. The "Japan premium" had first appeared back in 1974, when it seemed that the Japanese economy would be badly hurt by the Arab oil embargo and subsequent quadrupling of oil prices. It did not last long in the 1970s, but its reappearance in the mid 1990s, a few short years after Japan had been proclaimed the world's new economic superpower, was a humiliating comedown. And it was not even necessary; the banks could have turned to Japan's domestic holdings of excess dollars with the FESA to cover the gap created by the withdrawal of foreign funding. But not really grasping the way that money markets work, Japanese banks carelessly bid up interest rates on their deposit taking, aggravating their funding problems and reinforcing the notion abroad that something had gone badly wrong with Japanese finance.

The equity market, however, did provide for a short time another path for the inflow of foreign money and thus the outflow of Japanese capital. The authorities launched heroic efforts to boost the Tokyo stock market in the fall of 1992, leading to the desired influx of foreign money seeking quick profits from a "guaranteed" turnaround in Japanese stock prices. The Japanese media labeled the efforts PKO, a play on the acronym for "peace keeping operations" that saw Japanese soldiers sent overseas to such trouble spots as Cambodia; in this case, however, it meant "price keeping operations." Inevitably, the yen soared as a result, climbing in the early months of 1993 to new historical highs. While the MOF was successful in diverting the blame from itself to inexperienced officials in the incoming Clinton administration, it could not as easily divert the deflationary impact of its actions.[1] In the teeth of the yen's rise, the current account surplus continued its relentless climb, draining money from the domestic economy and deepening the deflationary trap. And the boost in equity prices proved short-lived; by the end of the decade, the stock market would be falling again to even lower levels.

## *The Life Raft of Deficit Spending*

In desperation, Japan's administrators turned to deficit spending. As they had done so many times before, American government officials wittingly or unwittingly provided a rationale for Japanese government action that helped deflect political heat away from the bureaucrats responsible for it. Since the late 1980s, under the label of the Structural Impediments Initiative, Washington had been pushing fiscal stimulus on Japan as a means of boosting Japanese growth rates and thus, it was hoped, increasing Japan's imports. The Clinton administration had taken office with a pledge to overhaul America's Japan policy and had ratcheted up the pressure, originally setting its sights on "results oriented" trade agreements. But as understanding of the implications of Japan's huge accumulated dollar position dawned on administration officials, as they watched with growing fear the seeming inability of their counterparts in Tokyo to cope with the burgeoning problems of the Japanese banking system, the White House abandoned its early goals of direct action to bring down the trade deficit with Japan. Instead, the administration began urging Tokyo to do whatever it took to keep Japan from plunging into recession and a full-fledged banking crisis. The suggested solution to Japan's trouble laid particular stress on fiscal stimulus—that is, deficit spending.

The shift in Washington coincided with the rising influence in the Clinton White House of Robert Rubin, who in early 1995 would be named secretary of the treasury. Rubin had come to Washington from Wall Street, where he had started his career on the bond-trading floor at Goldman Sachs and eventually become the firm's co-chairman before leaving to join the Clinton administration. Rubin's decades at the center of global finance had given him an acute understanding of the vulnerability of the U.S. economy to any significant collapse of confidence in the dollar, and no bond trader could be unaware of the key position Japanese entities played in dollar markets. Rubin succeeded in persuading the president to eschew the results-oriented approach, most importantly by folding the American hand in the auto-parts talks of September 1994. Instead, at Rubin's urging, the White House pushed upon Tokyo the need to restructure the Japanese economy, to reform the financial sector, and—most significant—to use deficit spending to prop up both the banks and the wider economy. Belligerent talk about Japan's trade surpluses disappeared as the administration sent tacit signals that it was prepared to accept an increase in Japanese exports provided that the Japanese used the fiscal tools necessary to revive the economy and stabilize the banking system.

But while pressure from the United States may have provided a politically useful excuse for what they set about doing, Japan's administrators had in reality no tool left other than fiscal reflation. The alternative of a genuinely radical overhaul of the economy was far too risky, particularly to their own control over the allocation of credit and income. With the drying up of bank lending in the wake of snowballing credit problems, deficit spending had become essential to push money into the economy; indeed, massive deficits were the only prop left to keep Japan from tipping over into recession. Any doubt about that disappeared when fiscal hawks in the MOF, worried about the burgeoning indebtedness deficits were naturally bringing in their wake, succeeded in forcing a regressive tax package on the country in the spring of 1997. The package, featuring a hike in the consumption tax and a cut in top marginal rates, seemed almost fiendishly designed to suppress Japan's anemic domestic demand while pumping yet more money into the vast, stagnant pool of savings desperately needed to fuel its capital exports. The economy promptly went into a downward spiral.

The prospect of the world's second-largest economy and its largest net creditor spiraling down into a black hole of depression and collapsing banks terrified Washington insiders. Rubin prevailed upon President Clinton to telephone then prime minister Hashimoto Ryutaro urging drastic action to halt what appeared from outside to be an imminent meltdown of the financial system.[2] It is not clear, however, whether Washington really understood the core problem of the Japanese economy: that it had become increasingly difficult for Japan to cope with its capital exports—that is, its huge pile of deflationary dollars. The American pressure nonetheless provided cover for a mammoth reflation-cum-bank-bailout package totaling some ¥72 trillion that passed the Diet in October 1998. The package broke the economy's fall but left the policy elite with no visible alternative but more deficit spending.

Most of this red ink took the form of public works that contributed little to Japan's real wealth and were in countless cases terribly destructive of the country's natural environment. The Japanese government has been roundly criticized for heavy reliance on such public works spending instead of, for example, tax reform that would boost consumption or the building of a social safety network that could help the Japanese public accept the inevitability of corporate restructuring and its effects on employment and job security. Economists point out that public works spending, like any other kind, brings with it diminishing returns; the more money funneled into public works spending, the less efficient such spending will be.

But all such criticism misses the real rationale for what the Japanese policy elite has been doing. The Japanese government allocates spending on construction and other government programs to each ministry through the Budget Bureau of the MOF, with the proportion going to each ministry essentially fixed, as discussed in chapter 2. Although MOF officials have well-deserved reputations for brilliance and hard work, it does not appear that the MOF conducts any kind of independent audit of the difference between the allocation sought for a particular project and what it might cost for a private sector entity to complete the project. We cited in chapter 2 a newspaper article that reported that of a typical ¥1.9 billion project, only ¥1.26 billion was actually needed to complete it; the rest of the money went to various middlemen. A front-page article in the January 9, 2002, issue of the *Nihon Keizai Shimbun* revealed that the former Ministry of Construction (now part of the MLIT) had long concealed an internal study that noted the sharply diverging unit costs for public works and private sector construction. In 1990, costs for both were roughly ¥200,000 per square meter, but within a decade public works costs had risen to ¥220,000, while the private sector had brought costs down to ¥130,000—a clear indication of how much was available for siphoning off as pure profit.

The widening divergence between public and private sector construction costs is not simply a result of market pressure producing greater efficiencies than those that bureaucrats can manage. Hasegawa Tokunosuke, a former Construction Ministry official and now a professor in the real estate department at Meikai University, has admitted that high public construction costs in Japan are welcome. They allow the relevant ministries to expand their budgets, permit politically important contractors to increase orders, and result in larger fees for "consultants" and architects. As Hasegawa explains, the government ultimately tries to maximize construction spending in order to induce economic growth.[3]

Indeed, this way of allocating money achieves two objectives—one political, the other financial. Politically, it directly enhances both the power of the MOF and that of what Tokyo's insiders call the *jigyo kancho*, literally, the "enterprise ministries"—ministries such as MLIT and MAFF that spread money aroud.[4] The money also buys political protection from the LDP, which relies on heavy rake-offs from construction projects to finance its expensive election campaigns. Financially, allocating money in this way helps create deposits to fund Japan's capital exports, thereby supporting the accumulated current account surpluses and keeping interest rates low. With the woes of the banking sector, the traditional means of creating deposits through bank lending have not been working well. Instead, the government now creates deposits through fiscal spending, and using most of that money to build useless and even destructive white elephants carries with it a perverse but compelling logic. Fiscal allocations without accountability ensure that 30 percent or more of the money spent on useless dams, seawalls, and tunnels can be pure profits—that is, money that is not paid out as wages. Those profits end up in the accounts of political fixers (usually with strong LDP connections), well-to-do construction executives, the part-time farmers these executives employ, and the farm families whose land is expropriated for the projects. The money these people receive is far in excess of their propensity to spend; indeed, in general they are careful to avoid too much conspicuous spending lest they invite tax audits. Instead, they put the money on deposit, where it finds its way into capital exports and the funding of Japan's dollar hoard.

## Endless Woes; Endless Scandals

While all the government's spending succeeded in keeping the economy from tipping over into a full-fledged recession, it did little more than that. The 1990s saw the Japanese system muddle through its worst decade since the 1940s, but at the end of the decade the woes besetting the economy seemed worse than they had at the beginning.

To start with, while the accumulated current account surplus kept climbing, foreign direct investment (FDI) by Japanese companies could not keep pace. Spending abroad on factories, resorts, office buildings, and corporate acquisitions is the most stable form of recycling the current account surplus because such investments cannot easily be liquidated and are far less subject to market shocks than portfolio investments. But much of the FDI in the 1980s turned out to be disastrous; repeatedly Japanese companies bought into foreign real estate markets such as those in Los Angeles and Bangkok at market peaks and then lost hugely when the markets tumbled. Corporations were understandably gun-shy about repeating their experiences, nor could they—only government-controlled entities such as Japan Tobacco and Nippon Telephone and Telegraph have made significant foreign acquisitions in recent years. The bank lending that had financed private sector acquisitions abroad disappeared with the drying up of fresh dollar deposits into Japanese banks. The losses suffered on investments outside Japan actually helped to keep the yen weaker than it otherwise might have been, which was, after all, the underlying rationale for the entire exercise in the first place. But the drought in financing for overseas projects and the publicity given to the huge losses precluded any new spate of vanity investing.

Meanwhile, developments in the real economy led to a dwindling demand for FDI that had a genuine economic rationale. Japanese firms were also-rans in most of the important technologies that arose in the 1990s (cellular phones being a major exception); the older industries they did dominate—automobiles, consumer electronics—were saddled with global overcapacity, precluding much additional FDI in plant and equipment.

Neighboring Asian countries, which absorbed the lion's share of Japanese FDI, turned out to have serious problems of their own in the wake of the 1997–98 economic crisis. Of course, there are many successful instances of FDI by such firms as Toyota, Honda, and the electronic component manufacturers. But those investments, as noted in chapter 1, tended to come at the expense of domestic production and employment. And there is a limit to how far they can go; the pressure to maintain lifetime employment protocols and avoid mothballing domestic production capacity is so great that companies cannot easily expand FDI by closing factories and laying off workers in Japan.

The slack left by dwindling Japanese FDI thus had to be taken up by dollars diverted instead into foreign securities and bank assets. Funding the current account deficits of Japan's major trading partners in this way proved to be highly unstable in the wake of the economic crisis of 1997–98 that started in Southeast Asia. We noted in the previous chapter the central role Japanese banks played in that crisis. With its onset, Japanese banks lost a great deal of additional money,[5] and even where they did not, local banks in the affected countries could no longer absorb Japanese credit.

The situation was exacerbated by the withdrawal of foreign deposits with Japanese banks, which, as we have noted, forced the banks to scramble to find money to pay off their international liabilities. Japanese banks had been financing long-term loans with short-term borrowings. Short-term liabilities abroad went down much faster than the loans outstanding that those liabilities had financed. Japanese banks had to shrink their assets elsewhere as a result. Figure 6-1 of chapter 6 demonstrates how rapidly the international assets and liabilities of the city banks overseas began to fall after 1995. Particularly after the onset of the Asian financial crisis, as Japanese banks pulled credit lines in one country after another, their overseas liabilities had to be liquidated by the remittance of money from Japan. Partly as a result, corporate borrowers inside Japan found themselves for the first time ever asked to follow the actual language of the loan contracts with their banks and repay borrowings. As we have mentioned repeatedly, while often those loans were technically short-term instruments, they had long been treated in effect as "evergreen" loans—in other words, more or less permanent borrowing that everyone assumed would be automatically renewed. But banks needed the cash. Paradoxically, in a country sitting on a vast pile of dollars, economic activity shrank because of a scarcity of credit.

Meanwhile, land and equity prices fell and fell again, as figure 8-1 indicates. The loans made during the bubble years therefore remained underwater because they were collateralized with assets worth only a fraction of the outstanding loans. The result has been to force partial liquidation of cross-shareholdings as banks sell shares to raise cash (see figure 8-2). We have already noted how any sale of cross-shareholdings puts extreme downward pressure on the stock market. To be sure, to date it has been the peripheral and unimportant cross-shareholdings that have been liquidated; core cross-shareholdings that keep the commanding heights of the Japanese economy immune from market forces and the pressure for profits will undoubtedly be maintained as long as possible. Indeed, there is talk of revising the commercial code to reduce the quorum at special shareholder meetings from shareholders representing 50 percent of outstanding equity to 30 percent. That will permit the amount of cross-shareholdings to decline by 40 percent without affecting the actual governance and control of Japanese companies. But even if revisions in the commercial code forestall a complete unraveling of cross-shareholdings, any bank sell-off of equity holdings at a time when bank loans are declining will result in a yet tighter credit squeeze because those who buy equity when banks sell typically do so by liquidating a bank deposit.

The government has, it is true, stepped forward to help banks and companies with the ¥72 trillion package mentioned above, part of which went into bank recapitalization. Existing programs that provide government guarantees to small and medium-sized enterprises were pumped up with an extra ¥30 trillion plus a significant easing of the eligibility criteria.[6] Meanwhile, Japanese government financial institutions were allowed to advance loans to financially weak companies to cope with the credit crunches of 1998 and 1999.

As a result, bankruptcies fell dramatically both in number and in gross liabilities during 1999. But the government had not solved the underlying problems that had driven the companies to the brink of bankruptcy in the first place; dealing with them had simply been deferred. Indeed, bankruptcies began to rise again in 2000. While large manufacturing companies in electronics, communications, and automobiles did, to be sure, begin to invest again in 2000, many were hit in 2001 by substantial losses. Meanwhile, most small and medium-sized companies are suffering worse than ever. Some of them would have gone out of business long ago without government help

**Figure 8-1.** *Equity and Land Prices*

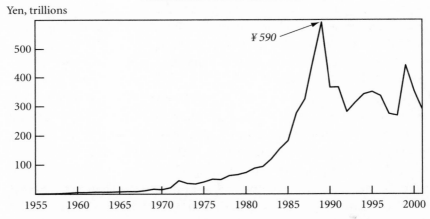

Total Market Value of Land

Yen, trillions

¥ 2,455

Total Market Value of Listed Stocks[a]

Yen, trillions

¥ 590

Sources: *Annual Report on National Accounts,* Cabinet Office; *Annual Securities Statistics,* Tokyo Stock Exchange. Calculated, arranged, and estimated by Mikuni & Co. © 2002 Mikuni & Co., Ltd.
a. Tokyo Stock Exchange, first section.

and subsidies, and many of them that provide crucial support to the LDP have seen their support rewarded. But they continue to bleed red ink. As a result, the aggregate net income (after taxes, without application of tax effective accounting) of the entire universe of Japanese companies excluding financial institutions shows three consecutive years of losses in the fiscal year

**Figure 8-2.** *Shares Owned by Financial Institutions as a Percentage of Total Shares Listed on the Tokyo Stock Exchange*[a]

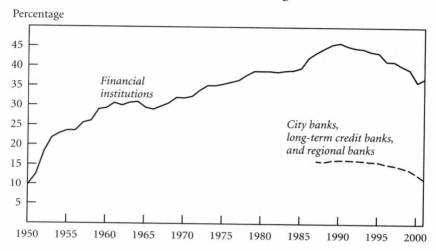

Percentage

Financial institutions

City banks, long-term credit banks, and regional banks

Sources: *Shareownership Listed Companies*, National Conference of Stock Exchanges. Calculated, arranged, and estimated by Mikuni & Co. © 2002 Mikuni & Co., Ltd.
  a. For years ending in March.

ending March 2001. Some 70 percent of corporate tax returns filed that year reported losses, compared with 30 percent thirty years ago.[7]

In the midst of escalating economic difficulties, scandal after scandal erupted. As Karel van Wolferen has noted, scandals play a crucial role in a Japanese system where neither markets nor courts are permitted to perform ultimate ordering functions.[8] Resorting to scandals instead of transparent legal proceedings in coping with corporate financial distress helps shelter Japanese finance from market forces; because outside investors have no meaningful legal recourse in such cases, they have no way to force management to manage corporate assets for profitability.[9] But scandals are not limited to spectacular bankruptcies. They constitute the primary means by which the Japanese system rights itself, copes with excess, and reassures an uneasy public. Scandals serve as object lessons to those whose personal agendas are seen to threaten overall stability. While scandals thus form an enduring feature of Japanese political and economic life, an excess of scandals can indicate that underlying strains and tensions have reached unbearable levels.

And that is precisely what the 1990s saw. The decade began in the wake of the Recruit and Sagawa Kyubin scandals, which engulfed the entire Japanese political establishment and led to the appointment of the unknown Kaifu Toshiki as prime minister. He would prove unexpectedly difficult for LDP puppet masters to control and had to be summarily shunted aside in favor of the aging ex-MOF stalwart, Miyazawa Kiichi. Kaifu's fate helped lead to a temporary loss of LDP control of the Diet in 1993 with the short-lived cabinet of Hosokawa Morihiro. Hosokawa himself was brought down by the scandal publicity machine of the Japanese media.

Paralleling what was happening in the political arena, the financial world saw virtually every one of Japan's top banks—the bluest of the blue chips—embroiled in scandalous upheavals, with spates of resignations, suicides, and probable murders in their wake. The securities industry was wracked by the so-called *eigyo tokkin* (brokers' discretionary accounts) scandals when the *Yomiuri Shimbun* revealed in June 1991 that Japan's top securities houses had been compensating their best-connected clients for market losses while deducting the payments as entertainment expenses.[10] That particular scandal ended an important link in the ability of the system to socialize risk. Brokers' informal guarantees on equity investments had permitted them to raise substantial funds that could be used to support and kick up share prices with the implicit approval of the MOF. But the decline in equity prices made it impossible to honor all the guarantees without destroying the industry. Brokers were allowed to walk away from some of their guarantees and were unable to make any more; those who had relied on the guarantees were "compensated" with the dubious pleasure of venting in the media their rage on the securities industry. The brokers were operating, of course, with the protection of other elements of the system, and it was the inability of the bureaucracy to support the market that triggered the scandal in the first place.

The biggest of the financial scandals—that of the *jusen*—was discussed in the previous chapter. Just as the *eigyo tokkin* scandal grew out of the inability of the bureaucracy to prop up equity prices in the wake of the deflating of the bubble economy, the *jusen* scandal stemmed directly from the loss of control over land prices. But the *jusen* scandals did not bring an end to the endless revelations of sleaze and chicanery; they seemed in fact more like a prelude. On the heels of the *jusen* scandals would come the bankruptcies of top Japanese financial institutions—Yamaichi Securities, the Hokkaido

Takushoku Bank, the Nippon Credit Bank, the Long Term Credit Bank of Japan, and Sanyo Securities, to mention just the biggest—scandalous events in a Japan where the MOF had long given tacit assurances that no bank or major securities firm would be allowed to fail. Insiders deliberately covered the bankruptcies with the cloak of scandal—complete with public resignations, humiliations of top officials, and lurid tales of misconduct—which replaced any sober and public accounting of what had happened in front of a disinterested judiciary. Executives and employees at failed institutions were given no rationale for why their employers were allowed to collapse while their competitors were kept alive. No publicly available information suggested that their competitors had done any better or worse than they had; objective, verifiable criteria regarding who went bankrupt and who survived were not available. Scandals provided the substitute.

The flames of scandal touched even the MOF itself, with theatrical raids on the MOF by the public prosecutor and tales in the press of lower-level MOF officials being entertained by the banks they were supposed to regulate at restaurants where the waitresses wore no panties. To anyone who knows the reality of Japanese business life, the amounts reportedly spent on such entertainments were ludicrously small. They provided, however, a titillating and diverting spectacle to ordinary people who understood by then that things had gone very wrong.

Before the 1990s, major scandals typically involved politicians taking bribes—usually the implicated politicians were men such as Tanaka Kakuei, who had risen to prominence from outside the bureaucracy. Bureaucrats and the top management of blue-chip companies used to escape scandals. But in the 1990s, scandals began to touch a wide spectrum of the ruling elite—a sign that at the very least, the legitimacy and prestige of the elite have sustained serious damage, pointing to potentially deadly rifts and the fraying of bureaucratic control.

## Losing Control of the Yen

Even more disturbing than loss of bureaucratic control, however, were signs that despite everything, the MOF might be losing its ability to control the exchange rate. The yen/dollar rate was, after the turbulence of the mid 1980s, reasonably stable in the first years of the 1990s. But the measures put in place to prop up the Tokyo stock market in 1992 saw the yen climb from the 125–140 range, where it had settled in the aftermath of the 1987 stock market crash, to a new 110–125 range. That to some extent had been foreseen, but the soaring of the yen in the spring of 1995 had seemingly come out of nowhere.

We touched on that event in the previous chapter. As noted, it did not start as a Japanese crisis at all—it began with the collapse of the Mexican peso and a vote by the global financial markets of no confidence in the Clinton administration, which appeared at the time to have been fatally weakened by the 1994 congressional elections. If the White House could not muster the congressional support necessary to bail out an ailing Mexico that was seen by the rest of the world as largely an American ward, if the United States could not cope with a financial panic in its own backyard, then, in the view of the markets, the Clinton administration was finished and the hegemony of the United States and its currency over global finance was at an end. But Robert Rubin, in his first major challenge as secretary of the treasury, found a way to circumvent partisan congressional opposition. He secured the necessary funds to halt the Mexican collapse, and the erosion of the dollar stopped.

Except against the yen. The Japanese currency continued to climb, rising to heights never imagined in the worst nightmares of Japan's policy elite, pushing past eighty to the dollar at one point, a rate at which most of Japan's exporters could not even cover variable costs. At eighty to the dollar, in other words, the manufacturers were losing money on each additional item made for export, although most kept on exporting despite negative cash flows. A desperate MOF broke the usual order of bureaucratic succession and brought in a relative outsider, Sakakibara Eisuke, as director general of the International Finance Bureau, largely on the strength of his purported personal relationship with Rubin's principal deputy, Lawrence Summers, who was then deputy secretary.[11] Sakakibara was successful in securing Rubin's and Summers's help in arranging a coordinated intervention in August of that year that brought the yen back down from its dizzying heights,[12] but not until the entire Japanese system had been shaken to its core.

Nor was that the only instance in which the MOF seemed to lose control of the currency. While the yen subsequently entered a period of weakness driven by a worldwide flight from Japanese assets when the outlook for the Japanese economy darkened in the wake of the April 1997 consumption tax hike, the yen would again spurt uncontrollably—climbing more than

15 percent against the dollar in two days—as hedge funds were forced to call in their yen-carry transactions at the time of the Russian debt crisis and the subsequent bailout of Long-Term Capital Management in October 1998. In both the 1995 and 1998 crises, overseas branches of Japanese banks hemorrhaged dollar deposits, deposits that had indirectly funded overseas portfolio investment. Japanese banks had, as noted, been forced to reduce credit to domestic borrowers as they called in dollar loans; overseas investments by Japanese investors were liquidated for yen, driving up the yen. Because of the damage suffered when the bubble burst, Japanese banks could not raise dollar funds abroad; with banks in Japan unable to create credit rapidly enough as foreigners withdrew their money, the MOF could not halt the sudden soaring of the yen.

## The Japanese Policy Elite at a Loss

Since 1998, the Japanese and American authorities seem to have succeeded—for the time being—in stabilizing the exchange rate. The Clinton administration had, after some early fumbling, sent clear signals that it would not use the exchange rate to rectify the trade imbalance. And the incoming Bush administration had—again after some initial ambiguity—followed suit. The United States continues to enjoy its "deficits without tears," while Japan seems to have reassured Washington that it can continue to export capital to finance those deficits.

But that has only postponed the day of reckoning for Japan. With money draining out of the financial system because of the chronic current account surplus, domestic demand has come under ever-heavier deflationary pressure, which destroys corporate profitability. All price indicators have shown downward movement, and there is no sign that that will change in the foreseeable future.

The Japanese government as a whole is therefore visibly at a loss. It does not know what to do other than continue to spend public funds and print money (figure 8-3). Such policies cannot continue forever, however, when one considers the size of the BOJ's balance sheet (see figure 3-6 of chapter 3) and the sharply rising total indebtedness of the government as a percentage of GDP—now more than 140 percent, up from 60 percent ten years ago. Despite all the efforts, self-sustaining growth has not been achieved. Production levels did recover a bit in 2000 thanks to the strong U.S. economy,

**Figure 8-3.** *Central and Local Government Indebtedness as a Percentage of Nominal GDP*[a]

Percentage

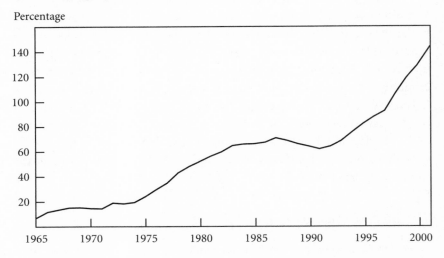

Sources: *Financial and Economic Statistics Monthly,* Bank of Japan; *Annual Report on National Accounts,* Cabinet Office; and *New Issue Volume and Value of Outstanding Bonds,* Japan Securities Dealers Association. Calculated, arranged, and estimated by Mikuni & Co. © 2002 Mikuni & Co., Ltd.
    a. For years ending in December and March.

the inventory buildup in Asia following the resolution of the Asian financial crisis, and the workings of the inventory cycle in Japan. Sales of personal computers, mobile phones, and digital products rose sharply, benefiting the electronics and IT sectors. Plant and equipment investment also began to increase. But all those indicators now have turned down again, while household income and consumer spending never showed any signs of recovery to begin with. Exports remain the critical demand factor in keeping the economy going—therefore the importance of stabilizing the yen/dollar rate.

Production costs in Japan are far above those of other Asian nations. Meanwhile, as has been noted, irresistible pressure on Japan's covert trade barriers has finally resulted in import surges of textiles, foodstuffs, and labor-intensive products. Supermarket prices have been falling at a time when declining income and fear of job loss have made Japan's consumers particularly price sensitive. The replacement of domestic goods by imports has reduced production in many industrial segments. But the growth of imports in volume terms has not been nearly enough to melt away the trade surplus. The deflationary impact of the current account surplus therefore persists and worsens, even as the volume of imports continues to rise. Japan is being hit at the same time by the deflationary effects of both the current account surplus and cheap imports.

Firms in industries that serve consumers have been suffering the most. Such firms have long played a central role in the de facto taxation of consumers through stupifyingly high prices that siphoned off household income and helped both to sustain Japan's vast distribution cartels and to funnel cash to manufacturers, where it subsidized the low prices abroad necessary to capture market share. But Japan's retail sector may be forcibly restructured as new retailers, taking advantage of falling land prices, build American-style malls on the outskirts of Japan's major cities, badly hurting old-line retailers and distributors. If the restructuring of the retail sector proceeds, the days when Japan's households can be exploited to support its industry may end.

We have already noted how bankruptcy rates have climbed to historical highs, but even that does not indicate the full extent of the problem. For a bankrupt Japanese company usually leaves behind much less of recoverable value than does its counterpart in the West. In the United States, well over half of the assets of bankrupt firms have, until the recession that began in 2001, typically been recoverable, but in Japan, as noted in the previous chapter, the figure is well under 20 percent.[13]

Japanese companies—and indeed the entire economy—are finally beginning to suffer the acute adjustment pains of decades of investments made without regard to profitability or return. The fact that companies have been allowed and even encouraged to borrow money in order to expand without any concern for profitability has inevitably left an enormous residue of bank loans funding facilities that do not pay for themselves. In the past, with borrowers rarely asked to pay back loans, any losses could be covered by having borrowers sell land to affiliates at orders of magnitude greater than book value, creating accounting profits. Actual sales to outsiders happened relatively rarely, helping sustain land prices. And if companies actually needed extra cash to plug gaps in their cash flow, they could easily borrow more as long as the nominal value of their landholdings continued to appreciate more rapidly than their indebtedness. But once land prices began to fall, capital gains could not be generated to conceal either speculative losses or losses on continuing operations.

Japan's corporate managers have never paid much attention to the profitability or even the viability of investments, assuming that at the national level the bureaucrat/banker nexus will always generate at least nominal GDP growth and that that growth will solve all problems. And as long as the economy grew, both banks and their borrowers did very well. But flat or negative real economic growth brings on losses, and the inability to create inflation makes it impossible to disguise them. Large, well-connected companies write off debt, reduce employment levels, and quit investing; the less well-connected go bankrupt, and the banks end up with awful loan portfolios.

For in today's Japan, the lion's share of the liabilities of bankrupt companies end up in bank loan portfolios. Most companies in Japan rely on bank loans for financing; the exceptions that go directly to capital markets are limited to the best-known Japanese names, which so far have experienced few bankruptcies. Even the bonds of those companies usually found their way into the portfolios of deposit-taking institutions. But the developers, speculators, and myriad of smaller second- and third-tier nonmanufacturers that have been going bankrupt at historically unprecedented rates have left their banks holding the proverbial bag.

Banks have long been expected as part of the natural course of their business to bear problem loans, and despite all the public talk, the MOF and FSA have never been serious about forcing banks to disclose such loans. As we have noted several times, MOF control of credit allocation required that the MOF have ultimate say-so over fiscal spending, loans and investments by government institutions, and loans by nominally private sector banks. American-style disclosure to the outside investment community is incompatible with that kind of credit allocation. The banks for their part were not expected to pressure borrowers. The bureaucracy wanted industrial borrowers to invest in capital formation regardless of profitability, and borrowers did not invest in order to make profits and generate cash flow to repay loans. While the banks, to be sure, had always been allowed to reserve a certain percentage of loans as loan loss reserves that could be deducted from taxable income, bankers had regarded them purely as tax shelters; no real provision for loan losses had ever been made. The result has been to saddle the Japanese banking industry with the largest pile of nonperforming loans ever seen without any accepted means of disposing of them.

## Muddling Through and the Chimera of "Reform"

Yet while problems mount and tools that once worked are now manifestly inadequate, Japan's administrators continue to give the impression that they believe that they can somehow muddle through, that the many banking and corporate failures of the past few years are exceptions representing only a temporary period of turbulence, and that, once they have gotten through it, they will be able to resume running Japan the way the country has been run since the dawn of the Meiji era.

That may seem to contradict all the talk streaming out of Tokyo in recent years of reform, of supposed "big bangs" that would transform Japanese finance into a replica of finance in the United States and Britain, of corporate restructuring and the breaking up of cross-shareholdings, of companies managed for profit rather than size, of impartial regulation replacing quid pro quo collusion between bureaucrats and businessmen. The letter of the reforms is, indeed, superficially comparable with practice in Western countries. From the much-hyped "big bang" to the imposition of new accounting standards, from the supposedly independent FSA to the welcome mat being laid out for foreign financial institutions, much new legislation has been enacted and carried out and new institutions set up, typically amplified in the Japanese media and trumpeted by the foreign press as evidence that Japan is finally and irrevocably changing.

But such breast-beating performances of "reform" and "change" have been staged periodically in Japan since the Meiji Restoration. The policy elite is acutely sensitive to Japan's image abroad and understands that to be taken seriously, Japan needs to project the image of an advanced country that conforms to international norms. As a result, superficial "reforms" are adapted very quickly, without discussion or testing. But in most cases, the reforms are permitted to proceed only as long as they do not undermine the foundations of the system. A good example is the so-called introduction of international accounting standards. The rest of the world has been shocked over the past decade to discover that Japanese banks are loaded with uncollectible loans; the banks are, after all, banks that had been pronounced AAA by the world's top ratings agencies. To cope with the international outcry and induce foreign-owned deposits to flow back into Japanese banks, the MOF and the FSA phased in a so-called "accounting big bang" during the late 1990s. The international press tended to take this at face value; a breathless article in *Business Week*, for example, predicted that the new standards would "radically change the way companies report earnings, fund their pension obligations, and value their stock portfolios."[14] But the new requirements are only the latest in a longstanding practice of importing accounting rules from abroad. The rules provide window dressing, but they have never been allowed to promote genuine disclosure to outside investors or to determine corporate viability.

It is well known, of course, that Japanese companies had long been able to disguise losses, that the treatment of consolidation was so vague that companies could consolidate the liabilities of their healthy affiliates while shunting out of sight those of their sicker wards. The fact of the matter, however, is that consolidated reporting has been required for twenty-five years now. To be sure, the new rules call for even more comprehensive consolidation, and the global investment community and the international financial press have praised them, assuming that it was the inadequacy of the old rules that permitted Japanese companies to escape being held accountable for their performance.

But it was the arbitrary and selective way that the old rules were enforced, not their inadequacy, that enabled Japanese companies to avoid outside scrutiny. Nakachi Hiroshi, the former chairman of the Japanese Institute of Certified Public Accountants, admitted as much when he remarked, "It used to be said that banks determined the amount of net income they would report; that in turn determined the level of charge-offs."[15] Until independently chartered accountants who do not depend for their livelihood on the favor of the bureaucrat/business nexus are permitted to make disinterested judgments of corporate financial performance, and until charges of misrepresentation brought by an independent SESC (Securities Exchange Surveillance Commission, Japan's formal counterpart to the American SEC) are actually pursued by the public prosecutor and enforced by an independent judiciary, the rules are simply window dressing.

The key issue, then, is not whether new rules are being introduced, but whether they will have any teeth to them. Will the MOF and the FSA permit investors to take companies and their accountants to court for misrepresentation of financial information? Will prison sentences and fines be imposed on managers who approved such misrepresentation and on accountants and regulators who let it pass? Even to ask such questions is to answer them. It is essentially impossible for any authority outside the MOF or the FSA—most particularly an independent accounting profession—to force a company to disclose insolvency because that would complicate efforts to rescue it. The ultimate misrepresentation here is the Japanese government's pretence that Japan's financial markets are regulated by the Securities and Exchange Act. Ochiai Seiichi, a professor at the University of Tokyo, has written that disclosure of the true financial condition of Japanese banks has always been subordinated to the perceived need to preserve confidence in the stability of the financial system.[16] At a 1998 symposium, Shibahara Kuniji, another Tokyo University professor, was reported to have said, "According to Commercial Code Article 498, misrepresentation of financial statements is subject to an administrative fine of ¥1 million ($8,300) or less. Violations of this law have rarely been assessed; the law is simply not implemented."[17] Disclosure requirements of the Securities Exchange Act are rooted in the accounting practices of the Commercial Code. Since violations of the Commercial Code are never seriously enforced, as Shibahara pointed out, prosecutions under the Securities Exchange Act cannot effectively be carried out. At the same symposium where Shibahara made his observations, Takehana Yutaka, a counselor in the General Director's Secretariat of the National Police Agency, remarked that misrepresentation of financial statements is not sufficient cause for initiating a police investigation; it is considered only a violation of formal procedures, not genuine theft or fraud.[18]

It is inconceivable that the MOF would voluntarily allow a disinterested accounting profession or judiciary to resolve questions of corporate financial distress. And even if the MOF were to concede such a key element of its power, the current Japanese accounting and legal infrastructure would make it impossible. A decade or more would be needed to construct a system with sufficient judges, lawyers, accountants, and physical facilities to cope with the volume of economic disputes inevitably engendered in an economy the size of Japan's. But surrendering the power to resolve such disputes is even more unimaginable. For neither such a judiciary nor an independent, disinterested accounting profession is compatible with continued

MOF control over Japanese finance through the ministry's unwritten "guidance" and the vast network of extralegal controls that it maintains. Inevitably, any investigation into an economic dispute by a judiciary with real power and authority would get back to the MOF, for in many if not most such cases, it would have been MOF policy that led to the dispute in the first place. How would a court with real power of subpoena react when, in explaining the misrepresentation of his organization's financial condition, a Japanese CEO or bank president said, under oath and facing prison if he perjured himself, that he had been following MOF guidance?

The question of MOF accountability to an outside entity cuts to the very heart of the exercise of power in Japan. The continued existence of the present Japanese system is simply incompatible with the notion that MOF bureaucrats would have to explain in court what they were doing and why they were doing it. The MOF has to ensure that its licensees follow its instructions in the absence of formal institutions that would compel them to do so. The MOF therefore needs to be able to demonstrate that it is the MOF and not some other entity that determines who does and who does not survive and that there is no appealing or second-guessing a MOF decision.

It is, of course, absolutely true that accounting and disclosure requirements are indispensable to a system in which market forces determine the viability of corporations and banks. But they are also incompatible with a system in which such matters are decided by bureaucrats and their licensees in the main banks who are, in turn, the principal providers of liquidity to corporate borrowers. In such a system, unprofitable borrowers can be kept alive for years—even decades—beyond the point that disclosure requirements would have automatically forced their demise. And as long as it is up to the government to ensure the solvency of corporations and banks, they need not transform themselves into profit-seeking enterprises. Profits are needed to counter risk, but the socialization of risk has been the essence of the Japanese system. Accurate disclosure is therefore not only unwelcome in this system, it must be avoided if the socialization of risk and its corollary—bureaucratic control over economic outcomes— is to be maintained. When journalists and other outsiders proclaim that international accounting standards have arrived in Japan, they are—unwittingly, to be sure—proclaiming the demise of a political and economic system that has survived and flourished for well over a century. Such a proclamation is, at the very least, premature.

## *The Sogo Bankruptcy and the Allocation of Money*

The way things actually work in Japan could be seen in the playing out of the bankruptcy of the Sogo department store in July 2000. As we noted in chapter 2, according to reports in the Japanese media, Nishimura Masao, the president of IBJ, Sogo's "main bank," testified in the Diet that the bank had known Sogo was insolvent since 1994—known, that is, that the company's liabilities exceeded its assets. That meant that not only IBJ but Sogo's management, union officials, accountants, closely tied companies, other lending banks, and bureaucrats supervising both IBJ and Sogo understood for five years that the company had been accumulating huge losses. Neither Nishimura nor the press thought it odd that that fact had not been publicly disclosed. The SESC said nothing about it; since it went unchallenged, it was implicitly approved. Under Japan's Securities and Exchange Act, misrepresentation of material information may technically be a criminal offense, yet it never even occurred to anyone that law suits and jail sentences might arise from the fact that as a matter of routine, Sogo's immense losses had been kept from public knowledge for five years.

Regulators in the FSA and SESC ostensibly charged with the oversight of securities markets quite obviously regard the guiding principle of the securities market as *caveat emptor*, not *caveat vendor*. "Let the buyer beware" still prevails, but of course that is not explicitly stated. If one studies simply the wording of the securities act, one might assume that Japan, like the United States, follows the principal of *caveat vendor*, with a plethora of zealously enforced regulations in place to protect the unwary outside investor. But while such regulation may exist on paper, outside investors have, in practice, no real recourse in the event of default. That had not mattered in an era when the bureaucracy could protect all its protégés. But it matters very much today.

If the SESC were asked actually to enforce the rules by which market players ostensibly are to abide, it could not do so. It lacks the sheer physical resources, not to mention the de facto authority. Of course, it can—and does—enforce rules selectively, and that is widely understood in Japan. When a company does go through bankruptcy proceedings—something that usually happens to a company not because its liabilities exceed its assets but because it runs into difficulty and is insufficiently well connected—it almost invariably comes to light that the company had been paying dividends out of capital stock. That, of course, is prohibited by Japan's Commercial Code; to make those payments, the company's managers would have had to resort to material misrepresentation. And that is the formal charge to which managers caught up in bankruptcy scandals often must answer—not because management was lying to the investment community but because paying dividends out of capital stock reduces the amount of recoverable claims. Charges of misrepresentation are never made, much less prosecuted, before bankruptcy occurs.

Banks have not even felt the need to require accurate financial statements from borrowers. In the case of small companies, they lent money only against the collateral of land to begin with. Before the air went out of the bubble, it was in fact very profitable for banks to allow some of their borrowers to fail; the realized value of the collateral was usually significantly higher than that of the loans extended. If borrowers were large enough and were well connected in the Japanese system, they borrowed whatever they believed they needed whenever they believed they needed it. Banks simply lent to such borrowers whatever was required to keep them going.

Japan has not developed workable procedures to recover loans because banks assumed that they would never need to use them against companies in good standing. Meanwhile, smaller companies could not get credit unless they offered land-based collateral that had, until the last ten years, always risen in price. The Japanese system really had no way of coping with the failure of large, well-connected companies, which was one reason that they were supported by the bureaucracy come what may. That was why the Sogo collapse was such a sensation; by Western standards the company had been bankrupt for years, but the decision to let it finally go under showed that somehow it had lost its stature as a member in good standing of the Japanese system. Sogo found that out without being directly informed and had no legal recourse to appeal the sudden withdrawal of bureaucratic support.

IBJ and its overseers at the MOF, the FSA, and the SESC had allowed the company to accumulate losses on the order of ¥550 to ¥700 billion. Sogo's banks knew that they were lending to an insolvent entity and that there was no chance that the loans could be repaid from Sogo's negative cash flow. In a market system operating under rules requiring genuine disclosure, banks would years earlier have stopped lending and initiated foreclosure proceedings. But Sogo's lenders were far more concerned with the stance of the bureaucrat/banker nexus, which determined whether Sogo would be allowed to continue or not; as long as Sogo was considered viable, no bank would voluntarily thwart the implied directive to keep Sogo afloat. Once the protection was withdrawn, banks operated under the assumption that the MOF would somehow make them whole because they had, after all, been lending in accordance with MOF policy. In such a system, a system in which banks do not seek to have their loans paid back from the borrower's cash flow, is there any need for financial statements?

Unless banks start calling their loans, borrowers who would be bankrupt in a market economy can survive by selling assets. But in effect, banks are not allowed to call their loans. The ruling elite demonstrated in the financial crises of 1997 and 1998 that it intended to support banks as well as borrowers. Small and medium firms were given, as noted, indirect government guarantees while the Development Bank of Japan backed up large bond-issuing companies when they encountered financial difficulties. With such measures, the government made it explicit that such big borrowers and banks would not go bankrupt. Until such things change, accounting and disclosure remain window dressing.

The same could be said of all the other much-trumpeted "reforms" and "changes" that have supposedly swept over Japan in the past decade. Yet while the ruling elite very obviously intends to continue to manage the core of the economy the way it always has, events are working against them. Change probably *is* coming to Japan—wrenching changes with consequences that will extend far beyond Japan's borders, consequences that in many cases will not be pretty. But that change will not come through the superficial implementation of "reforms" by a Japanese elite that does not believe in them and has no intention of enforcing them. It will come from the force of events.

# 9

## The Anomalies of
## Contemporary Japan

In the fundamentals of its political and economic order,
Japan differs so greatly from the West that the conceptual framework through which Westerners view political
and economic reality can itself interfere with understanding
the country. The very terminology Westerners use to discuss Japan makes it difficult to bring it into proper focus. A
host of seemingly unproblematic terms—terms that cannot
be avoided in discussing political and economic arrangements in Japan—must nonetheless be used with the utmost
care. Words and phrases such as "company," "board of
directors," "political party," "bureaucracy," "cabinet," "prime
minister," "stock market," "equity," "private" and "public"
sectors, "bank," "entrepreneur," and "fiscal spending," to give
only a few examples, can communicate images and ideas to
the Western reader that risk distorting and even subverting
what actually goes on in Japan.

Things become most treacherous when attempting to
describe the Japanese system as a whole—its government
and its economy. Karel van Wolferen has argued that Japan
does not really have a government—that what looks like a

government is in fact a collection of quasi-independent fiefdoms operating without what he termed a "center of political accountability." From a distance, such an assertion can sound preposterous. Japan's electoral campaigns seem at least as noisy and vital as those in other countries; newspaper accounts of the Japanese political scene are filled with the platforms and reform plans of particular prime ministers. But as one scholar noted, "The weakness of [Japan's] elected government never ceases to shock on first encounter."[1] And whether Japan does or does not have a government, to label a country a "democracy" when neither the voters nor their representatives can remove the senior officials who actually make policy seems to mock the meaning of the word.

The same is true for the Japanese economy. The word "capitalist" is used to describe it, albeit sometimes with qualifiers—for example, "Japanese" capitalism—but if "capitalist" is to mean anything other than "not Leninist," it has to refer to an economic system in which the means of production are bought and sold by private sector entities operating under the profit motive. Yet as we have seen repeatedly, that is precisely what does not happen in Japan. Control of the most important assets in the Japanese economy is not for sale; politically important prices are set by bureaucrats, not by markets.

During the 260-year period in which Japan closed itself off from a world in the throes of the early modern era, the country underwent an economic transformation in many ways comparable to that taking place at the other end of the Eurasian continent. Great cities took shape, an emerging urban proto-bourgeoisie instituted centralized markets for commodities and money, the construction of a national infrastructure of roads and shipping lanes fostered movement of people and goods, growing literacy permitted the widespread dissemination of the written word.

But Japan missed out on many of the lessons learned during the same centuries by Western nations. Europe had to endure decades of social upheaval and economic catastrophe before the continent's elites understood that real wealth comes not from hoarding gold but from engaging in trade. People slowly came to the realization that unaccountable rulers could not ultimately be trusted with important decisions—and they then displaced those rulers. Long years of intellectual ferment were required before economic thinkers grasped that rather than allocating peasants amounts *"ikasanu yo ni; korosanu yo ni"*—not enough to give either life or death—as the shoguns had, economic policies aimed at ensuring that ordinary people had the means to spend were the key to soaring prosperity and national wealth.

Instead of participating in the struggles that seared those lessons into the Western mind, Japan's rulers worked to stymie the development of any body of thought that assumed a critical stance toward existing political reality while closing the country from virtually all contact with the outside.[2] Once that was no longer possible, once Japan's rulers could no longer isolate their country from an outside world threatening uncontrollable political, economic, ideological, and military upheavals, they engineered a forced march into rapid industrialization. As discussed in chapter 2, they had a single goal: accumulating so much production capacity and so many claims on foreign countries that the world would simply have to accommodate them on their terms.

Their relative success to date, however, obscures the almost certain ultimate failure of their aim: the continued ability to determine economic and political outcomes. Indeed, the jig appeared to be up in 1945, when desperate attempts to impose direct Japanese rule on neighboring countries disintegrated in the ruin of defeat. Japan's elite had come to believe that military conquest was the only way to secure the resources and markets necessary to sustain its hold on power. Instead, Japan found itself occupied by a far stronger conqueror whose intention was to dismantle the Japanese system and replace it with a series of institutions modeled on its own.

But the United States had only the vaguest inkling of what a monumental task it had undertaken. Americans had neither the knowledge nor the stamina to see the task through to completion, and the project was quickly abandoned once Japan's rulers grasped how easily the Americans could be deceived about Japanese reality. The surviving elements of the Japanese elite realized that if they could make themselves useful to the Americans, the Americans would for the most part leave them alone. And they were greatly helped by the fortuitous onset of the Cold War, which made a pliant, orderly, heavily industrialized Japan a great asset to the American alliance. Early dreams of genuine economic and political democratization were forgotten as a conservative political elite returned to power with active American encouragement, including covert funding from the Central Intelligence Agency. That elite would provide political protection for the policy officials who would resume the unfinished task of the war years: the nearly complete bureaucratization of the Japanese economy.

A long half-century of illusion then set in, illusion about what made for the peculiar set of circumstances that permitted Japan to achieve dazzling levels of success while running an economy that violated every accepted tenet of Western economic orthodoxy. Having escaped what seemed the near-certain destruction of their system, enjoying the indulgence and protection of American economic and political power, and with living memory of any alternative order gradually dying out, Japan's rulers appear to have forgotten the origins and purpose of the postwar alliance between the United States and Japan. Today it is too often taken as simply a given.

Meanwhile, the intellectual capacity for conceiving of a world without a protective cocoon provided by the United States has atrophied since 1952 and the formal end of the American Occupation. One might even call the last half of the twentieth century a second *sakoku*—the term used to describe the enforced isolation of Japan by the Tokugawa shoguns, but this time imposed by what John Dower calls the "almost sensual embrace" of the United States.[3] Japan has not participated in any of the great debates of the past fifty years about either global security or global economic arrangements. The Bretton Woods system was, as we noted, conceived—and understandably so—without any input from Japan. But no Japanese voices were heard in the discussion of the system's viability that began as early as the mid 1950s. No Japanese economists joined the ranks of the Jacques Rueffs and Robert Triffins ringing warning bells about the system's fatal flaws or advising their government on the proper policy response. Tokyo simply chugged forward as if the system would endure forever and then, when it collapsed, scrambled to recreate as much as possible the Bretton Wood certainties by endeavoring to suppress the value of the yen.

On security issues, Tokyo takes its cues from Washington. Allowing another country to make fundamental security decisions permits the Japanese elite to avoid the question of political control of the bureaucracy. For the military is, of course, a bureaucracy par excellence, distinguished from its counterparts that handle such activities as finance and construction by having physical coercion at its disposal as a means of enforcing policy. Today, the extralegal tacit agreements that allocate fixed shares of the national budget to each bureaucratic entity restrain the Japanese military. But remove American protection in what is still a manifestly dangerous world, and Japan would have to confront a question it has never properly answered: how to ensure institutionally that bureaucrats serve the national interest rather than the interests of their own particular bailiwicks. If the Japanese military were freed of the heavy shackles that now keep the so-called Self-Defense Forces little more than an American adjunct, only a strong national revulsion at the memory of the war years would be left to prevent a revitalized military from embarking on a course that could again lead the country and the world down into a sea of flames. The Japanese military—like any bureaucracy anywhere, most obviously including the Pentagon—would surely, unless subject to institutional restraints, act to increase its sway over policymaking and to secure its freedom to make decisions without accounting to outsiders.

The Japanese elite knows that and almost on autopilot works to preserve the current system. But it may no longer understand that it would be impossible to continue in the post-1955 fashion following the withdrawal or crumbling of American protection—whether that were to happen through the deliberate decision of American policymakers or through the force of events. Because the United States conducts for Japan several of the essential functions by which a state is commonly identified—most particularly providing for national defense—other areas of public policy can be carried out without a central governing entity that sets priorities. The quasi-independent bureaucratic fiefdoms that characterize Japanese political life can carry on under the facade of democracy. But the disappearance of American protection would force Japan to resolve the question of where the right to rule lies; as suggested by the example of the 1930s, when endless wrangling among segments of the Japanese elite permitted mid-ranking officials in the Japanese army to start a war on their own initiative, a struggle to determine the answer might not be pretty. It would be inevitable, however, for no conceivable alternative to today's global political order would allow Japan to accumulate endless production capacity and claims on foreigners while taking no steps of its own to ensure that its capacity could be defended or its claims exercised. Absent American protection or a beefed-up military of its own, Japan as a nation would find itself in the position of the great Osaka merchant houses that bankrolled the samurai and the shogunate. When the warriors grew restive, they simply reneged on their loans and expropriated the merchants' wealth. Today, Japan may be China's most important source of capital and technology, but that would count for little if a future Chinese government believed that

Japan was frustrating its national goals and Japan had no way to defend itself.

The modern world makes dealing with foreigners an unavoidable if distasteful necessity for Japan. The Japanese elite believed, however, that by building production capacity far in excess of domestic requirements, by piling up a vast hoard of claims on other countries, those dealings could be made predictable. The uncertainty and danger that foreigners posed to carefully calibrated domestic power balances could be reduced to manageable levels. But the Japanese elite has again miscalculated, as it did in the 1930s. No matter how much capacity you have accumulated, no matter how many claims you have the theoretical right to exercise, unless you control the currency of your international trade, investments, and finance, you are at the mercy of those who do control that currency. The Japanese elite has been unable to grasp the implications of a huge buildup of external assets in the form of claims on foreigners denominated in a foreign currency: that those assets make them more, not less, vulnerable to the shifts of global economic forces and comparative advantage. The great fortress of industrial capacity and dollars built up so laboriously since 1955 rests on sand.

For Japan is seeing its industrial competitiveness slip. The United States has reasserted leadership in state-of-the-art technology while other Asian nations—most particularly China—put increasing and relentless pressure on Japan in mass-produced goods. It is common in Tokyo to hear industrialists and bureaucrats blame Japan's loss of industrial preeminence on an American conspiracy, on globalism, on envious foreigners who do not appreciate the service Japan has performed in providing the world with a flow of capital.

To be sure, Japan's elite officials are not the only policymakers to be caught flat-footed by the undermining of existing hierarchies of comparative advantage by newly globalized financial markets and the rise of outlier powers such as China. Even American triumphalists have been humbled by the popping of the NASDAQ bubble and the swift implosion of such citadels of market fundamentalism as Long-Term Capital Management and Enron. The high priests of economic orthodoxy at the International Monetary Fund got their comeuppance with what is widely seen as their botching of the developing world crisis of 1997–98 that began in Asia. But having provided the world with its premiere object lesson in the last half-century of just how radically a determined nation can shift comparative advantage in its favor, the Japanese elite has been blind to the reasons why the latest shifts have worked so decisively against it.

For Japan's policy elite never allowed the floating rate system to function as it is supposed to. Had Japan accepted the logic of floating rates back in 1973, inefficient and internationally uncompetitive industries would have been phased out, with capital moving to those sectors of the economy in which Japan's comparative advantage is the most pronounced. A balanced growth economy led by domestic demand could have spurred Japan to develop its own cutting-edge technologies suited to its own culture and endowments. Instead, Japan embarked on a policy of suppressing the yen and mitigating the effects of what yen strengthening did occur. That meant running surpluses, denominating those surpluses in dollars, and re-exporting those dollars. The money went to permit the United States to rack up several decades of "deficits without tears" while enjoying surges of liquidity that financed the emergence of Silicon Valley and other avatars of American high technology. The insatiable American market—a never-never land where consumption could always exceed production—provided the demand needed to fuel the take-off of Japan's Asian rivals, which financed their own factories with Japan's dollars.

The Japanese elite is not, however, alone in its miscalculations. The United States has forgotten how much its hegemony depends on the role its currency plays as the world's money. The relative success of the American economy in the past decade has fatefully obscured something that may soon be all too obvious: that success rested to a very large extent on the ability of the United States to exploit its role as the issuer of the world's currency in order to run those vast external "deficits without tears." Ever since the 1960s, when the United States financed the Vietnam War by using its central position in the Bretton Woods system to export inflation, the United States has been seen by many as what international relations theorists call a "predatory hegemon." A hegemonic power maintains international public goods such as a universal currency and an open market into which all countries can sell their surplus goods, plays lender of last resort, and anchors global security. A hegemon can be distinguished from an imperial power, so goes the theory, because it acts with the voluntary cooperation of other powers in the system and will play system-sustaining functions, even if doing so entails some domestic political cost. But as the

United States racks up external deficits with impunity, as it escapes the disciplines to which ordinary countries are subject—disciplines that impose a limit on capital imports and the running of current account deficits—the case that the United States is simply exploiting its position for its own benefit becomes ever more compelling.

One can take things too far. Much of the developing world—particularly China—benefits from the ability and the willingness of the United States to run endless deficits. But at each crisis point in the last thirty years, when it appeared that upheavals in foreign exchange markets might finally force the United States to live within its means, it has been the Japanese elite that has acted to support the dollar and, by extension, the continuation of American hegemony. The elite has not done so because of any particular affection for Washington, but because it identifies its own survival with the continuous buildup of piles of dollars in the American banking system. That has gone on so long now that neither the American nor the Japanese elite seems to recognize any more how odd it is for a country to exchange real wealth and real purchasing power for the fiat currency of a foreign country that it would never seek to repatriate or exchange. Nor is there much recognition of what an enormous price Japan has paid in its reduced standard of living and loss of economic vitality in order to maintain the dollar's supremacy in global finance. Japan's monetary authorities continue blandly to assert that Japan's endless exports of capital are a consequence of the economic slowdown; there is no acknowledgment or perhaps even awareness that the entire policy apparatus has been rigged to allocate credit to support those exports—or that the economic slowdown might be a consequence, not a cause, of a regime devoted to earning and retaining dollar-denominated claims.

The era of illusions is now coming to an end. Economic well-being has always ultimately depended, as Keynes pointed out, on "animal spirits," on confidence in the future. In capitalist economies, that confidence derives from the perceived earning power of corporations. In Japan, it stems from the perception that the bureaucrat/businessman nexus that manages the economy knows what it is doing. But the anomalies that have piled up inside the Japanese system have simply become too great to disguise. And with those ever-more-visible anomalies and the inability of the bureaucracy to cope with them, it has become manifest that Japan's administrators no longer know what to do.

## Anomalies upon Anomalies

The Japanese economy today exhibits anomalies piled upon anomalies. First and perhaps the biggest of them: the yen is both too strong and too weak. Viewed through the prism of its current economic and banking conditions, not to mention purchasing power parity (PPP), the yen is manifestly too strong, conclusive evidence that despite the many leaks that have sprung in the protectionist dikes surrounding Japan, the country is still far from being an open economy. According to the OECD, PPP would have put the yen at ¥152 in 2000 as opposed to the average market exchange rate that year of ¥107.78. At the same time, however, when viewed from the perspective of the current account surplus, the yen is far too weak. That tells us that the floating exchange rate regime does not, at least in the Japanese case, work. Floating exchange rates should long ago have taken the yen to levels that would have forced a reduction in the Japanese surplus.

Second, at a time when Japan has run up the highest government debt as a percentage of GDP among all the OECD countries, the Japanese government offers the lowest interest rates of any of its OECD peers on the bonds issued to finance that debt. Yields typically reflect the credibility of the issuer and the scarcity value of the issuer's bonds. Japan has no realistic plan to reduce—much less retire—its government debt, and it floods its financial system with government paper even while the yields on that paper are next to nothing. Very obviously, therefore, yields on Japanese government bonds are not being set by market forces, notwithstanding talk of a Japanese bond "market" and associated calls for the authorities to deluge that so-called market with reams of additional government paper. Such talk overlooks the intermediation of virtually all savings by the Japanese banking system (together with the post office); JGBs do *not*, as we have stressed repeatedly, end up in the portfolios of final investors. The banking system exists to marshal deposits in order to support JGBs as well as land, equities, dollars, and real economic activity. The last decade may have demonstrated that vast as the deposits are, they are not sufficient to support all of those assets at the desired price levels. But they are still adequate for the time being to support JGBs at current high prices and low yields.

Third, the Bank of Japan is running a demonstrably expansionary monetary policy, but inflation is nowhere to be seen. While there are those who urge the BOJ to do even more—setting inflation targets and buying assets such as equity, problem loans, and land that typically do not appear on a central bank's balance are two oft-heard suggestions that we have examined—there is no getting around the fact that the BOJ has lowered interest rates to practically zero with little to show for it. Certainly there has been no inflation. Furthermore, the BOJ balance sheet contains only a relatively small portion of the financial assets controlled by the MOF. Equity, problem loans, and land have *all* been bought directly or indirectly by government-controlled entities in an attempt to push money into the economy. But there has been no discernible stimulative effect. That is not supposed to be possible except in the unusual circumstances that Keynesian economists label a liquidity trap. The Japanese government is using precisely the measures Keynes recommended to escape from that trap—deficit spending—but the economy continues to sit dead in the water with prices sagging on all sides.

To be sure, a number of commentators have argued that Japanese fiscal stimulus has actually been considerably less than the government's press releases would suggest.[4] And it is undoubtedly true that any effects of fiscal stimulus have been undermined by frequent reversals—most notably the consumption tax hike of 1997—and the lack of a clear government commitment to spending whatever it takes to get Japan moving again. But those policy reversals and the manifest unease at Japan's snowballing public debt do not stem from mindless worship of out-of-date economic doctrine. They stem from the fear that at some point too much borrowing will force the Japanese government to pay market-driven rates of interest and destroy the MOF's control over interest rates and the flow of credit.

Fourth, despite a decade of ostensible measures to revive it, domestic demand remains completely flat and shows every sign of continuing to stay that way and even of worsening. Corporations are being forced by both banks and their own apprehensive managers to reduce indebtedness. The government is reluctant to increase public sector debt for fear of losing control of the JGB market and the subsequent collapse of bond prices. But the household sector cannot be expected to pick up the slack. Tax incentives continue to work against household sector borrowing, and with the economy burdened by excess capacity in almost all industries, inflation cannot be created. Wages have continued to rise slowly over the past decade, but as profitability deteriorates with the economy falling back into recession, wage growth is likely to halt altogether and even to fall.

Finally, despite the widespread publicity given to the woes of the banking system, there has been only modest liquidation of deposits and no flight of capital out of Japan. There may be little real equity left inside Japanese banks; if they were Western banks, Western regulators would surely have taken over or shut down many of them long ago in order to avert a possible panic. Yet most Japanese households continue to put their savings on deposit with banks and the post office. The bleeding of cash around the edges, as it were, into the proverbial mattress or into foreign currency and mutual funds does not begin to add up to any kind of run on the system or anything that resembles genuine capital flight.

Any one of these anomalies could at some point blow up the Japanese economy—pushing it from the stagnation of the last decade into a full-fledged crash and taking much of the world down with it in the process. And if that happens, it will probably take place through the currency markets.

## *The Yen as Achilles' Heel*

Fear of a Japanese economic collapse is no longer confined, of course, to a handful of pessimistic Japan watchers and American treasury officials. Finance ministers, central bankers, investment analysts, and economic observers worldwide wring their hands over the possibility of a Japanese economic crash and the collateral damage it would wreak.

The most common scenario sees a collapse starting with a run on the yen. The scenario is superficially convincing. It is rooted in what we noted above—that according to PPP criteria and the manifest woes of the Japanese economy, the yen is already far too strong. It assumes, and probably correctly, that the holes in Japan's protectionist dikes will only continue to widen. But the scenario then goes on to postulate that as more and more sectors of the Japanese economy become subject to foreign competition, the Japanese economy will finally begin to function like a "normal" open economy with a floating exchange rate. Imports would, according to this line of thought, rise to the point that the currency would begin to weaken.

The scenario also assumes that foreigners will react to the seeming inability of Japan's leaders to extricate the country from the current policy trap by refusing to buy or hold any yen-denominated equity or debt instrument. And the scenario takes as a given that the Japanese authorities will finally conclude that they have no choice but to issue vast quantities of new debt and then monetize it, thereby bringing on inflation.[5] Inflation is simply a word to describe the reduction in value of a given unit of currency.

The scenario ignores, however, the continued ability of the Japanese authorities to protect key sectors of the economy—particularly those on which Japan's export performance depends. We noted that although bankruptcy rates are at historical highs, manufacturers have largely been spared. Small manufacturing subcontractors may be going out of business, but they are not going bankrupt at anything like the rate of their nonmanufacturing counterparts. In an economy operating under market principles, manufacturing would surely be experiencing the same trends as other sectors, but it is not, as shown in figure 2-1 of chapter 2, which illustrates bankruptcy rates in different sectors of the economy. Protection is not the only reason. Manufacturers during the bubble years had not, unlike nonmanufacturers, bought much of the land that had come on the market and thus tended to avoid the more immediate effects of the steep, post-bubble drop in land prices; further, most well-established manufacturers carry their land on their books at a value of practically zero because they have held it for upward of a century or more. Even at today's depressed prices, they can sell land in a pinch and generate substantial, albeit declining, capital gains. Nonetheless, the Japanese bureaucracy seems committed to continuing to ensure that manufacturers can sell things abroad even if the companies are not profitable.

And while imports have, it is true, brought on waves of "price destruction," as long as demand in Japan remains flat, the aggregate value of Japan's imports (excluding petroleum) will not increase meaningfully. The current account surplus—and thus upward, not downward, pressure on the Japanese currency—will continue to expand as long as Japan can finance the current account deficits of its trading partners. Since early 2001, the trade surplus has been declining, but that is mostly a function of declining demand in Japan's major trading partners, not any fundamental restructuring of the Japanese economy. And the wider current account surplus, which had also been declining, began to rise again in 2002 under the strength of investment income. Unless and until a significant reduction in manufacturing capacity occurs in Japan through a string of visible bankruptcies, production will continue to flow, resulting in a continued surplus, particularly under any weak-yen scenario.

Meanwhile, expectations of an inflationary surge run into overwhelming pressures pushing the opposite way. We noted in the previous chapter that the bureaucracy's inability to guarantee the solvency of all its protégés is the root cause of the drying up of lending. Unless lending resumes, inflation cannot be created through the banking system. Creating inflation through the bond market requires that Japan have a deep and liquid bond market. The government therefore has to spend and spend even to maintain current price levels, not to mention spark inflation. But local governments, which are responsible for part of the spending, are putting up more and more resistance to further increases because they understand that they will eventually be forced to take the politically difficult and dangerous step of raising local taxes. The national government's fiscal policies transfer income from the wage-earning majority to a relative handful of people whose propensity to spend is low, further thwarting any inflationary upsurge. Rising bankruptcy rates further depress purchasing power. And a bureaucracy that continues to be solicitous of a manufacturing sector already under tremendous pressure is not going to increase that pressure by raising utility prices—a means often used in the past to spark cost-push inflation. We expect that those anticipating a wave of inflation to cheapen the Japanese currency will be proved wrong.

To be sure, foreign portfolio managers have grown so wary of Japan and have been burned so often that a dwindling number are willing to hold yen-denominated securities. That poses a major hurdle to reviving a stock market that has been repeatedly propped up in the last decade by foreigners who—like the villagers in the folk tale who kept responding to the little boy who cried wolf—wanted to believe Tokyo's regular pronouncements that the Japanese economy has finally rounded the corner. But foreign holdings of yen instruments have little to do today with the yen/dollar rate. For the yen to fall steeply in value, Japanese yen holders themselves—households and businesses—would have to abandon the Japanese currency. Fear of tax audits, however, remains a major deterrent to capital flight. And the experience of the past three decades has taught Japanese households to anticipate not a weakening of the yen but a strengthening. Practically every Japanese family knows someone who borrowed money to buy a plot of land or invest in an equity venture during the bubble years and was then wiped out. As a consequence, households have become extremely risk averse. The last thing they will do now is send their money overseas into markets that they do not understand, piling up currency risk on top of every other kind. Instead, they will continue to keep their money in yen and on deposit in Japan. The post office might be as risky as the NASDAQ, but Japanese households do not know that and the authorities will do everything they can to keep them from finding out.

Indeed, far from worrying over it, the authorities show every sign of encouraging a weak yen. The dynamics of the yen carry trade, discussed in chapter 7, were driven at least in part by the conviction that ultimately the Japanese government supports a weak yen policy. And the spate of bad news late in 2001 suggested that yet again the government, with tacit American cooperation, was seeking to drive the yen down.

Although it cuts against conventional wisdom, we find a catastrophic surge in the yen's value a more likely scenario than any sudden and precipitous fall. As we believe we have amply demonstrated, the overriding foreign exchange policy goal of the Japanese monetary authorities has been to suppress the yen. This policy, as we saw in chapter 4, goes back as far as World War I, when Japan first faced the problem of the accumulating current account surplus driving up the Japanese currency. The MOF and its International Finance Bureau have single-mindedly supported the dollar except when specifically asked not to by the United States (for example, during the mid 1970s or at the time of the Plaza Accord). That support has tied up more and more high-powered money, exercising a deflationary effect in Japan while it simultaneously increases available liquidity in the United States.

An implicit bargain has long been in place between Japan and the United States in which Japan exports high-powered money to the United States— money that helps maintain American prosperity—in return for which Japan enjoys the protection of the U.S. military umbrella and open access to the U.S. market. The continuous suppression of the yen has in turn played an absolutely essential role in maintaining bureaucratic control of the Japanese economy. A cheap yen helps companies maximize production capacity without having to worry about profits, and a lack of concern for profits removes profit-seeking outside investors from the picture. That leaves the bureaucracy rather than capital and labor markets in control of credit and income allocation. We do not see how bureaucratic control of credit allocation could survive an economy reorganized around the profit principle, and we see the suppression of the yen as central to preventing any such reorganization.

Of course, profit seekers—including foreign investors—have recently appeared in such areas as high-tech products, consumer goods, and non-bank financial services. But two-thirds of the 1,500 companies (excluding banks) covered by Mikuni Ratings received ratings of BB or below, meaning that they do not enjoy sufficient cash flow to retire indebtedness and leave profits to be distributed to investors. Such companies have survived not because of financing from profit seekers but because they could go to banks that would lend against the collateral of land. But any sustained rise in the value of the yen will destroy the credit systems that keep so many profitless companies alive.

We believe that the day is not far off when the Japanese authorities will again be confronted with precisely that—a surge in the yen's value. The banking system is less and less able to support and fund Japan's vast pool of dollars, putting more and more pressure on the Bank of Japan to take up the slack. But the ability of the BOJ to expand its balance sheet is reaching a limit. The clearest evidence is the return of BOJ bills, discussed briefly in chapter 5, which were first authorized in August 1971 as a way of sterilizing the inflationary effects of the BOJ's heavy dollar buying in its ultimately fruitless effort to stave off a revaluation of the yen. But the BOJ's renewed use of these bills beginning in the late 1990s as a tool of monetary policy demonstrates that the BOJ has, with the collapse in general demand, been unable to create sufficient currency to support its expanding assets. It is forced to rely on the bills instead. The bills, however, have the pernicious effect of absorbing liquidity and thus putting upward pressure on interest rates—in direct opposition to the BOJ's stated goals. In a manner of speaking, the rapid expansion of the BOJ's balance sheet has pushed the monetary authorities into a corner—to support that balance sheet, they have to resort to involuntary sterilization.

A central bank should be able to put liquidity into the banking system by expanding its assets. If the policy works as expected, currency in circulation should rise, reflecting the rise in economic activity. But the BOJ's efforts to expand its assets have not resulted in corresponding increases in currency in circulation. Therefore the BOJ has to fund its assets by selling liabilities such as the bills under discussion; in credit terms, they are government bills and they are being bought by the same MOF-licensed institutions from which the BOJ is buying JGBs. The BOJ ends up essentially buying and selling what amounts to the same instruments, buying JGBs from the banks and issuing bills to fund its purchases. In the past, as we have seen, the BOJ expanded liquidity in the system by effectively ordering the banks to lend more. But in the post-bubble era, window guidance no longer works. The BOJ has been trying to satisfy Western observers by emulating the open-market operations of Western central banks, but their efforts will go nowhere unless banks can expand loan volume.

The BOJ has, in response to this dilemma and as we noted at the beginning of the book, allowed current deposits with the BOJ by the nation's banks to rise. The deposits yield the banks no interest, but the banks have no other place to put their money. JGBs, BOJ bills, and bank deposits with the BOJ go back and forth in a seemingly endless loop without putting much new money into the economy or stimulating real economic activity. The tools of monetary policy are manifestly not working. Meanwhile, the FESA's dollar holdings spiral upward, even as Japanese banks retreat from the international arena. At the end of 1998, the FESA's dollar assets totaled $223 billion; three years later they had climbed to $402 billion, a full one-tenth of Japan's GDP. The buildup in yen liabilities necessary to fund the FESA's holdings puts ever more deflationary pressure on the Japanese economy as that portion of the money supply that supports all the rest of Japan's assets is relentlessly squeezed.

Nor does fiscal policy offer much hope. Since 1990, fiscal policy has become, as we have noted, the primary instrument in supporting dollar holdings. As banks were frozen out of dollar markets and banks stopped lending, deficit spending had to create the deposits necessary to fund Japan's accumulated dollar-denominated current account surpluses. As we mentioned above, however, Japan's government debt has skyrocketed while interest rates remain absurdly low. Many policy analysts believe this situation cannot continue much longer.[6] Given the difficulties the BOJ is having in creating sufficient liabilities even to support existing assets, it is hard to see how it could fund a flood of new JGBs without simply adding to the vast pool of liquidity currently sloshing uselessly back and forth between the BOJ and the banks. Banks, for their part, already hold JGBs in large quantities, violating some of the oldest rules in the book of prudential asset/liability management to do so. They fund their JGB purchases with short-term deposits; if, for any reason, those deposits are not renewed or the rates on them rise, banks' JGB holdings would be under water. More JGB purchases would simply increase the banks' vulnerability.

Waves of new government debt therefore would at some point have to be bought by outside investors responding to price signals. If yields on JGBs were to rise to the level necessary to attract new investors, then widespread disintermediation would likely take place as depositors pulled their money out of the banks and the post office and bought JGBs. That is what happened in the United States in the early 1980s with the direct purchase by households of U.S. government securities and the introduction of money market funds whose assets consisted primarily of those securities. The U.S. banking system saw its relative size as a repository of household savings permanently diminish and its role in the American economy shrink.

A fully intermediated system helps the government control interest rates because it can essentially dictate the rates banks pay depositors. But if JGBs start paying reasonable rates of interest, depositors can be expected to leave the banks and post office in droves and use their savings to purchase government paper. That would worsen the already dire straits of the banking system as it bled deposits and saw higher interest rates depress the value of its existing bond holdings. Not only would the advent of a genuine market for household savings threaten bureaucratic control of credit allocation, such a market would make it that much more difficult to engineer inflation—the widely recommended cure-all for Japan's troubles. Free markets in bonds and money tend to be anti-inflationary, as any attempt to flood an economy with bonds immediately depresses the value of existing debt securities, thus driving up interest rates and counteracting the extra liquidity. To create inflation with impunity, monetary authorities need a banking system as a repository for most household savings. Deposits are not "marked to market" every day; their nominal values do not fluctuate in response to the vicissitudes of monetary policy—or, for that matter, to widespread bankruptcies and defaults. Japan's policy officials understand that full well, which is why they have long worked to ensure that no genuine bond market takes root in Japan. Furthermore, the higher interest rates necessary to attract outside investors to purchase Japanese government paper would surely push the yen up, assuming that the infrastructure of the JGB market (for example, withholding tax and settlement procedures) is overhauled to promote foreign participation.

And if the Japanese government reverses course and instead of issuing floods of new debt introduces fiscal austerity—whether by increasing taxes or reducing government spending—the result will be highly deflationary, as it was back in April 1997. With neither monetary nor fiscal policy supporting Japan's dollar hoard, that hoard will begin to melt. Like Japanese exporters of old "dumping" their excess production, Japanese financial institutions will have no choice but to dump their dollar holdings. The only entity left to absorb all those dollars—the buyer of last resort, as it were—would be the FESA, whose dollar holdings already, as noted above, account for some 10 percent of Japan's GDP. In order to fund a sudden leap in dollar purchases, the Japanese government would have no choice but to issue a flood of JGBs, with the consequences noted above. Banks would be caught in a Catch 22: if the FESA stops buying dollars, the yen will go through the roof, destroying many of the banks' best customers and their ability to service debt. But if the FESA's dollar purchases are funded by waves of new JGBs that drive up interest rates, the effects will be the same: a steep climb in bankruptcies and a new inundation of bad debt. Sooner or later, the yen could climb to levels never seen or even imagined—levels that will destroy whatever is left of corporate profitability, with bankruptcies and unemployment soaring. Japan's real growth rate will turn negative, capital outlays and net exports will decline sharply, and the holes in Japan's protectionist dikes will become yawning gaps as imports pour into the country. Only the strongest and most competitive Japanese companies will survive easily.[7]

## The Absence of Genuine Debate

The analysis above does not, we believe, require unusual insight or rely on information unavailable to the typical economist, journalist, or policy analyst. There may be flaws in it, but if so it is difficult to know what they are, because in Japan the issues involved are not really discussed with the depth and openness necessary to permit policy errors to be exposed and corrected. The government resorted to low interest rate policies and public construction spending to support economic activity without any real examination of either their implications or sustainability.

While few officials in the economic ministries are economists per se, many of them are familiar with current trends in economic thinking and have been sent abroad for graduate study in the field. Plenty of bona fide economists can be found in financial institutions and think tanks. They have advanced degrees from the best universities in Japan and the United States and a command of the tools of economic analysis. But neither they nor ministry officials can use these tools effectively, and if they are too persistent in contradicting what the Japanese call "common sense," they are shunted aside and treated as disruptive oddballs. Foreign economists need not fear such treatment and freely offer loud advice from the pages of the world's major financial journals. They are invited to Japan, paid large sums to give lectures, and heard with every appearance of attention. But their advice is not followed—it cannot be followed.

Part of the problem rests with the conceptual basis of contemporary economics, which postulates as a given profit seeking and a direct correlation between profit and risk. Neither assumption is valid for Japan. Of course, Japanese individuals, like people anywhere, will respond to monetary incentives. But the entire institutional structure of the Japanese economy has been designed to suppress the profit motive and to transfer risk from individual entities, whether corporation, bank, or working family. The applicability of economic analysis of Japan that fails to acknowledge those realities is often limited.

Another reason for what can seem to be the deliberate deafness of Japan's policy establishment to "obvious" remedies for Japan's economic malaise: Japan's economy not only functions differently from the economies of Western countries but also from its own publicly trumpeted principles, which inevitably affects the ability of Japan's policymakers to come to grips with the country's problems. In the Japanese system, as we have stressed, risk is socialized. Politically well-placed manufacturers adamantly demand that things be arranged so that they can expand production without having to concern themselves much with the real costs of profitless production; the bureaucracy for its part responds to such demands by creating bubbles and spending money heedlessly on useless monuments. Each ministry strives zealously to protect its own interests and those of its protégés without considering the consequences for Japan as a whole, and no policy official is charged with grasping the totality of the system or thinking through its problems. Because such thinking would by its very nature allow for the competing claims and interests of others, anyone who voices such thoughts publicly cannot remain a member in good standing of the ministry or other "public sector" entity with which he is affiliated—he is seen as betraying the interests of his own employer. And the taboos are not limited to policy officials; the pervasive socialization of risk blinds every player in the economy to understanding how it functions. The handful of politicians who have from time to time shown signs of wanting to construct an entity that can ultimately grapple with the systemic dilemmas Japan faces are pilloried in the press for their supposed arrogance.

The system has thus attenuated not only the appreciation of risk but also the understanding of cause and effect. James Callaghan, the former prime minister of Great Britain, remarked after the collapse of the Soviet Union that "one of the great difficulties that Russia is left with, following 70 years of communism, is that there is little understanding of the relationship between cause and consequence."[8] The same phenomenon in Japan had been remarked on by the prewar economic historian Nomura Kentaro, whom we encountered briefly in chapter 2. For nearly a century now the bureaucracy has blunted any perception among the citizenry of economic cause and effect while the cocoon of American protection has had a comparably pernicious effect on the cognitive abilities of the Japanese elite in the arena of power politics and international relations.

Members of Japan's policy elite will react with injury and even outrage when Japan is described as a socialist country, as a society without real property rights or as one not governed by the rule of law. Yet the moment that a concrete suggestion is made that assumes the existence of property rights and the performance of ordering functions by courts rather than bureaucrats—for example, one requiring a written record of all bureaucratic directives affecting financial transactions, a record that would permit judicial scrutiny—one is met with vague talk of "Japanese culture" and the "warm, wet" nature of Japanese human relations as opposed to the "dry, cold, mechanical" nature of such relations in the West. The mounting problems of the system are blamed on the more or less passive recipients of Japan's capital exports—the Americans, the Chinese. That may be understandable—taking responsibility for one's own problems is not easy, particularly when an entire system has fostered dependency relations (*amae* is the Japanese word) and muffled sensitivity to risk and reward—but it also is dangerous.

For the truth of the matter is that the Japanese economy is based on a social infrastructure permeated with unacknowledged military values that are antithetical to the underpinnings of democratic capitalism: equality of all persons before an impartially administered law. That infrastructure has survived largely intact since shogunal times; indeed one could argue that it was strengthened in the wake of the Meiji Restoration as Japan's new rulers, drawn almost entirely from the shogunal samurai class, set about inculcating samurai—that is, warrior—values into other social strata, such as the peasant and merchant classes, which had until that time largely been free of them.

Military values do not include the notion that ordinary people have any innate right to relax and enjoy life. Spending by ordinary people on anything but essentials still seems to disturb Japan's self-appointed guardians of public morals—witness the endless hand wringing in the Japanese media over the lax ways of the nation's youth or the consumption habits of single female office workers. Like their shogunal ancestors, Japan's elite officials often act as if they believe it best that ordinary people be "squeezed like seeds," as a traditional proverb had it. In the practical terms of macroeconomic policy, that translates into never-ending encouragement of saving and suppression of consumption—different ways, of course, of saying the same thing. What was probably the single most important strand of economic thinking to emerge in the twentieth century—Keynes's refutation of Say's law that "Supply creates its own demand," his democratic and empowering notion that demand is the ultimate engine of economic progress and the corollary that "excess" savings can bring on suboptimal economic equilibrium—falls on deaf ears in the corridors of Japanese power. The notion that changing the consumption habits of millions of Japanese consumers so that they spend more could have an immense and salutary effect on the economy undermines the entire worldview of Japan's ruling elite and their assumptions about the proper roles of ordinary people.

The official explanation for Japan's persistently high savings ratio relies on supposedly "innate" cultural traits supplemented, in recent years, by demographics and the rise of insecurity related to job restructuring. Those factors naturally have some relevance. But the government has never made clear that for decades it has deliberately pursued the maximization of savings as a matter of policy. Because that policy is either unacknowledged or dismissed with largely irrelevant talk of "inborn" cultural predilections, its merits cannot easily be discussed nor the reasoning behind it questioned.

To be sure, during World War II it was clearly understood that the suppression of consumption played a central role in the war effort; keeping domestic prices under government control gave Japan's military a priority claim on resources. In the postwar period, however, such explicit justification disappeared. Land prices soared in value as Japan entered the export-led high-growth years. High land prices played, as we have seen, a critical role in the transfer of real purchasing power from consumers to landowners. Landowners ended up reaping unearned benefits from Japan's "economic miracle" while the industrial workers who built that miracle paid the highest prices in the world for housing and food. The industrial associations into which Japanese corporations were herded during the buildup to the war survived the end of the war despite efforts by Occupation authorities to disband them, giving the bureaucracy ready-made tools with which to cartelize nearly the entire economy and to suppress price competition. Meanwhile, the antitrust laws introduced by the Occupation existed only as a formality.[9] Indeed, in 1977 the law was revised to legitimize what was in fact going on, requiring the Fair Trade Commission, theoretically responsible for "enforcing" the law, to "consult" the relevant ministry before launching any investigation.

While Japan's consumers were systematically exploited, the land-linked credit-pumping machine we have described enabled the authorities working through the banking system to ratchet land prices ever higher, creating huge windfall capital gains for land sellers. Landowners could jack up rents for living space, office buildings, and commercial properties virtually at will, resulting in the further accumulation of savings. Meanwhile, the proceeds of fiscal spending could be and were directed to those who would squirrel most of it away as deposits.

The tax system further encouraged the wealthy to save by effectively exempting interest income from the marginal taxes applied to working income. While rich people in Japan can and do lead more comfortable lives than their fellow Japanese, ostentatious displays of wealth have long been both openly and covertly discouraged—with the possible exception of a few years in the late 1980s during the height of the bubble—not least through the threat of tax audits. Instead, the rich were encouraged to save in officially approved ways. Indeed, one could argue that the principal benefit of being rich in Japan is the ability to dwell with satisfaction on a fat bank account and the concomitant sensation of economic security. Interest income, for example, was, until quite recently, wholly exempt from taxes. Even today, it is taxed at a flat and separate withholding rate of 20 percent. A variety of savings instruments come in bearer form, making them impossible to trace and allowing investors to enjoy anonymity if they wish to escape taxes. High-income and high-net-worth households therefore have every incentive to save. The result is to lower the general interest income level to the equivalent of a quasi-tax-exempt rate; that is to say, the entire financial system in Japan ends up resembling in crucial ways the U.S. market for tax-exempt securities.

In the United States, tax-exempt municipal securities are regarded as an appropriate investment only for rich people in high tax brackets, who buy them, even though the interest income is lower, in order to escape the full marginal tax rate. Meanwhile, fully taxable government bonds are purchased by pension funds and working people in lower tax brackets. But in Japan, ordinary working people who pay relatively low income taxes have effectively no choice but to put their savings into the bank or the post office, where they receive what amounts to a low, tax-exempt return on their savings. They are not in a position to benefit much from the low 20 percent tax on interest income since their income taxes are fairly low or nonexistent to begin with. In other words, they are forced to buy investments that are really appropriate only for the rich. And pension funds have no option to invest in securities that would yield the equivalent of fully taxable income streams. As far as we know, this simple analysis has never been discussed by any of the *shingikai* (councils of handpicked "experts") advising the government on tax policy.

As a final insult, as it were, mortgage interest expenses typically have not been tax deductible, with some minor exceptions for inexpensively constructed houses. The tax credit available for housing loans extends only to a house worth some ¥50 million. That equals about $400,000, which is enough to purchase a nice house in much of the United States, if not in New York City or San Francisco. In Japan, however, it will get you little more than a "rabbit hutch" (the notorious term used in a 1970s European Commission study to describe Japanese housing; given the policy objectives of Japan's elite, the term could be taken as a back-handed compliment). Further, the deduction is good only if you actually live in the house. Because most Japanese "salarymen" can expect to be transferred often during their working lives and will need to rent out the houses they own, they will be forced to forego the credit. And while corporations may never have been expected to pay back their loans, individuals enjoy no such indulgence on mortgages or any other kind of consumer borrowing. The fact of the matter is that the MOF is adamantly against the interest expense deduction for spacious dwellings because it fears that the better off will no longer act like good Japanese; they might instead spend the money on large and comfortable houses rather than buy deep discount securities or put it on deposit in a bank or the post office, where it can be allocated by MOF officials. Meanwhile, Japanese savers and saving institutions such as insurance companies and pension funds receive such miserable returns on their investments—interest rates being based on the quasi-tax-exempt structure of Japanese finance—that the entire infrastructure for financing the retirement of Japan's aging population is essentially bankrupt.

## The Control of Asset Prices

The notion that profits should determine the allocation of credit and the viability of corporations also does not sit well with the militarized values held by Japan's elite, values that leave little room for the inherently "selfish" nature of profits. With both credit and market risks socialized and controlled by the government, investment and lending decisions are not made by any criteria recognizable in a profit-driven, capitalist economy. Accounting therefore has never played an important role in the economy other than as bookkeeping. Because Japanese companies do not seek profits and profits do not determine the allocation of capital, no objective, market-driven means of establishing asset prices really exists. Asset prices therefore have to be determined by the bureaucracy, giving rise to the public quotation systems used in so many areas.

We noted in chapter 5 that the wartime economic mobilization effort gave the MOF the power to promulgate the *Kabushiki Kakaku Toseirei* (stock price ordinance), which permitted the MOF to fix stock prices and required all transactions to quote the official price. The ordinance was canceled following the war. But the philosophy of share pricing has survived, not only in the stock market but also in other markets. Because Japan wants to be seen as a capitalist country, it does not openly fix share prices any longer. But in contrast to the American SEC, the SESC does not pay any meaningful attention to the way that stock prices are formed. The media reported extensively on MOF manipulation of the market to support prices in 1992 with what journalists labeled price-keeping operations; many, including former MOF vice minister Sakakibara Eisuke, suggest that those operations went back in force in March 2001 when the market slid to a new post-1985 low in the wake of the NASDAQ crash.[10] Through their informal guidance, the MOF and the FSA can put pressure on financial institutions to purchase specified stocks, and while MOF officials probably believe that they are simply acting to correct market failures, most Westerners would regard that level of manipulation as inconsistent with a capitalist system.

We have noted several times the Official Public Land Price Quotation System, which helps ensure that all real estate transactions within a designated area are consummated within certain price limits. Both short- and long-term prime interest rates are set by the banks as spreads over rates decreed or controlled by the government. In 1947 the *Rinji Kinri Choseiho* was enacted specifically to exempt the fixing of interest rates from antitrust law, and it is still on the books. Prices and yields on JGBs have historically been controlled by the MOF's Trust Fund Bureau and MOF-licensed financial institutions; the Trust Fund Bureau has ostensibly been phased out, but all that has really disappeared is a set of intermediate accounts. The functions of the Trust Fund Bureau in allocating the assets of the postal savings system and government pension funds have supposedly devolved to the managers of the money themselves rather than being turned over to the MOF. But the amounts involved are far too large and simply cannot be deployed outside the traditional recipients: *zaito*, JGBs, and government banks. The ministries that collect the funds and the MOF continue to allocate them in a manner that ensures bureaucratic discretion. Meanwhile, a small portion of outstanding JGBs are traded in the secondary market, where their prices can easily be manipulated by the authorities working through their licensees.

Economists properly regard the level of interest rates as a key factor in helping to set asset prices and in determining the balance between savings and consumption and between investment and debt repayment in a national economy. But interest rates in Japan exist independent of what goes on in the real economy, another example of the severing of a connection between cause and effect, of a system with no brakes. That is why the Japanese government can run up the largest public sector debt in the world and pay next to no interest on it.

## Turning Capitalist?

Commentators call on Japan to "free up" its economy, to allow profits and market forces to determine profits and allocate capital. But the obstacles are enormous. As we noted in the previous chapter, simply importing state-of-the-art accounting and auditing rules from the United States does not, in the absence of an enforcement mechanism, mean very much. According to newspaper reports, before it went bankrupt, the Sogo department store was negotiating with a bank syndicate over whether certain affiliates could be consolidated in order to avoid insolvency. It was just assumed that the company and its bankers could arbitrarily report what they wished, that the SESC would take no action.

For Japan to become a capitalist economy, functioning markets have to be established and policed and transaction costs reduced; purchasers of securities, houses, and land need to have post-sale recourse to sellers for misrepresentation and fraud; and a functioning legal system must be created that can rule on litigation in a reasonable time frame. The growing chorus of commentators—both outside and, increasingly, inside the country—imploring Japan to implement these reforms are, in fact, calling for something akin to a revolution: for the replacement of bureaucratic rule by market capitalism. Unless Japan's ruling elite defies the entire record of human experience and becomes the first such elite ever to voluntarily surrender power and commit collective suicide, such a revolution will not be implemented from above.

The key question, then, is whether Japan's economic troubles will destabilize the existing order. For serious dislocations could see the birth of a coalition of other forces—new politicians mobilizing ordinary working people, frustrated entrepreneurs, creditors holding defaulted debt, bureaucratic protégés that do not get the protection they seek—coming together to replace Japan's current governing elite.

# 10

## *The End of the Japanese System?*

The accumulated ills of the Japanese economy would seem to promise either change or continued decline. Excess capacity across so many industrial sectors drives down prices, reducing the profitability of the entire economy. Surging bankruptcies among nonmanufacturers will hurt manufacturers in the capital goods sector because nonmanufacturers account for almost 70 percent of total private capital spending. Japan's decades-long policy of maximizing production without regard for profit or return may run aground and the economy may founder under the dead weight of too much capacity that cannot generate sufficient revenues even to cover wages and other operating costs.

An economy managed solely to increase production is not, of course, an altogether unknown phenomenon in the West; that is the kind of economy run by countries at war. Indeed, it has become a commonplace observation that Japan has had what amounts to a war economy for the past sixty years.[1] Demobilization of the Japanese economy, however, will not—cannot—occur as an orderly process.

Increasing production without profitability required both credit and market risks to be socialized; Japan's fully intermediated, centrally directed financial system has served that purpose. But demobilization implies privatization. It implies a return to the pre-war status quo, in which companies and entrepreneurs sought profits and markets by employing strategies they devised for themselves; it implies the existence of private sources of financing that decide whether or not to support the business plans of companies by independently determining risk and return.

Japan, however, has no antebellum period to which it can return. The country has been something of a garrison state since at least 1600, when the Tokugawa *bakufu* (literally, military government) was installed, and in the late nineteenth century the Meiji leaders militarized broad sectors of society that had managed to escape under the old regime. And while soldiers were demobilized in 1945, the economy was not. The far-reaching cartelization and bureaucratization that the economy underwent during the war years was never reversed—if anything, it intensified straight through the Occupation and into the decades of the "economic miracle."

The major corporations and banks that dominate the uppermost levels of the Japanese economy may be private sector institutions in name, but like military contractors in a war economy, they are to a large extent bureaucratic entities that depend on bureaucratic support. Bureaucrats determine whether or not such entities survive, and they do so by socializing credit risk. Japan has been able to survive and flourish in a wider world governed by very different principles because of the factors we noted in the previous chapter: American protection and an external market that cushioned and mitigated the imbalances spun off by the Japanese industrial machine's drive to expand. As the imbalances become too large to be absorbed by other countries, even the United States, those days are coming to an end. The United States has permitted Japan to flood its economy with exports provided that Japan is willing to accept dollars as payment and reinvest those dollars back in the United States. Once Japan can no longer do that, American hospitality to Japanese imports will wane.

But the Japanese ruling elite does not have the power to overhaul the fundamentals of the Japanese economic system, short of committing collective suicide. The privatization of Japanese finance and the end of the socialization of credit risk would, to be sure, spell the end of Japan's war economy. It would also spell the end of the power and privilege of the ruling elite—and it is unrealistic to expect that the elite will, in short, "privatize" themselves out of existence.

The demobilization of the Japanese economy and the resolution of the contradictions that bedevil it and prevent its recovery will be more difficult, drawn out, and arduous than many commentators realize. When the dimensions of the policy trap first became clear ten years ago, no one—not even the worst pessimist—expected that well into the new millennium Japan would still be mired in the same old rut of bad debt, falling prices, and stagnant demand. But as we have tried to demonstrate in this book, Japan stumbled into the trap long before the collapse of the late 1980s bubble— indeed, the jaws first closed with the end of the Bretton Woods system a full thirty years ago. And while elite administrators have been thrashing about trying to escape the trap ever since, they have succeeded only in tightening its grip. They cannot escape, but neither will they expire easily.

## Survival Mechanisms of the Japanese System

The key to the system's survival lies in the diffusion and allocation of sovereign power to each of the ministries rather than to an elected prime minister who could be held accountable for actual policy decisions. Because the true power holders cannot easily be identified, there is no effective way of removing them. Because their decisions cannot be scrutinized, there is no room for reversal.

Ordinary Japanese voters understandably tend to think of themselves as subjects rather than citizens because they have held little in the way of real political power. Never having experienced it, they cannot easily conceive of a world in which their rulers have to account for decisions, a world in which voters can choose actual instead of de jure rulers. As a result, most tend to react with ambivalence toward the lonely voices raised from time to time against particularly arbitrary exercises of power—toward those who protest, for example, environmental devastation or corporate malpractice. The protesters may evoke sympathy, but they are just as often thought of as useless troublemakers who lack sufficient maturity to accept the inevitable. Japanese are brought up to think that way from early childhood, assisted by an educational system and media that consistently portray and treat nonconformists as unattractive deviants.

Sometimes, however, even the most prominent of figures—CEOs, television personalities, politicians, and, increasingly these days, elite bureaucrats—can find themselves on the receiving end of flagrant and unfair abuses of power, forced to "take responsibility" for failed policies that they did not determine or, often, even know about; for following accepted practice that is suddenly deemed "scandalous." In the Japanese system, the person nominally in charge at the outbreak of a scandal is expected to assume ritual responsibility. That involves bowing deeply, looking contrite, and making heartfelt public apologies. Provided that the minister, executive, or senior bureaucrat in question performs his part with a suitable show of sincerity, his "apology" is accepted and the scandal ends there. Investigations into the underlying institutional arrangements that gave birth to the scandal typically do not occur, nor do criminal indictments usually ensue. The individual in question ordinarily reemerges after the hullabaloo has died down; the "black mist" of scandal, to use a common Japanese term, has touched at one point or another nearly every important politician in the country, yet only rarely do scandals permanently derail individual careers.

Meanwhile, the Diet, constitutionally established to enact laws, does not function in the manner it theoretically is supposed to; it has instead given the bureaucracy carte blanche to formulate policy and laws to protect the bureaucracy from democratic scrutiny. Tanaka Kakuei, the great genius of modern Japanese politics, was known for his disdain for policy debates and his insistence that legislating amounted to the skillful negotiating of the political payoffs necessary to assemble majorities.[2] The newspapers and the Sunday morning talk shows are filled with ruminations on ostensible policy choices while leading politicians speak of the need to write off bad loans or restructure economic institutions. But nothing actually happens. In the words of an anonymous MOF bureaucrat, "Real decision making to change the course or direction of an established policy must be discussed among a selected few without any publicity or disclosure."[3]

Ordinary people are made to believe that they must follow a plethora of laws, but the government itself enforces laws only selectively. An article in the *Asahi Shimbun* detailing the miserable experiences of hundreds of victims of deceptive sales practices by financial institutions openly acknowledged that "the court system is biased against ordinary citizens."[4] These people had been assured that their investments were safe, but with the collapse of the bubble they discovered that they had lost their savings, and their houses were seized as collateral. After years of attempts, only 5 percent of the plaintiffs obtained any redress; the article describes judges as "acting like mere agents for banks and life insurance companies."

Ordinary Japanese have effectively no legal redress against powerful entities. Japan appears to be a modern country with a functioning legal system, and it can and does enact laws in response to foreign criticism of such things as trade barriers, collusion, and corporate financial misrepresentation. Study groups are sent to Europe and the United States to find out what is happening there to provide models for new legislation. But putting new laws on the books has little impact on what actually happens. The laws are treated as *kakashi*, or scarecrows—there to give the illusion of the rule of law to outsiders.

A great deal of attention has been paid both in Japan and abroad to the restructuring of parts of the Japanese bureaucracy. But the fundamental character of a functioning system such as Japan's, with its deep roots in the country's history and the vast network of dependents it has fostered, cannot be altered simply by rewriting laws or regrouping certain administrative organizations. Those who call for wholesale and revolutionary changes in the system as if it were a simple matter of rethinking Japan's economic policies by a "new generation" of political and business leaders display an uncertain grasp of the lessons of history. For the same system survived utter defeat in war and a seven-year occupation by a foreign power determined to dismantle that system. Those who run it, whose status and livelihood are intertwined with its perpetuation, are not going to abandon it willingly to the whims of an electorate they distrust and the vicissitudes of a market they do not understand.

Japan's decisionmakers have long regarded profits as secondary to the maximization of production and efficiency as simply the speed of production. They do not see the value of prices and profits as signals regulating economic activity. Trade associations that every company in a given industry has little choice but to join act like a single company in setting the conditions under which business is done. Their purpose is to reduce, not foster, competition. The term "excessive competition" is often used by Japanese analysts when discussing their own economy; what that actually means is that excessive capital spending risks lowering prices unless cartels can be made to function and policed. Competition aimed at weeding out weaker players is openly discouraged. The waves of mergers that have taken place recently in such segments of the economy as the banking, paper and pulp, and non–life insurance industries did not take place as a result of intensified competition. They were fostered to head it off.

Michael Porter and his colleagues have made the case that the Japanese economy would be strengthened by competition. No doubt it would. "[The Japanese] government should abandon its prevalent anti-competitive policies", they write.[5] But to the Japanese elite, competition carries with it the deadly whiff of disorder and loss of control. Asking Japan's governing elite to embrace competition is like asking the Pentagon to embrace radical pacifism.

Real decisionmaking in Japan appears to take place among a handful of powerful current and former officials associated with each of the major ministries. To a very large extent, these officials are almost unknown to the general public. Their decisions are disseminated informally through the various hierarchies of the system through extensive webs of personal ties usually stemming from a mixture of family connections and common experience in elite schools. Sometimes directives are explicit, sometimes implied; but in either case they are not written down and are issued without explanation. Lower-ranking officials and managers who do not follow both explicit and implicit orders can be almost sure that their careers will suffer. But if one makes ones best efforts to do what one is told, one will usually be compensated even if failure is the result.

When officialdom cannot bail out everyone who has done what he is supposed to do—and today it cannot, because the economy has stopped growing—the determination of who gets saved and who does not is not subject to external review. As with the failures of the Hokkaido Takushoku Bank and the Sogo department store, the determination is made according to seemingly arbitrary criteria rooted in hierarchical principles. The ability to determine who does and who does not survive without accounting to courts, accountants, investors, or politicians enables elite officials to reduce the costs of bailing out their dependents to an affordable level. Priority goes to political supporters of the Liberal Democratic Party—manufacturers and their banks on the one hand and the agriculture/construction nexus that provides voting power on the other. Those who find themselves abandoned, even though they have done what they are supposed to, have no way of forcing any kind of public explanation. The bankers at Takugin, brokers at

Yamaichi Securities, and managers at the Sogo department store who had understood that they were protected have no recourse, no way of demanding that the elite fulfill its side of the implied social contract.

The bureaucracy's power to determine on its own who survives and who does not has two important implications. First, the bureaucracy can conserve resources. The very arbitrariness of the bureaucracy's decisions increases its control of subordinates and dependents, who are fearful that even the appearance of defiance will result in the severing of the credit lifeline. Second, the bureaucracy can nonetheless claim that bankruptcies are now allowed in Japan, that the "creative destruction" held by economist Joseph Schumpeter to be the touchstone of progress in a capitalist economy is working. But as we have seen, bankruptcies in Japan take place at the whim of the bureaucracy, not as the direct result of insolvency.

The near monopoly of resources by the elite gives the Japanese system a resilience and strength that, amid all the attention given to Japan's economic woes, is too little appreciated. Because no explanations are given, there is no way to measure how policies are decided and implemented. Nobody is identified with particular policies. When the government appears to reach a policy impasse, prime ministers or other cabinet ministers are available to "take responsibility" without an accounting because no one really blames them, ensuring that the bureaucracy is not identified with failure. That is why Japan has had eleven prime ministers since 1989; so many policy initiatives have failed that they have all had ritualistically to resign.[6] Few of the men had much inkling of the policies being carried out in their name, but they fulfilled their role in the Japanese system, leaving office to assume "responsibility" for failure.

## *The Deception of "Politics"*

Japan has all the trappings of democracy, with elections, competing candidates, and opposition parties. But many protective walls insulate actual governance from the will of the voters. Newspapers rarely discuss policy in any detail; political coverage concerns itself instead largely with the ups and downs of factional struggles. Politicians simply attach labels to various platforms, and it is difficult for voters to determine any real differences among candidates. During campaign season, candidates and their supporters are allowed to cruise the streets in sound trucks, shouting their names repeatedly, but they are not given much chance to discuss details of policy. Most Japanese politicians perceive their primary responsibility to be prying spending out of the bureaucracy for favored constituents. Many Japanese voters thus regard politics as a joke; they do not bother to vote, or they vote as they are asked to by their employers and local patrons.[7]

Even if urban voters should show some signs of wanting to use the political system to force change—something that, despite everything, has in fact occurred—the gerrymandered system blocks it. Voters in rural areas, whose livelihoods are sustained almost entirely by government subsidy, cast ballots, as we have noted, that carry from 2.5 to 5 times the weight of those cast in Japan's wealth-producing cities. And most of the so-called opposition works covertly to perpetuate the existing system—as was made abundantly clear back in 1993, when it appeared for a few tantalizing months that an opposition government might actually take charge and run things. The LDP had been turned out of "power" for the first time since 1955, replaced by a coalition of opposition parties under the nominal leadership of the uncharacteristically stylish and telegenic prime minister Hosokawa Morihiro. But just as the mainstream press doomed Hosokawa with the usual Japanese tactic of scandal-manufacture, the Socialist Party—for decades Japan's leading "opposition" party, long known for striking a public pose of unyielding enmity to the LDP—revealed its true colors by torpedoing the coalition and joining hands with its ostensible "opponents" to restore the political arrangements that had prevailed since 1955.

The fact of the matter, notwithstanding a handful of courageous politicians who now and again make a genuine effort to impose some kind of political control over the bureaucracy, is that Japan has no real opposition party. The network of think tanks, ex-officials, policy experts, commentators, university professors, campaign consultants, lawyers, bankers, and managers that constitute the infrastructure of a Democratic or Republican Party out of power does not exist in Japan. Nothing comparable to the first elections of Margaret Thatcher or Tony Blair could conceivably take place there. Those individuals assumed office at the head of cadres of policy experts ready to take the reins of government and lead Britain in a new direction. But any conceivable opposition government coming to "power" in Japan would be as dependent on the existing bureaucracy as the current LDP—probably more so. Japanese voters do not have the option of throwing out the government in power.

## The Appearance of Change

Despite its apparent unassailability, Japan's ruling elite is nonetheless acutely aware that over the past decade it has made a hash of things. It cannot do what is necessary to set Japan right, but it has responded to the barrage of criticism—both abroad and increasingly at home—by striking a visible posture of great concern and implementing many superficial reforms. A few highly visible bankruptcies that in earlier decades would have been unthinkable have been allowed to proceed, creating the impression that market forces are finally being given free rein. Such gestures may buy a bit of time for the system by convincing outsiders that real change has arrived while relieving some of the pressure building up on the economy. But they do not amount to genuine reform or to the displacement of bureaucratic by market norms in determining economic outcomes. Elite officials may have lost the ability to run an advanced industrial economy, but they continue to be masters of creating the facade of change. Perhaps no regime in world history has been as accomplished in the use of diversionary tactics to deflect pressure for a fundamental realignment of power.

Such tactics date at least as far back as the late nineteenth century, when the Meiji oligarchs needed to create a facade of legally accountable government that was sufficiently convincing to persuade the Western powers to lift what the Japanese called the Unequal Treaties. The treaties, which subjected Japan to extraterritoriality and stripped it of control of its own tariff regime, understandably stuck in the craw of the leadership. But the oligarchs had not the slightest intention of constructing a government genuinely subject to the rule of law; instead they built a very good facsimile thereof, writing the so-called Meiji Constitution, founding the Diet, sponsoring political parties, and so forth. The oligarchs used the new democratic institutions for their own ends, never allowing those institutions to determine outcomes.

Such tactics, seen again during the Occupation, are employed just as zealously and deftly today as they were in the early 1890s or the late 1940s. A growing chorus of outrage at the overweening power of the bureaucracy is met by the reshuffling, merging, and renaming of certain ministries. The MOF finds itself "stripped" of its supervisory powers over banks; such powers are now lodged with the FSA, an agency staffed almost entirely by bureaucrats—most of them MOF graduates. The Ministry of Education solicits opinion on how to ensure that Japanese children become more creative and independent, all the while tightening curriculum requirements and issuing more rules. Japan takes part in various global "green" initiatives while the MLIT (the former Ministry of Construction) fights tooth and nail against the cancellation of a single dam project and the MAFF, with a huge landfill boondoggle, destroys the country's primary source of *nori*, a type of seaweed that plays an indispensable part in Japanese cuisine. The obvious institutional weakness of the office of the prime minister is "corrected" by having that office "determine" the agenda of cabinet meetings. (Previously, the agenda had been decided in *jimujikankaiji*, meetings of administrative vice ministers from each of the ministries that are theoretically the highest summit meetings of the bureaucracy. But in fact even those meetings are just for show; each ministry determines its own real agenda.) Then shadowy power brokers whom no one can identify install in the job the barely known Mori Yoshiro, who provokes media ire by his obvious impatience with the expectation that he pretend to be a prime minister with any command of or even input into policy decisions.

Beyond the smokescreen of "reform" and "change," one finds actual policymaking going on as it always has. The ruling elite keeps trying the same old initiatives in the hope that somehow they will work like they used to. We noted in the previous chapter that bankruptcy rates in the manufacturing sector have not risen, evidence that bankruptcies are not being determined by market forces. The elite continues to believe that manufacturing capacity is the key to Japan's control over its own destiny, and it continues to protect manufacturers from the pressure for profits or return. Each March, as the fiscal year end approaches and appropriations have to be spent, the countryside becomes a hive of activity as perfectly good roads are torn up for repaving, tunnels are blasted through mountains, gurgling brooks are encased in vast concrete trenches, and more coastline is ruined with seawalls.

And the authorities are still trying to produce bubbles. On February 12, 1999, the BOJ lowered the overnight call rate to almost zero by buying government bonds aggressively. The extra money released into the economy went straight into the stock market, taking the market, measured by the Nikkei average, from 13,000 in late 1998 to just over 20,000 by early 2000. Brokers' loans for margin transactions increased fourfold, clear evidence that money was moving into the market. The easy money policy coincided with the U.S. NASDAQ bubble and pushed to astronomical levels the prices of IT-related shares of companies such as Hikari Tsushin and Softbank. Coinciding as it did with the widely trumpeted government policy of turning Japan into an "information society" and overtaking the United States in IT-related industries within five years, the surge in IT-related asset prices provided clear evidence that the elite had latched onto the hope that an IT boom could lead Japan out of its troubles.

But it was the same old policy recipe: BOJ credit pumping, MITI "visions" to steer the credit, and surges in asset prices to inflate the economy. It didn't work. By early 2001 the micro-bubble had burst; the market had given up all its gains and was back where it was in the fall of 1998, dead in the water again. Another prime minister was preparing to walk the plank, and the BOJ began yet one more time to try to pump the liquidity machine with zero interest rates.

## The Continuation of American Protection

Such failed initiatives would seem almost amusing if the results were not deadly serious, chewing up the ravaged Japanese countryside and saddling Japan's public with more and more debt. But if the Japanese elite is not going to replace them with the kind of overhaul the economy truly needs, neither is it realistic to expect the United States, through the dogged continuance of *gaiatsu*—foreign pressure—to bring it about. True, if the American economy were becalmed in a long, deep recession, if the dollar were to plummet in value and the U.S. current account deficit to shrink, the impact on Japan could be great enough to crack the Japanese system. But that would not happen through a conscious choice of the American policy elite. In the end, any American president or treasury secretary who wants to keep his job will come around to supporting the continuation of Japan's economic policies.

Endless American talk of "reform" notwithstanding, the fact of the matter is that the Japanese system has produced incalculable benefits for the U.S. economy. There was a time when it appeared that Japan threatened American technological supremacy, but those days are past. Instead, Japan has taken over process industries, from machine tools to automobile components, driving costs down and quality up, while leaving the United States with the high-value-added, cutting-edge sectors. Japan supplies the "new American economy" with components and the "old economy" with manufactures at lower prices than American manufacturers can offer, freeing up capital and resources for the IT and service sectors, where the U.S. comparative advantage is so pronounced. Even more important, Japan's willingness and ability to hold vast quantities of dollars in the American banking system has enabled the United States to live in a never-never land of endless "deficits without tears," a strong currency, and vanishing capacity restraints.

To be sure, changes of power in Washington sometimes bring in policymakers who do not grasp the underlying dynamics of the economic relationship between the United States and Japan: treasury secretaries who "talk down the dollar," presidents who make a market-rattling fuss over the trade deficit with Japan. But usually some scary bond market tremors and a roller-coaster ride for the dollar are enough to wake them up. When they get a glimpse of just what it might mean if the Japanese economy really did go through the wringer on its way to "reform" or what might happen if Japanese financial institutions were forced to liquidate all those dollars they hold, they find their way back to the position every U.S. administration since Nixon's has ultimately ended up assuming: lip-service calls for "reform" in Tokyo and concrete help in maintaining the existing order.

## A Moment of Truth?

But despite the Japanese system's strength and resilience, despite de facto American support, despite the political passivity of Japan's populace and the lack of any immediately available alternative to the existing order, the system's days may be numbered. To begin with, we do not believe that Japan's ruling elite really understands its current predicament. That may be a matter of political necessity. George Orwell identified the ability to spot and avoid politically disturbing trains of thought before they gain momentum as essential to members in a ruling elite that perpetuates itself through non-democratic means. And real analysis of Japan's swollen current account surpluses—analysis that treated them as the problem they are—would surely be politically dangerous. Such analysis might lead to the conclusion that Japan needs to allow greater room for market forces, forces that would destroy existing power alignments. But the trained inability to think through the problem of Japan's surpluses makes it harder and harder for the elite to cope with the effects. There is little recognition that Japan's structural and accumulating current account surpluses are the root cause of both past bubbles and the seemingly eternal stagnation that has gripped the economy since 1990. Instead, the elite gives every appearance of believing its own propaganda: that exports of financial capital stemming from the current account surplus are a natural byproduct of Japan's demographic development.

Back in the early 1970s, just before the "Nixon shock," the possible side effects and collateral damage of what was then an emerging current account surplus were still discussed openly by Japanese scholars. But since that time, no material discussions of the issue, to the best of our knowledge, have taken place in policy circles. Yoshino Toshihiko, the former director of the BOJ whom we met in chapter 4, wrote in his book *The Yen and the Dollar* of his anger on coming across statements from his former colleagues that they had had misgivings about the BOJ's implacable opposition to yen appreciation. Yoshino states that the entire organization had been united in its conviction that come what may, the yen had to be suppressed, and that no objection had been raised at the time.[8] There are stories of economists told by their employers not to discuss yen appreciation, on orders from the MOF; the well-known journalist Tachibana Takashi specifically complained in 1987 about MOF "guidance" to foreign exchange dealers not to discuss projections with the media.[9] As a result, the current account surplus is now treated as the macroeconomic equivalent of oxygen: necessary for easy money, higher production, and higher growth. Economic analysis is used after the fact to justify the current situation, not as a means of evaluating policy options.

The inability to analyze the sources of its difficulties makes things harder for the elite, which is now confronting the potential for economic dislocations on a scale not witnessed since the late 1940s. We discussed in the previous chapter why we expect that at some point in the near future the yen will surge beyond its already strong levels—strong, that is, from the standpoint of the cost structure of Japanese industry. Its strength already has destroyed the profitability of most companies except the larger export manufacturers. With a further ratcheting up of the yen, they too would be unable to escape; even more losses, bankruptcies, and unemployment would be in the offing. That would finally bring on a sharp reduction in both the current account surplus and in the concomitant export of funds needed to finance the current account deficits of trading partners. The U.S. current account deficit would fall as a result, not because of any increase in exports, but because the United States would experience tighter money and declining asset prices. That would make Americans less able to afford imports.

Japan's real GDP then might shrink for several years as capital outlays and net exports declined substantially, finally forcing revolutionary change in Japanese corporate finance. As we have repeatedly emphasized, banks historically have paid no attention to what Westerners would consider credit analysis. Bankers have not demanded accurate financial statements because they have never had to assess the capacity to repay loans; loans were essentially "evergreen." Corporate borrowers were expected to increase production capacity per se, without considering profitability. That worked well enough when overall economic growth could be taken for granted. As long as sales increased, debt could be serviced. But the recent stagnation already is changing the picture; even companies enjoying bureaucratic support are finding themselves unable to reverse declining profits.

If the Japanese economy truly plunges into a protracted, real recession with the GDP shrinking for several consecutive years and prices continuing to fall—a prospect that we believe is quite possible—the situation will worsen dramatically. No matter how much prodding they receive, banks cannot lend to borrowers suffering from negative cash flow. Banks will have to confront the reality that such borrowers are reducing the very assets against which loans have always been made. They cannot be considered going concerns, and bankers will understand that lending to them is simply pouring money down the drain. With the government no longer able to guarantee the viability of even the largest banks, banks will have no alternative but to maximize profits and minimize losses. When the government cannot control risk, both borrowers and lenders will be forced to seek profits as a hedge against risk.

That could be the moment of truth for the Japanese financial system. Because once banks become serious about being repaid, borrowers will be unable to expand capacity unless they can demonstrate the ability to turn a profit. Both the corporations that make capital investments and the bankers that finance them will be forced to become more discriminating about capital expenditures, treating capital not as manna from the sky provided by an omnipotent bureaucracy but as what it actually is: the precious product of the toil and sweat of the Japanese people. As capital is treated with the respect it deserves, capital expenditures will become more conservative, and capital outlays will decelerate. Three decades of unprofitable and excessive capital investments could finally begin to unwind.

Japan's already ruined banking system will not be able to provide the long-term money necessary for future capital outlays. Banks themselves are having to reduce assets in light of the collapse of their stock prices. The entire Japanese financial system is finally learning at great cost one of the oldest lessons of finance: that the payback period for an investment should match the maturity of the instrument that finances it. Inventory that turns over quickly can be financed out of here-today, gone-tomorrow funds—current deposits, commercial paper. But a factory that takes years to construct and a decade to earn back the money spent on it needs to be financed by stable, long-term capital. Japan's entire glittering manufacturing infrastructure has been financed with what amounts to mobile current deposits and cash. That is the heart of Japan's financial dilemma, and escaping it will require the mobilization of securities markets to fund the investments of the future. But such markets price securities by fully discounting credit risk. In order to do that, they need transparent corporate financial reporting, disinterested ratings agencies, impartial enforcement of disclosure requirements, and independent accounting and legal professionals of sufficient numbers and expertise.

Today, banks are not only lenders but the primary investors in their customers' debt and equity securities. If Japan's banks expect to return to health, they will need to match their lending to the maturity of their own funding bases. A bank using its own balance sheet to make loans and whose funds are primarily demand and short-term deposits ought to restrict its business to the financing of working capital requirements. Long-term debt and equity securities are far too risky. If and when Japanese banks learn to control risk, bank credit will be instrumental in normalizing prices. To date, bank loans have been extended regardless of profitability, and in the process they provided extra purchasing power. That was needed, as we believe we have demonstrated, to fund the external assets acquired in order to suppress the value of the yen. With banks acting like genuine banks and managing risk properly, that no longer will be possible and the yen will appreciate as a result. The strong yen will encourage imports and discourage exports, finally reducing production capacity in Japan to a level low enough to ensure a reasonable rate of return. Corporate profits would eventually turn around and start to rise. In such a world, asset prices would be determined by the profits they generate; asset prices would thus recover as profitability recovers.

But for that to happen—for genuine securities markets to take root and function as the primary sources of long-term financing; for banks to engage in proper credit oversight and institute adequate risk controls; for investment decisions to be determined by analysis of risk/return tradeoffs—the Japanese bureaucracy will have to be stripped both of its power to determine corporate viability and its control of credit. It will never surrender those powers voluntarily because that would end its ability to purchase political protection. But a serious worsening of Japan's economic predicament threatens to bring it about anyway. As it becomes clearer that the bureaucracy can support fewer and fewer of its dependents, the stronger of those dependents may acquire the courage to look out for themselves. And the ranks of those dependents will not be just banks that are afraid to make loans and companies that would have no prayer of survival in a market economy. They also will include Japan's working people, particularly the participants in the so-called lifetime employment system. And any hope for a political awakening that could lead to the replacement of bureaucratic authoritarianism with the institutions of an accountable government probably lies with them.

## The Coming of a Labor Market?

Most of the analysis in this book has been devoted to Japan's financial trap. But the suppression of the labor market went hand in hand with the suppression of market forces in the financial arena. The Japanese bureaucracy has long worked to control the allocation and price of labor, just as it has the allocation and price of credit—and for the same reasons. The free movement of people in and out of jobs and organizations as they seek to better their lives is no more compatible with a bureaucratized economy than is the free movement of money seeking the highest return.

The bureaucratization of Japan's labor markets can, like that of its financial system, be traced back to the war years, when the Total Mobilization Act of 1940 banned the free movement of labor and ended freedom in hiring and job-seeking. The shift to war production reduced the production of consumer goods while labor markets tightened as most able young men went into the military. To head off inflationary pressure on wages and prices, the bureaucracy fostered the formation of company unions to control wages and reduce purchasing power. First-year salaries were fixed according to the employee's level of education, wage hikes were limited to annual across-the-board increases, and promotions and higher salaries were awarded on the basis of seniority only. With such measures the bureaucracy ensured that companies in essential war-related industries had first access to labor at prices they could afford.

Just as with bureaucratic control of money, those labor practices continued with minor modifications into the postwar period. To be sure, bureaucratic control of labor endured a stronger challenge. While no entity ever really tried to wrest control of money from the MOF, Japan did go through a fifteen-year period of labor militancy. Early Occupation reforms and a revitalized Communist Party led to a nascent trade union movement, complete with a series of bitter and prolonged strikes that culminated in the strike at the Mitsui Miike coal mines in 1960. That represented the last hurrah for a genuine labor movement or any real labor market in Japan. Management locked out the workers, and the presidents of the other major coal mines agreed to help Mitsui Miike financially and not to poach the company's market share. A bank consortium stood ready to lend whatever was needed. The strike was broken and with it any alternative to central bureaucratic control of labor.

The key element in the system was the establishment of a lifetime employment norm for core male employees. In the same way that profits became irrelevant for large companies and banks that knew that they were protected, Japan's workers and managers accepted controlled wages and the absolute right of employers to determine job content because their livelihoods were guaranteed. The lifetime employment protocol did not cover the entire economy; it extended only to male heads of household in well-connected companies. But it was a norm to which every company aspired. A company that cannot guarantee the livelihood of its core male employees is, by definition, beyond the pale of protection in Japan. Just as the inability of a company or ministry to bail out affiliates is a sure sign of trouble, so is the inability to keep core male employees employed.

Lifetime employment is another reason why the restructuring urged on Japanese companies by the outside world is so resisted. Profits and returns on investment simply cannot increase unless unneeded workers are laid off.

But despite all the lip service given to reform, despite all the talk in management circles and the financial press of the need for profits, nothing much has really happened where it matters: reducing employment levels. Presumably managers have been sitting tight waiting for a return to growth that would enable them to meet their wage costs without significant layoffs. But growth has remained elusive.

For Japanese companies cannot easily terminate employment contracts. The letter of the law requires only thirty days' notice or a lump-sum payment equal to thirty days of wages, but a string of court cases has effectively required companies to respect the lifetime employment protocol and the seniority system. Dismissal is one of the few instances in which individuals can actually expect to use the legal system to seek redress against large entities. The reason is obvious. The socialization of risk has to involve ensuring minimal standards of living for Japan's working population. Rather than accomplish that through a publicly funded welfare system, the Japanese system places the burden on corporations—another example of the use of an ostensibly private sector institution to accomplish a public sector goal, thereby sensitizing the nominally private entity to bureaucratic rather than market norms. And of course lifetime employment also serves to suppress the formation of a labor market and to enhance social control because this "welfare" benefit is in practice available only to male employees who stay with a well-connected company for their entire working lives.

The courts have accordingly established a series of precedents that make it exceedingly difficult to fire core employees or *seisha-in*, as they are known in Japanese (women and temporary workers do not typically qualify as *seisha-in*). Before a company can fire such a man, it must either be on the verge of bankruptcy or have exhausted all other measures, including transfers and requests for "voluntary" retirement. And comprehensive rationales are required; a simple explanation that the employee in question is not suited for a job or has delivered subpar performance is not deemed adequate. To all intents and purposes, management cannot reduce its workforce, scrap the seniority system in favor of merit-based pay, or bring in more productive outsiders to replace current employees.

Profit and return-on-investment goals are largely meaningless in such a managerial environment. Therefore, for example, announcements by major electronics manufacturers in response to rapidly deteriorating conditions in the mobile phone and personal computer industries have emphasized that workers are not being laid off. And even when companies find their backs against the proverbial wall, the Ministry of Labor (now part of the Ministry of Health, Labor, and Welfare) has provided funding to major companies to enable them to avoid layoffs.[10] The bureaucrats take this tack because they understand full well that just as banks will balk at making loans the bureaucracy can no longer guarantee, people whose jobs are not secure may no longer easily accept wage rates, job content, and working conditions without explanation or accountability. But as the troubles of the economy deepen, companies are being forced to renege on their implicit guarantees or go under. The bureaucracy can no longer protect all established companies or all their lifetime employees.

It is much too early to say that the lifetime employment system has unraveled. Demographic trends project a shortfall in younger workers that threatens to introduce unwanted market forces into the all-important hiring of new recruits, and large established companies are doing their best to combat pressure for higher entry-level compensation by continuing to promise lifetime job security. But we do not see how lifetime employment could survive a prolonged and deep recession. The lack of an implicit guarantee of lifetime job security would complicate efforts to prevent the emergence of a labor market as people begin to negotiate compensation packages rather than simply accept whatever they are offered. With Japan's pool of younger workers shrinking, market power could even begin to shift away from established Japanese companies and toward workers and entrepreneurs in new industries less beholden to the bureaucracy. With people changing jobs in response to market forces, bureaucratic control of labor allocation could weaken just at the time its control of credit weakens.

## Possibilities for Change?

As we consider various aspects of the Japanese system, we discern a basic pattern repeating itself over and over. Anything that can be traded, anything that can give rise to competition, is forced into what amounts to a single system of institutions subject to bureaucratic control. Prices are accordingly divorced from market forces. The banking system functions in essence as one gigantic institution with interest rates and lending conditions set by central decree. All companies in particular industries are herded together into trade associations that determine how business is done and define the limits of allowable competition so corporate viability is never endangered. Salaries and labor conditions are set with scant regard to the supply and demand for workers in different industries.

But a period of serious economic distress will impose an ever-increasing strain on bureaucrats' ability to isolate prices from market forces. Workers abandoned by their companies may be radicalized. Younger people entering the work force may see what is happening to older workers and begin to look more closely at compensation and job content. Households receiving no return on their savings may begin to study alternatives to depositing their funds with the bank or the post office. Pensions that are inadequate to finance retirement will cause tomorrow's retirees to be much more careful today about balancing risk and return. Consumers faced with the reality of job loss and restructuring will continue to seek value for their money, flocking to stores like Uniqlo that offer high-quality apparel imports at a fraction of the cost of Japanese-made clothing. Companies noticing that the likes of the Sogo department store are left to twist in the wind will begin paying more and more attention to profits, building financial cushions against bad times and coughing up capital only for projects that promise high returns. Financial institutions will begin to lend again only when they are reassured that the money is going to finance profitable business that will generate the cash to pay them back.

In short, prices may begin to matter. It has often been said that Japan's consumers, savers, and workers do not understand the relationship between price and quality, risk and return, contribution and compensation. Prices have been set by bureaucratic fiat, not market forces. Once prices are fixed, there has been no room for negotiation. The absence of market pressure has been an indispensable prerequisite in the ability of Japanese producers to maximize production without concern for profits. But once prices start to matter, things will start to change—and change will accelerate in the event of a serious and prolonged downturn. Contrary to widespread impressions, however, change of this type is not in and of itself an alternative to the existing order. It is true that the credibility of the Japanese bureaucracy is fast eroding, and it is true that that credibility has long served to keep Japan's nonmarket system intact. But as long as the non-elite sectors of Japanese society accept exploitation—and that is what they have been brought up to accept—liberal capitalism operating under the rule of law has no chance of replacing today's system.

Market fundamentalists like to say that capitalism is what you get when you leave people alone. They are wrong. What you get is intimidation and rule by force. A healthy capitalist system can flourish only within a framework of strong, accountable, legal and political institutions that enforce contracts; provide for the security of persons and property; establish transparent, impartial, and universally applicable regulations; and issue a reliable currency that retains its function as a store of value.

As the Japanese elite loses the ability to control economic and political outcomes, the real question is whether the Japanese population can and will undertake the arduous and difficult task of building the institutions of accountable government. The alternative would see the faux-paternalism of today's authoritarian bureaucracy replaced by more exploitation and more naked displays of power. If bureaucrats can no longer handle the settlement of corporate financial distress, courts will not automatically spring forth like Venus from the sea to perform that function. Gangsters—*yakuza* is the Japanese term—may do it instead. The meaning of *yakuza* is now understood worldwide, and it is neither a coincidence nor the result of a few Hollywood movies. It stems from the increasing visibility of organized crime in Japan as bureaucratic control weakens.

To be sure, that is not the whole story, and the situation in Japan is still very far from the "gangster capitalism" said to prevail in Russia. Some voters are beginning to demand more from politicians, asking for realistic policy proposals to lead Japan out of its morass. However, most LDP politicians, being largely dependent on the bureaucracy for policymaking and implementation, have no real way of responding to their demands. They have neither the training nor the power to do very much.

The bureaucracy cannot, as an institution, change fundamental policy. Because each ministry is essentially a sovereign power, there is no mechanism for setting overriding priorities. Each ministry is responsible for its own protégés, not for the public at large. The bureaucracy will not tamper with the core of the economic system because that system is part and parcel of a wider political and social system that gives power to the ruling elite. It is a de facto, informal system that has been neither comprehensively mapped nor analyzed, one largely immune to democratic political scrutiny and control. So-called deregulation has been allowed to take place only when it did not change the core of the system. But some hope lies in the simultaneous existence of what is after all a comprehensive, if inadequate, de jure system of the rule of law through an accountable government. The institutions are all there in embryonic form, even if they function primarily as facades, even though they may never have been really tested.

People are conservative by nature. They generally will not act unless they are forced to do so. We believe that the current doldrums may well end with a prolonged and severe recession that will subject the Japanese system to more strain than it may be able to endure. For the power of the ruling elite lies in its ability to create income without labor for its protégés, to shift wealth from one sector to another at its own discretion. That power gives the ruling elite enormous political clout. But without economic growth, power shrinks. Wealth that does not exist cannot be redistributed. When a shrinking pie is divided anew, some will suffer actual loss of wealth, forming the nucleus of a potential opposition. Meanwhile, those who have grown accustomed to more wealth than their economic contributions merit will be outraged when they receive less. The government is piling up indebtedness in its efforts to maintain existing patterns of wealth distribution. It cannot persuade its protégés to reconcile themselves to smaller outlays, and those who have been deprived of their wealth are becoming increasingly vocal.

In the last two years, independent candidates won gubernatorial elections in Nagano and Tochigi. The new governors have yet to prove that they can take charge of the machinery of government and put it to work for the benefit of the public at large rather than favored constituencies, but they give every indication of understanding that that is what they should be doing. And more and more voters realize that the real benefits they will receive if politicians can muster the power to take charge outweigh the value of the subsidies they have been receiving. More and more of them now know that those subsidies are not free, that they are being paid for in the stupifyingly high prices for daily necessities and in a stagnant economy drowning in debt. Increasingly, one finds politicians at the national level who grasp the danger for Japan of rudderless, unaccountable bureaucratic rule and seek one way or another to impose political control on the bureaucracy. Isolated cases suggest that a number of judges and lawyers want to live up to their professional calling and help bring about a society governed by the rule of law. Many editors and journalists display unease at the cartelized, propagandistic nature of reporting in Japan, leading to conflict in editorial rooms. And an increasingly cosmopolitan group of entrepreneurs, managers, and bankers long for the chance to compete in a free economy and are doing what they can to bring that about. For the sake of Japan and the sake of the world, one wishes them the best.

# Notes

## Chapter One

1. The current account measures a country's trade in goods and services plus dividends, transfers, and interest payments flows with the rest of the world. The current account balance captures more fully the country's economic relationship with the outside world than does the simple trade balance.

2. An example translated from the *Asahi Shimbun* ran in the newspaper's English edition October 12, 2001: "Losing the Edge: Imports from Japan's Overseas Plants Shrinking Trade Surplus."

3. Ibid.

4. As any economics textbook will state, the trade balance can be calculated not only by toting up exports minus imports of goods and services but also by subtracting what a country consumes from what it produces. (If a country produces more than it consumes, it exports the difference and vice versa.) That difference is the level of savings. If savings exceed domestic investment needs, they will flow overseas and, again, vice versa. A country like Japan that saves more than it invests will have a current account surplus, while a country like the United States where investment exceeds domestic savings will have a current account deficit.

5. C. Fred Bergsten, "The U.S.-Japan Economic Problem: Next Steps," in Hugh T. Patrick and Tachi Ryuichiro, eds., *Japan and the United States Today: Exchange Rates, Macroeconomic Policies, and Financial Market Innovations* (New York: Center on Japanese Economy and Business, Columbia University, 1986), p. 83.

6. The definition of high-powered money can vary, but the Bank of Japan defines it as the equivalent of its monetary base, that is, currency in circulation plus bank deposits with the BOJ. In this book, we will use the term "high-powered money" in accordance with this definition.

7. According to the Ministry of Finance, in the latter half of calendar year 2000, 36.1 percent of Japan's total exports were settled in yen and 52.4 percent were settled in dollars. Of Japan's exports to the United States, 86.7 percent were settled in dollars, while 48.2 percent of Japan's exports to other Asian countries were settled in dollars and 50 percent in yen. We believe that these figures actually overstate the extent to which Japan's exports are settled in yen because the yen-denominated settlements appear to be accounted for largely by trade between Japanese companies and their Japanese affiliates/subsidiaries domiciled abroad.

8. According to the MOF, in the latter half of calendar year 2000, 23.5 percent of Japan's imports were paid for in yen and the rest almost entirely in dollars. One of the authors recalls from his days as a banker trying to persuade large Australian mining companies to take advantage of low yen interest rates by borrowing in yen and using the proceeds of their sales to Japan to service the debt. The Australians responded that they had been attempting for years to persuade Japanese trading companies to denominate long-term supply contracts in yen, but the firms refused and insisted that the contracts be denominated in U.S. dollars. Unless the Australians could denominate their supply contracts in yen, they were unwilling—correctly in retrospect—to take the currency risk of denominating their borrowings in yen.

9. Ichinose Atsushi, *Kotei Soba Seiki no Nippon Ginko Kinyu Seisaku* (BOJ's Monetary Policy under the Fixed Exchange Rate System) (Tokyo: Ochanomizu Shobou, 1995), p. 7.

10. In his landmark study of Japan's industrial policy and the Ministry of International Trade and Industry (MITI), which is responsible for its implementation, Chalmers Johnson describes MITI's control over foreign exchange allocation to industry as "the heart of the matter" in carrying out industrial policy. See Chalmers Johnson, *MITI and the Japanese Miracle: The Growth of Industrial Policy, 1925–1975* (Stanford University Press, 1982), pp. 16–17.

11. Jacques Rueff, *The Monetary Sin of the West* (New York: The MacMillan Company, 1972), pp. 192–193.

12. Alex Kerr, *Dogs and Demons* (New York: Hill and Wang, 2001) provides a comprehensive picture of Japan's public works "monster."

## Chapter Two

1. Alex Kerr, *Dogs and Demons* (Hill and Wang, 2001), p. 104.

2. Kan Naoto, *Daijin* (*Minister*) (Tokyo: Iwanami Shoten, 1998). The affair is discussed on pages 82–92.

3. Only Karel van Wolferen to our knowledge has really grappled with the question of how it is possible for a power structure to function so well without any visible center or explicit legal foundation. See *The Enigma of Japanese Power* (Alfred A. Knopf, 1989), particularly chapters 8, 9, 12, and 13.

4. Hirose Michisada, *Hojyokin to Seiken-to* (*Subsidies and the Ruling Party*) (Tokyo: Asahi Shimbunsha, 1993), p. 257.

5. Ibid., p. 17.

6. Kan Naoto discusses this in *Daijin*, pp. 150–156.

7. Igarashi Takayoshi and Ogawa Akio, *Gikai: Kanryoshihai o koete (The Diet: Beyond Bureaucratic Hegemony)* (Tokyo: Iwanami Shoten, 1995). Pages 68–69 specially discuss bureaucratic control of policymaking.

8. The concern among sectors of the Japanese elite over the danger of bureaucratic rivalry to Japan's war efforts can be seen in a book written in the early 1940s by Yamazaki Tansho, a high-ranking official of the *Hoseikyoku* (Legislative Bureau) in the prewar system that, despite its name, played a quasi-judicial function in the bureaucracy by interpreting law. Yamazaki recommended strengthening the powers of the prime minister as a means of curbing the rivalry. See *Naikaku Seido no Kenkyu (Study of the Cabinet System)* (Tokyo: Takayama Shoin, 1942).

9. Chalmers Johnson had back in 1982 documented the prewar and wartime origins of MITI's industrial policies: *MITI and the Japanese Miracle: The Growth of Industrial Policy 1925–1975* (Stanford University Press, 1982). John Dower writes in his magisterial study of the Occupation years, "it is now clear that the structural legacies of wartime Japan to the postsurrender decades were enormous": *Embracing Defeat: Japan in the Wake of World War II* (W.W. Norton, 1999), p. 559. In Japan, the eminent economist Noguchi Yukio argued that Japan's supposedly "postwar" economic and financial system was actually the "1940 System" in his book of that title: *1940-nen Taisei* (Tokyo: Toyo Keizai Shinposha, 1995). Igarashi and Ogawa, *Gikai,* also discuss the survival of prewar bureaucracies under new names in the postwar period.

10. Dower, *Embracing Defeat,* and Herbert P. Bix, *Hirohito and the Making of Modern Japan* (HarperCollins, 2000), chapters 14–16 document in relentless detail the success during the late 1940s of elements of the prewar conservative elite in reasserting their control over Japanese political and economic life. They were greatly—even crucially—helped by an Occupation that by 1947 had become far more worried about purported Communist influence in Japan than any resurgence of "militarism."

11. "Hashimoto Remark Triggers Sharp Plunge In U.S. Stocks," *Asia Pulse,* June 25, 1997.

12. Frank Upham in *Law and Social Change in Postwar Japan* (Harvard University Press, 1987), p. 16, writes,"The identification of litigation as a threat to the political and social status quo is implicit in all writing on Japanese law and society, and recent scholarship argues persuasively that self-interest has led the Japanese elite to take deliberate steps to discourage litigation."

13. Bank of Japan Research Department, *Nihon Ginko no Hoteki Seikaku: Shin Nichigin ho o fumaete (Legal Character of the BOJ: Based on the New Bank of Japan Law)* (Tokyo: Kobundo, 2001) discusses the new law.

14. Thomas Cargill, Michael M. Hutchison, and Ito Takatoshi, *Financial Policy and Central Banking in Japan* (MIT Press, 2000), p. 104.

15. Article 4, clause 59, of the 1999 law governing the MOF (*Zaimusho settchi ho*) states that "appropriate management of the BOJ's business organization is to be secured by the MOF except for functions given to the FSA." Clauses 60 and 61 have similar statements with respect to reserve deposits and interest rate adjustments. Article 4, clauses 11, 12, and 13 of the 1999 law establishing the FSA (*Kinyu cho settchi ho*) grant comparable authority over the BOJ to the FSA.

16. Ikeda Hayato, *Kinko Zaisei: Senryo ka San Nen no Omoide (Balancing the Budget: Memories of Three Years under the Occupation)*, new edition (Tokyo: Chuokoron-Shinsha, 1999), p. 149. The original edition was published in 1952.

17. Igarashi and Ogawa, *Gikai*, pp 68–69.

18. See, for example, Minobe Tatsukichi, *Nippon Gyoseiho Satsuyo* (*Description of Japan's Administrative Law*), vol. 1 and 2 (Tokyo: Yuhikaku, 1936); original edition published in 1909. Minobe was arguably the most important legal scholar of Japan's entire modern period. As Marius Jansen points out in *The Making of Modern Japan* (Harvard University Press, 2000), p. 542, Minobe's "books in which he laid out his views became standard texts."

19. Gavan McCormack notes that "Japan outspends the United States on construction by a ratio of 2.6/1, or in proportion to relative land area, 32/1." *The Emptiness of Japanese Affluence* (Armonk and London: M.E. Sharpe, 1996), p. 33.

20. Kerr, *Dogs and Demons*, p. 155.

21. "Marunage de rizaya sanoku hassen man" ("Whole Contract Farmed Out with Spread of 380 Million Yen"), *Yomiuri Shimbun*, February 21, 2001, p. 1.

22. The Ministry of Public Management, Home Affairs, Posts, and Telecommunications announced at the end of 2001 that the discrepancy in voting power among single-seat lower-house districts reached a maximum of 2.55, while in the upper house it was as high as 5.7 times. "Ippyo no Kakusa" ("Weight of One Vote"), *Nihon Keizai Shimbun*, December 28, 2001, p. 2.

23. Shiozaki Yasuhisa, "Nihonban SEC o Sosetsuse yo" ("A Japanese SEC Should Be Established"), *Toyo Keizai*, October 21, 2000.

24. According to Kuribayashi Yoshimitsu, in 1992, 114 retired MOF bureaucrats occupied senior management positions in Japanese commercial banks, while another fifty or so could be found in comparable positions of influence inside securities firms and insurance companies: *Okurasho: Fushin no Kozu* (*The Ministry of Finance: A Profile of Distrust*) (Tokyo: Kodansha, 1992), pp. 360–63.

25. The incident is described in *Okura Shihai* (*Rule of the MOF*), a compilation of articles written on the MOF by eighteen journalists in the *Asahi Shimbun's* economics department (Tokyo: Asahi Shimbunsha, 1997), pp. 25–26.

26. "Authorities Tell Shinsei to Ease Up," *Asian Wall Street Journal*, September 26, 2001, p. 1.

27. Frank Packer and Mark Ryser, "The Governance of Failure: An Anatomy of Corporate Bankruptcy in Japan," Working Paper Series 62 (New York: Center on Japanese Economy and Business, Columbia University, 1992), pp. 20 and 26.

## Chapter Three

1. Paul Krugman, *The Accidental Theorist* (W. W. Norton, 1998), p. 125.

2. Adam Posen, *Restoring Japan's Economic Growth* (Washington: Institute for International Economics, 1998), pp. 122–25.

3. According to Hamada Koichi and Horiuchi Akiyoshi, between 1947 and 1981, private sector banks provided from 71 to 83 percent of all external financing requirements of Japanese corporations, with government financial institutions such as the Japan Development Bank providing an additional 8 to 14 percent. "The Political Economy of the Financial Market," in Yamamura Kozo and Yasuba Yasukichi, eds., *The Political Economy of Japan*, vol. 1, *The Domestic Transformation* (Stanford University Press, 1987), p. 173.

4. The *tanshi gaisha* make markets (that is, they use their own balance sheets) in Japan's interbank market, known as the call money market, which functions as Japan's equivalent of the Fed Funds market. The biggest *tanshi gaisha* are Ueda Tanshi and Tokyo Tanshi.

5. The operations of the call money market are described in detail in Yoshio Suzuki, *The Japanese Financial System* (Oxford: Clarendon Press, 1990), pp. 112–17. The role of the *tanshi gaisha* is also described there (pp. 269–73).

6. The three long-term banks had a monopoly on the issue of fixed-rate five-year debentures, which were their principal funding vehicles. Until the mid 1960s, the MOF arranged for the direct purchase of the debentures, and the coupons on the debentures were set by negotiation between the MOF and the three banks. The key long-term lending rate, the Long Term Prime Rate, was always set at a fixed spread over the debenture coupon rate.

7. Ogihara Kiyoto and Masubuchi Minoru, *Nippon Ginko* (*The Bank of Japan*) (Tokyo: Zaikei Shohonsha, 1986), pp. 74–75. Also see Suzuki, *The Japanese Financial System*, pp. 325–26.

8. Toyooka Tomiei, *Jisho Kinyuron* (*On the Theory of Finance*) (Tokyo: Kinyu Zaisei Jijyo Kenkyukai, 1975), p. 148.

9. Ikeda Hayato, *Kinko Zaisei: Senryo ka San Nen no Omoide* (*Balancing the Budget: Memories of Three Years under the Occupation*), new edition (Tokyo: Chuokoron-Shinsha, 1999), pp. 149–50.

10. We estimate that current cash in circulation, per capita, is five to six times that in the United States.

11. The book has been translated into English by Simul International as Tanaka Kakuei, *Building a New Japan: A Plan for Remodeling the Japanese Archipelago* (Tokyo: Simul Press, 1972).

12. Nakayama Ichiro, *Sensokeizai no Riron* (*The Logic of a War Economy*) (Tokyo: Nippon Hyoronsha, 1942), especially pp. 251–68.

13. Makino Hiroshi, *Nichibei Gaiko no Hikakubunseki* (*Comparative Analysis of Japan-U.S. Currency Diplomacy*) (Tokyo: Ochanomizu Shobou, 1999), p. 134.

14. Robert C. Angel, *Explaining Economic Policy Failure: Japan in the 1969–1971 International Monetary Crisis* (Columbia University Press, 1991), p. 272.

15. Makino, *Nichibei Gaiko no Hikakubunseki*, pp. 172–73, describes the opprobrium that descended on the group. Many of Japan's academic economists at the time were Marxists and could be expected to oppose automatically whatever the government did; that non-Marxist economists would do so was significant.

16. Ibid., p. 175.

## Chapter Four

1. Richard Katz, *Japan: The System That Soured* (Armonk and London: M.E. Sharpe, 1998), p. 75.

2. Michael Porter, Takeuchi Hirotaka, and Sakakibara Mariko, *Can Japan Compete?* (Cambridge, Mass.: Perseus Publishing, 2000), p. 143.

3. Fukai Eigo, *Kaiko 70 Nen* (*Memoirs of 70 Years*) (Tokyo: Iwanami Shoten, 1942).

4. Ibid., p. 84.

5. Suzuki Toshio, *Japanese Government Loan Issues in the London Capital Market* (London and Atlantic Highlands, N.J.: Athlone Press, 1994), p. 168.

6. The history of Japan's external specie holdings can be found in Yamazawa Ippei and Yamamoto Yuzo *Choki Keizai Tokei*, vol. 14, *Boeki to Kokusai Saishushi* (*Estimate of Long-Term Economic Statistics of Japan since 1868*, vol. 14, *Foreign Trade and the Balance of Payments*) (Tokyo: Toyo Keizai Shinposha, 1979), pp. 62–67. On page 57, Yamamoto notes that Britain informally requested that the Chinese gold reparations be kept within the United Kingdom in order to avoid disturbing the London gold market. Russia, France, and Germany had all pressured Japan—the "Triple Intervention," as it was known—not to insist on the Liaotung territorial concession by the Chinese; the indemnity was partial compensation for Japan's giving up the concession. Japan may have felt a debt of gratitude to Britain for not joining the Triple Intervention and thus amenable to suggestions that the Chinese gold be left in London.

7. The speech was made April 15, 1915, at the Tegata Kokanjyo Rengokai (Federation of Bill Exchanges) and quoted in Tanaka Ikuo, *Nippon Ginko Seisaku Shi* (*History of Monetary Policy of the Bank of Japan*) (Tokyo: Yuhikaku, 1989) p. 17.

8. BOJ Research Division, *Honpo Zaikai Doyoshi* (*History of Japan's Business Fluctuations*) (Tokyo: Bank of Japan, 1923), p. 48.

9. Takahasi Kamekichi, *Taisho Showa Zaikai Hendoshi* (*Economic History of the Taisho and Showa Periods*) (Tokyo: Toyo Keizai Shinposha, 1954), pp. 113–19.

10. Speech given April 22, 1919, at the Tegata Kokanjyo Rengokai (Federation of Bill Exchanges), quoted in Tanaka, *op. cit.*, p. 25.

11. Between March and July of 1920, for example, the value of inventories stored in Japan's major warehouses rose from ¥980 million to ¥1.280 billion. Since that buildup occurred in a macroeconomic environment of declining prices, the volume of buildup was even greater than the numbers would indicate. Meanwhile, dishonored bills on the Tokyo Bill Exchange were ten times greater in May 1920 than they had been the previous January. BOJ Research Division, *Honpo Zaikai Doyoshi*, pp. 291–92.

12. Nomura Kentaro, "Meiji Shoki Keizaishi Kenkyu" (Study of Economic History of the Early Meiji Era"), *Bulletin 1 of the Keio Gijyuku Economic History Society* (Tokyo: Ganshodo, 1937), p. 17.

13. Peter F. Drucker, "Economic Realities and Enterprise Strategy," in Ezra F. Vogel, ed., *Modern Japanese Organization and Decision-Making* (Berkeley: University of California Press, 1975), pp. 232–33.

14. During periods of prosperity, Japanese depositors—like depositors anywhere—have acted purely as creditors with a first claim, through deposit-taking institutions, on corporate debt service payments. But during times of economic difficulty, depositors have often been forced into the role of equity holders, indeed taking a backseat to the ostensible equity holders in the distribution of claims. After World War II, banks had to be reorganized because they could not collect the loans they had made to industrial borrowers; the government could not or would not compensate the latter for war losses. It was depositors, however, who were written off first through bank reorganization, not ostensible equity holders. No official documentation exists that establishes smoking-gun evidence of the government's policy of treating depositors' claims as subordinate to those of equity holders, but Takaishi Suekichi, a former MOF official, discusses this and—perhaps unwittingly—makes the case that depositors took a back seat to equity holders in

his *Oboegaki Shusen Zaisei Shimatsu* (*Memorandum on Settlements of Public Finance after the War-End*), vol. 16 (Tokyo: Okura Zaimukyokai, 1971), pp. 759–98.

15. The amalgamation is discussed in *Manshujiken igo no Zaisei Kinyushi* (*Fiscal and Monetary History Since the Manchurian Incident*) (Tokyo: Bank of Japan Research Department, 1948), p. 264.

16. One of the most interesting of these measures lay in the currency arrangements made for Japan's newly conquered colonies and their intertwining with the financing of the Japanese military. For financial purposes, eight different colonial areas were established, each with its own central bank authorized to issue currency. The Japanese military needed to purchase goods and services from the local economy in these jurisdictions, but the Japanese government did not want to pay for the purchases in a manner that would reduce Japan's hard currency or gold reserves. Instead, the colonial central banks (CCBs) issued local scrip to the Japanese Army that the army could use for local procurements. The army paid for the scrip by depositing yen funds into the accounts of the YSB in Tokyo with the BOJ. The YSB then made counterbalancing deposits into the accounts of the CCBs with the YSB.

The arrangement was called *azukeai*, or duplication, and it enabled Japan to carry out its war efforts without transferring purchasing power from Japan to the colonies. For while the funds on deposit with the YSB were nominally the assets of the CCBs, the CCBs were required to leave the funds on deposit with the YSB. Naturally, the arrangement led to severe inflation in the colonies. The extra local scrip issued to the Japanese Army was not backed up by funds available for investment in the colonies because those funds were kept idle in Tokyo; demand therefore increased without any concomitant increase in supply. Japan financed World War II by running huge deficits that were made up for by capital imports from the occupied areas and reserve deposits of the CCBs. The available materials are, alas, too scant to permit a full analysis. But the situation seems to bear eerie parallels with the financial arrangements that would prevail in the postwar era between Japan and the United States. For a half-century now, the United States has procured goods from Japan—partly to finance the Korean, Vietnam, and Cold Wars—but most of the dollars that paid for those goods never left the U.S. banking system, just as the yen that was theoretically supposed to pay for the Japanese Army's colonial procurements never left Tokyo. Having run a similar system, the Japanese ruling elite may have had a surer grasp of the monetary dynamics of the postwar U.S.-Japan relationship than their American counterparts. Among other things, to forestall inflation, the YSB was under strict orders to leave idle the CCB deposits. But Tokyo never warned Washington that American financial institutions should avoid using deposits by nonresidents to fund additional lending.

17. Suzuki Takeo maintains that the 360 rate overvalued the yen. *Gendai Nippon Zaiseishi* (*History of Modern Japan's Fiscal Policy*) (Tokyo: Tokyo Daigaku Shuppankai, 1960), p. 169. The weight of conventional opinion, however, is that the 360 rate significantly undervalued the yen. John Dower writes, "[Joseph] Dodge virtually single-handedly established a fixed exchange rate of 360 yen to the dollar, undervaluing the yen somewhat to stimulate exports by making Japanese manufactures cheaper on the world market." *Embracing Defeat: Japan in the Wake of World War II* (W.W. Norton, 1999), p. 540. Dodge was the "economic czar" sent by Washington to Japan in 1949, supposedly to set right a deficit-prone Japanese economy.

18. Dower, *Embracing Defeat*, p. 542.

19. Ikeda Hayato, *Kinko Zaisei: Senryo ka San Nen no Omoide* (*Balancing the Budget: Memories of Three Years under the Occupation*), new edition (Tokyo: Chuokoron-Shinsha, 1999), p. 68.

20. The United States in 1934 established the Exchange Stabilization Fund (ESF), also modeled on Britain's Exchange Equalization Account. Set up to facilitate foreign exchange interventions and defend the dollar, the ESF was most recently in the news during the Mexican peso crisis of 1995. The ESF is under direct control of the Secretary of the Treasury and was used by Robert Rubin, then the secretary, to circumvent congressional opposition to funding the Mexican bailout. See C. Randall Henning, *The Exchange Stabilization Fund: Slush Money or War Chest?* (Washington: Institute for International Economics, 1999). Needless to say, the histories of the American ESF and Japan's FESA are very different.

21. Ikeda, *Kinko Zaisei*, p.149.

22. The *tokushu hojin* play a critical role in the ability of the bureaucracy to direct funds to favored parts of the economy and as retirement posts for former bureaucrats. For a detailed account of the founding and early postwar activities of the *tokushu hojin* and their financing by *zaito*, see Chalmers Johnson, *Japan's Public Policy Companies* (Washington, D.C. and Stanford, Calif., AEI-Hoover Policy Studies, 1978). Johnson stresses that while the modern *tokushu hojin* and *zaito* date from 1953, they are based on wartime and pre-war institutions.

23. See particularly Robert C. Angel, *Explaining Economic Policy Failure: Japan in the 1969–1971 International Monetary Crisis* (New York: Columbia University Press, 1991); and R. Taggart Murphy, *The Weight of the Yen* (W.W. Norton, 1996), chapter 4.

24. Yoshino Toshihiko, *En to Doru* (*The Yen and the Dollar*) (Tokyo: Nippon Hoso Shuppan Kyokai, 1996), p. 219.

## Chapter Five

1. Alvaro Cencini, *Monetary Theory* (London and New York: Routledge, 1995), p. 150–51.

2. Richard Katz, *Japan: The System That Soured* (Armonk and London: M.E. Sharpe, 1998), p. 169.

3. Sakakibara Eisuke, *Beyond Capitalism: The Japanese Model of Market Economics* (Lanham, Md.: University Press of America, 1993).

4. Toyooka Tomiei, *Jisho Kinyuron* (*On the Theory of Finance*) (Tokyo: Kinyu Zaisei Jijyo Kenkyukai, 1975), p. 21–22; 69–84. Price cartels are discussed on pages 24–29.

5. *Nippon Ginko Hyaku Nenshi* (*Hundred Year History of the Bank of Japan*), vol. 6 (Tokyo: Bank of Japan, 1982), p. 226.

6. Fujiwara Hidejiro, president of Shimamua, a leading clothing store chain, was quoted as saying "There are many who sold land and equity at high prices which contributed to gigantic financial asset holdings by individuals." Keizai Kansoku (Economic Outlook Regular Column), "Iriyohin wa sagedomari" ("Prices Bottoming") *Nihon Keizai Shimbun*, March 10, 2002, p. 3.

7. Hisatsune Arata, *Kosureba tochi wa ugoku* (*Reviving the Real Estate Market*) (Tokyo: Nihon Keizai Shimbunsha, 1999), p. 170.

8. Among the better discussions of the deliberate creation and fostering of stratospheric land prices in Japan is Robert L. Cutts, "Power from the Ground Up: Japan's Land Bubble," *Harvard Business Review* (May-June 1990), pp. 164–72.

9. See Karel van Wolferen, *The Enigma of Japanese Power* (Alfred A. Knopf, 1989), pp. 127–38, for a concise history of Tanaka's career and significance. Jacob Schlesinger, *Shadow Shoguns* (Simon & Schuster, 1997), describes the political dynasty that Tanaka built, which has dominated Japanese politics since the 1970s.

10. Robert C. Angel, *Explaining Economic Policy Failure: Japan in the 1969–1971 International Monetary Crisis* (Columbia University Press, 1991), p. 51.

11. William Greider, *Secrets of the Temple: How the Federal Reserve Runs the Country* (Simon and Schuster, 1987), p. 342.

12. Keynes had, in his original blueprint for the Bretton Woods system, incorporated measures that would force surplus countries to bear some of the adjustment burdens to payment imbalances by increasing their growth rates. In one of history's ironies, however, he had been overruled by the American delegation.

13. Nixon believed that he needed the industry's help in blunting the electoral appeal of third-party candidate George Wallace, particularly in the southeastern states where both Wallace's popularity and the industry were concentrated. See the account in I. M. Destler, Haruhiro Fukui, and Hideo Sato, *The Textile Wrangle: Conflict in Japanese-American Relations, 1969–1971* (Cornell University Press, 1979), particularly pages 68–70. Chapter 5 discusses the Nixon-Sato summit of November 1969.

14. Although "Marshallian K" did not originate in Japan, one encounters it far more widely in Japanese economic writing than in Western.

15. *Nippon Ginko Hyaku Nenshi*, p. 372.

16. Ibid.

17. Noguchi Yukio, *Tochi no Keizaigaku* (*The Economics of Land*) (Tokyo: Nippon Keizai Shimbunsha, 1989), pp. 29–47; 134–38. Also see Kan Naoto, *Tochiseisaku* (*Land Policy*) (Tokyo: Shin Hyoron, 1992), pp. 35–39.

18. Kato Izuru, *Nichigin wa Shindanoka?* (*Is the Bank of Japan Dead?*) (Tokyo: Nippon Keizai Shimbunsha, 2001).

19. *Nippon Ginko Hyaku Nenshi*, p. 399.

20. At the beginning of the decade, Japan's government debt stood at 6.5 percent of GDP versus 7 percent and 11.2 percent for West Germany and France, respectively; at the end of the decade, Japan's would reach 26 percent, while West Germany's and France's stood at 15.5 percent and 9.7 percent, respectively.

21. R. Taggart Murphy, *The Weight of the Yen* (W.W. Norton, 1996), chapter 5.

## Chapter Six

1. See in particular Yoichi Funabashi, *Managing the Dollar: From the Plaza to the Louvre* (Washington: Institute for International Economics, 1989); and R. Taggart Murphy, *The Weight of the Yen* (W.W. Norton, 1996), chapter 6.

2. Among the most important pieces of evidence: the sales pitches of Japanese banks such as the Bank of Tokyo and the Industrial Bank of Japan with close MOF connections urging sovereign borrowers in the early 1980s to consider denominating syndicated

loans in yen rather than dollars. The interest rate differential was on the order of five to six whole percentage points in favor of yen; borrowers who rightly worried about the potential for yen appreciation were told that the yen would have to strengthen beyond 180 for it to be more cost effective to borrow in dollars and that the Japanese government would never allow the yen to strengthen beyond that rate. An even more compelling piece of evidence was the purchase by Japan Air Lines (Japan's flagship airline, which had close connections to the Ministry of Transportation) of $3 billion of forward foreign exchange contracts at the 180 rate in 1985. The company sustained losses of more than $1 billion as a result. See "JAL's Battle against Red Ink Highlights Cost of Strong Yen," *Asian Wall Street Journal*, August 10, 1994, p. 8.

3. Robert Gilpin describes Hume's price-specie flow theory as "the first great contribution to the science of economics and the basis for the development of liberal economics. . . . Hume responded to the mercantilist states' obsession with amassing specie through a trade surplus and their fear that a trade deficit would cause a dangerous loss of specie. He demonstrated that if a country gained specie in payment for an excess of exports over imports, the consequent increase in its money supply would cause its domestic and then its export prices to rise. This in turn would discourage others from buying its goods. At the same time, its own citizens would be able to import more because the relative value of their currency had risen and foreign prices would have fallen due to the decreased money supply abroad. As a result, the nation's exports would decline and its imports would increase." *The Political Economy of International Relations* (Princeton University Press, 1987), p. 121.

4. Dennis Encarnation, *Rivals beyond Trade* (Cornell University Press, 1992), p. 46.

5. As a fledgling investment banker back in 1982, one of the authors worked on the first-ever acquisition of a controlling interest in a Japanese company listed on the first section of the Tokyo Stock Exchange by a foreign entity: the purchase by British Oxygen of a major stake in Osaka Sanso, then Japan's third-largest manufacturer of industrial gases. The principals and senior investment bankers involved in the deal were far more concerned about the stance of three ministries—MOF, MITI, and the Ministry of Health and Welfare—than about any other single factor. The deal went forward because British Oxygen, sensibly, refused to make its cutting-edge technology available to Japanese industry on any terms other than a controlling interest.

6. Susan Strange, *Mad Money: When Markets Outgrow Governments* (University of Michigan Press, 1998) discusses on p. 160 "the political pressure from U.S. banks to make sure, through international agreement, that they were not unfairly handicapped in competitive international business" that began in 1983 and led to the 1988 Basle Accord on bank capital ratios.

7. In May 1984, as an outgrowth of the so-called Yen/Dollar Committee negotiations between the MOF and the U.S. Treasury, limits on dollar/yen conversion amounts were lifted, euroyen (yen issues floated outside Japan by non-Japanese issuers) were permitted, and swaps could be attached to eurobond issues by Japanese issuers. The last was particularly significant because it gave birth to the Tokyo swap market. The swap market played a key role in the late 1980s in undermining the funding distinctions among classes of financial institutions, which the MOF may not have anticipated.

8. Kan Naoto, *Tochiseisaku (Land Policy)* (Tokyo: Shin Hyoron, 1992), p. 36, stresses in particular how capital gains tax rates are subject to arbitrary changes without solid or rational explanations.

9. Fujii Yoshihiro, *Kinyu-zaisei no Gosan* (*Miscalculation of Financial Revival*) (Tokyo: Nihon Keizai Shimbunsha, 2001).

10. Murphy, *Weight of the Yen*, pp. 229–35, discusses the role of the MOF in arm-twisting Japanese financial institutions to hold and purchase dollar-denominated instruments. See also Richard Koo, "Japanese Investment in Dollar Securities after the Plaza Accord," supplement to *U.S. Foreign Debt: Hearing before the Joint Economic Committee*, 100th Cong., 2d sess. (U.S. Government Printing Office, 1989), p. 73.

11. One of the authors worked at Chase between 1983 and 1989.

12. A warrant is an instrument that gives its owner the right to buy an underlying share of stock at a predetermined price, called the exercise price. Investors buy such warrants because they believe the market will rise and bring the warrant "into the money"—in other words, make it profitable. The exercise prices on Japanese warrants were a little higher than the current underlying prices, but everyone assumed that the stock market would keep going up. Demand for warrants soared. Investment bankers would strip the warrants from the bonds. The stripped bonds would be sold to garden-variety bond investors, both Japanese and foreign, at discounts steep enough that the yields were similar to what other comparable bond issuers were paying. But the warrants were sold almost entirely to Japanese investors who believed the Tokyo stock market would go in only one direction: up.

Corporations issuing the bonds also believed the market had but one way to go. They fully expected that before the bonds matured, the warrant holders would exercise the warrants—in other words, buy the company's stock at the exercise price—giving the company the money it needed to repay the bondholders. Meanwhile, thanks to the swap markets, the extremely low dollar coupon payments could be swapped into yen receipts; in other words, instead of paying out interest, the company would receive interest.

Most of the warrant holders ultimately found themselves holding worthless pieces of paper. The Japanese stock market began to drop dramatically in the early 1990s. The exercise price of the warrants ended up, in most cases, above the actual market price when the warrants expired. And the industrial companies that thought that they never need worry about paying off the bondholders went scrambling for funds in the early 1990s when the expected proceeds of stock sales to warrant holders failed to materialize. But from the perspective of the Japanese corporate treasurer, raising capital in the late 1980s had become a matter of helping yourself to whatever you needed; in fact, the companies thought that they were being paid to take it. Thus, in their view, it cost nothing to build a factory, acquire machinery, buy foreign real estate, or snap up foreign companies. All they needed to do was float an equity warrant bond. And floated they were—in amounts upward of several hundred billion dollars.

13. This point was made by Arai Atsuko in "Kakushite, Nippon ni Infure wa Okoraji" ("Nevertheless, Inflation Cannot be Generated in Japan"), *Kinyu Business*, February 1999, pp. 74–77. Until publication of the article, many had argued behind closed doors that inflation was the only means left to deal with Japan's mountain of bad loans. There has long been a hesitancy to discuss inflation publicly in Japan; the first scholar to write openly about inflation as policy, Kimura Kihachiro, had been jailed when he came out with a book entitled *Inflation* in 1939. But Arai demonstrated that creating inflation had become practically impossible in the Japan of the late 1990s. She contended that people believe that the MOF could deliver inflation if it wanted to and that because they have never concerned themselves with how policy is actually determined, they do not

understand that the option is no longer available. Arai argued that MOF's inability may plunge Japan into depression and that companies ought to take measures to protect themselves rather than expect the MOF to bail them out; the MOF may turn out to be unable to help any entities other than its closest affiliates. Arai is an economic analyst at Mikuni & Co.

## Chapter Seven

1. Charles Kindleberger, *Manias, Panics, and Crashes: A History of Financial Crises* (Basic Books, 1989).

2. Mikuni & Co. had projected at the beginning of the 1990s that liabilities of bankrupt companies would climb to more than ¥10 trillion in the near future. See Arai Atsuko, "Kigyo Tosan 10cho-en Jidai to Ginko" ("Banks and the Rise of Liabilities of Bankrupt Companies beyond Ten Trillion Yen"), *Kinyu Business*, May 1991, pp. 52–55.

3. An account of the Itoman saga can be found in R. Taggart Murphy, *The Weight of the Yen* (W.W. Norton, 1996), pp. 257–58, and in the Japanese mass media in the fall of 1991 (see, for example, *Asahi Shimbun*, October 9, 1991, morning edition, page 1). Ito Suemitsu, a mobster, had become a director of Itoman, where he looted the company of some half-trillion yen. Much of Itoman's senior management, including its president, ended up in jail while one secondee from the Sumitomo Bank committed suicide.

4. Mikuni & Co. had projected that the MOF would be unable to support all the banks due to the rapid expansion of bank assets in comparison with tax revenues. See Mikuni Akio, "Kinyu Chitsujyo Kiban no Hokai" ("Collapse of the Foundations of the Credit Order"), *Kinyu Business*, July 1991, pp. 103–07.

5. In 1984, Riccar defaulted on a Swiss franc convertible bond. That was the first time in the postwar period that investors suffered a loss on any kind of debt security; in any case, convertible bonds were purchased primarily as equity plays.

6. According to the Bank of Japan, during the fiscal year that ended March 31, 2001, straight bonds worth a total of ¥7.64 trillion were issued. City banks bought ¥0.15 trillion; top-tier regional banks, ¥0.36 trillion; second-tier regional banks, ¥0.12 trillion; trust banks, ¥0.61 trillion; *shinyo kinko*, ¥0.91 trillion; Norinchukin and nokyo-affiliated credit organizations, ¥0.43 trillion; insurance companies, ¥0.86 trillion; individuals, ¥0.86 trillion; and others, including investment trusts, ¥3.33 trillion.

7. Niwayama Keiichirou, "Jutaku Kinyu Judai" ("Ten Points Concerning Housing Loans"), *Kinyu Zaisei Jijyo*, August 25, 1975.

8. Author Murphy worked on and helped develop the first such financing, a ¥30 billion placement for the Malaysian Highway Authority guaranteed by the Malaysian government that when it was signed in early 1985 constituted the longest-term fixed-rate yen financing ever done by any borrower in any market. The deal was structured as an installment sale agreement rather than a loan to avoid MOF restrictions on nonbank cross-border lending. The asset being sold (gold in the Malaysian case and most subsequent such deals) was simultaneously bought back by the nonbanks so that no actual asset remained in the hands of the borrower—thus the term *kagonuke* (literally, "escape from the palanquin," or a palanquin with nothing in it). Malaysian government entities did four more such large deals, and they were followed by a rash of borrowers in Algeria, Turkey, Greece, Spain, Oman, Hungary, and several other countries, usually with gov-

ernment guarantees. While the financing technique survived (most of the billions of dollar-denominated subordinated debt raised by European and Australian banks from Japanese sources in the late 1980s were structured as *kagonuke* leases), the era of un-hedged, cross-border yen borrowing would end by 1987 as the yen climbed in the eigh-teen months following the September 1985 Plaza Accord.

9. See John Judis, "A Dollar Foolish," *New Republic*, December 9, 1996, for an account of the meetings between Sakakibara and Rubin.

10. See Roger Lowenstein, *When Genius Failed: The Rise and Fall of Long-Term Capital Management* (Random House, 2000). On page 135, Lowenstein notes that Long-Term had bet "exactly the opposite" on yen bond yields—that is, interest rates.

11. Quoted in Paul Blustein, *The Chastening* (New York: Public Affairs, 2001), p. 124.

## Chapter Eight

1. See R. Taggart Murphy, *The Weight of the Yen* (W.W. Norton, 1996), pp. 288–90; also David Asher, *Dissecting the Yen Bubble: Price Keeping Operations and the Inflated Price of the Yen* (Washington: Mike Mansfield Center for Pacific Affairs, 1995), p. 13.

2. See the account in Jacob Weisberg, "Keeping the Boom from Busting," *New York Times Magazine*, July 19, 1998.

3. Hasegawa Tokunosuke, *Fudosan Kinyukiki: Saigo no Shohosen* (*The Final Prescription for Resolving the Crisis of Real Estate and Financial Circles*) (Tokyo: Diamond Sha, 1998), chapter 10.

4. Muramatsu Michio, a professor in the Faculty of Law at Kyoto University, discusses this jargon in *Nihon no Gyosei* (*Japan's Public Administration*) (Tokyo: Chuo Koronsha, 1994), p. 224.

5. We have been unable to ascertain the precise extent of Japanese bank losses stem-ming from the Asian crisis, but good circumstantial evidence suggests that it was in the $10 to $20 billion range. The evidence lies in the sudden sharp increase in lending from the Export-Import Bank of Japan, most of which would find its way onto Japanese com-mercial bank balance sheets because it typically would go to help foreign borrowers ser-vice their loans. Loans from the Export-Import Bank of Japan rose from ¥10.2 trillion yen to ¥12.1 trillion yen—nearly a 20 percent increase—in the period from June 1998 to June 1999.

6. The program, *Shinyo Hosho Kyokai Ho*, set up in 1953, established in each prefecture credit guarantee corporations that issue guarantees accepted by the Small and Medium Enterprise Credit Insurance Corporation, which in turn is backed by the central govern-ment; banks are thus assured that lending to specified companies is guaranteed.

7. Sources: Aggregate losses from the MOF's *Hojin Kigyo Tokei Nempo* (*Annual Sta-tistics of Enterprises*); tax returns from the National Tax Agency's *Kokuzei Tokei* (*National Tax Statistics*).

8. Karel van Wolferen "Sukyandaru ni yotte Nihon Kenryoku Kikou wa Ikinobiru" (The Structure of Japanese Power Depends on Scandals"), *Chuo Koron*, October 1991, pp. 186–94. Also see van Wolferen's *The Enigma of Japanese Power* (Alfred A. Knopf, 1989), pp. 136–38.

9. The Japanese distinguish between *jiken*—scandals that involve litigation (for exam-ple, the Itoman case)—and *fushoji* or *sukyandaru*, in which matters never end up in

court (for example, the *eigyo tokkin* scandals in which securities firms were compensating their best customers for losses). Even with *jiken*, however, litigation is a consequence of the scandal and usually ensnares only lower-level officials.

10. "Nomura Shoken ga Hojin Sonshitsu 160 oku en anaume; Saiken o takane Kaimodo shi; Shotori hou Ihan no Utagai" ("Nomura Securities Deducts ¥16 Billion in Losses; [for] Securities Bought at High Prices; Violation of Securities Law Suspected"), *Yomiuri Shimbun,* June 20, 1991, p. 45.

11. An account of Sakakibara's career and his appointment as director general of the International Financial Bureau ran in *Shukan Bunshun,* November 23, 1995, pp. 42–45 under the title "Sakakibara kyokucho madamada tobidasu 'Dai-hogen'" ("Director General Sakakibara Still Shoots His Mouth Off").

12. Inevitably, some will argue that the yen would have weakened anyway without the intervention, as indeed it had started to do so before the intervention. At the time, however, it was seen as one of the most successful cases of intervention by government authorities ever.

13. Marc Lasry, senior managing director at Amroc Investments, a specialist in distressed companies, was quoted in *Business Week,* September 10, 2001, p. 40, as saying, "It used to be that you got at least 50 cents on the dollar" of the assets of defaulting companies.

14. Emily Thornton, "Japan's Financial Secrets Pour Out," *Business-Week International On-Line Edition,* August 2, 1999 (http://www.businessweek.com/1999/99_31/b3640152.htm [April 29, 2002]).

15. Quoted in "Kosei na Shijo e" ("Toward Fair Markets"), a regular column in *Nihon Keizai Shimbun,* September 13, 2001, p. 14.

16. See Ochiai Seiichi, "Ginko no Furyo Saiken no desukurojya" ("Disclosure of Bad Loans"), *Juristo,* September 15, 1993, pp. 16–22.

17. Transcript of the symposium can be found in "Kigyo no Ihokodo: Sono Taio" ("Illegal Corporate Activities: Countermeasures"), *Juristo,* March 1, 1998, pp. 4–33. Shibahara's remarks are quoted on p. 32.

18. Ibid., p. 15.

## Chapter Nine

1. Bertell Ollman, "The Emperor and the Yakuza," *New Left Review,* March/April 2001, p. 74.

2. The career of Ando Shoeki (circa 1703–62), a satirist and agitator against official corruption, is a case in point. His *Animal Court* has been compared with Orwell's *Animal Farm.* But absent a base of opposition to existing power alignments—opposition that could draw strength from religious and philosphical traditions that taught the possibility of an alternative order—Ando's works fell on barren ground and he is seen as an isolated figure. See E. H. Norman, *Ando Shoeki and the Anatomy of Japanese Feudalism: Transactions of the Asiatic Society of Japan,* 3d series, vol. 2, December 1949 (reissued in hard cover by University Publications of America,1979); and Yasunaga Toshinobu, *Ando Shoeki: Social and Ecological Philosopher in 18th Century Japan* (Tokyo: Weatherhill, 1992).

3. John Dower, *Embracing Defeat: Japan in the Wake of World War II* (W.W. Norton, 1999), p. 23.

4. Adam Posen contends that fiscal stimulus has been "only mildly countercyclical" and "the result of the downturn and not of any discretionary response to it." *Restoring Japan's Economic Growth* (Washington: Institute for International Economics, 1998), p. 34.

5. Paul Krugman, for example, writes that "since any recovery strategy in Japan will involve printing lots of yen, it will almost surely drive the currency down even further." *International Herald Tribune*, April 2, 2001, p. 6.

6. See, for example, David Asher, *Japan's Financial Mount Fuji: Threatening Economic Stability* (Washington: American Enterprise Institute, December 2000) in which Asher notes in the opening summary that "Japan's public finances have entered unsustainable territory by any standard."

7. Kodama Mariko, manager in charge of credit ratings at Mikuni & Co., argues that despite widespread sentiment in Japan that most large manufacturers will survive come what may, polarization of stronger and weaker manufacturers already has occurred and the latter will not easily survive a shakeout. See "Can Industry Withstand Reform?" *Japan Echo*, December 2001, pp. 29–34. The article originally appeared in *Bungei Shunju*, September 2001.

8. Remarks made March 11, 1992, at a seminar to commemorate the seventy-fifth anniversary of the establishment of the insurance system run by the Japanese Post Office.

9. Former Japanese government officials describe the weakening of the antitrust laws and the reversal of the Occupation's attempts to disband the trade associations in Ashino Hiroshi, *Jigyo Dantai Ho (The Trade Association Law)* (Tokyo: Nihon Keizai Shimbun-sha, 1948); Izumoi Masao, *Shin Dokusen Kinshihou no Kaisetsu (Explanation of Revised Antitrust Law)* (Tokyo: Jijitsushinsha, 1948); and Imamura Narikazu, *Jigyo Dantai Ho (The Trade Association Law)* (Tokyo: Kobundo, 1950). Ashino served as commissioner of the Fair Trade Commission, Izumoi had been a MITI official, and Imamura had been on the staff of the Fair Trade Commission and a law professor at Hokkaido University.

10. Sakakibara Eisuke, former vice minister of finance, noted that "toward the end of March [2002], if the government would continue to manipulate equity prices, the market would bottom out after April," acknowledging that manipulation was happening. See "Koizumi Honebuto Kaikaku-ha Hatanshita" ("Koizumi's Fundamental Reform Plan Has Failed"), *Bungei Shunju*, April 2002, p. 103.

## Chapter Ten

1. The case has been made most compellingly by Yukio Noguchi in *1940-nen Taisei (The 1940 System)* (Tokyo: Toyo Keizai Shinposha, 1995).

2. Jacob Schlesinger, *Shadow Shoguns* (Simon & Schuster, 1997), p. 129, notes that "Tanaka's own creed of pragmatism and horse trading was improbably applied to the most fundamental philosophical differences."

3. Sakai Mitsuhide, *Yuichi-kun Monogatari: Aru Zaimukanryo no Showashi (The Tale of the MOF: Elite Finance Bureaucrats during the Showa Era)*, vol. 2 (Tokyo: Zaikei Shohosha, 1995), p. 689. We believe this book, written under a pseudonym, to be one of

the best descriptions of the inner workings of the MOF. The book has been quoted by Satake Goroku, a former elite bureaucrat at the Ministry of Agriculture who served as head of the Fisheries Agency, in *Taiken teki Kanryoron* (*The Theory of Bureaucracy as Experienced*) (Tokyo: Yuhikaku, 1998), p. 24–26—as clear an indication as possible that Sakai's book is reliable.

4. Ogawa Akio, "How the Elite Took Their Clients to the Cleaners," *Asahi Shimbun,* English edition, November 23, 2001, p. 28.

5. Michael Porter, Takeuchi Hirotaka, and Sakakibara Mariko, *Can Japan Compete?* (Cambridge, Mass.: Perseus Publishing, 2000), p. 140.

6. Except Obuchi Keizo, who died in office.

7. Hirose Michisada, *Hojyokin to Seiken-to* (*Subsidies and the Ruling Party*) (Tokyo: Asahi Shimbunsha, 1993), discusses the way in which the LDP "purchases" votes by distributing patronage.

8. Yoshino Toshihiko, *En to Doru* (*The Yen and the Dollar*) (Tokyo: Nippon Hoso Shuppan Kyokai, 1996), pp. 248–49.

9. Tachibana Takashi, "Joho Wocchingu" ("Media Watching"), regular column, *Shukan Gendai,* November 28, 1987, pp. 56–57.

10. The program is known as *Koyo Chosei Kin*, literally, employment adjustment payments.

# *Index*